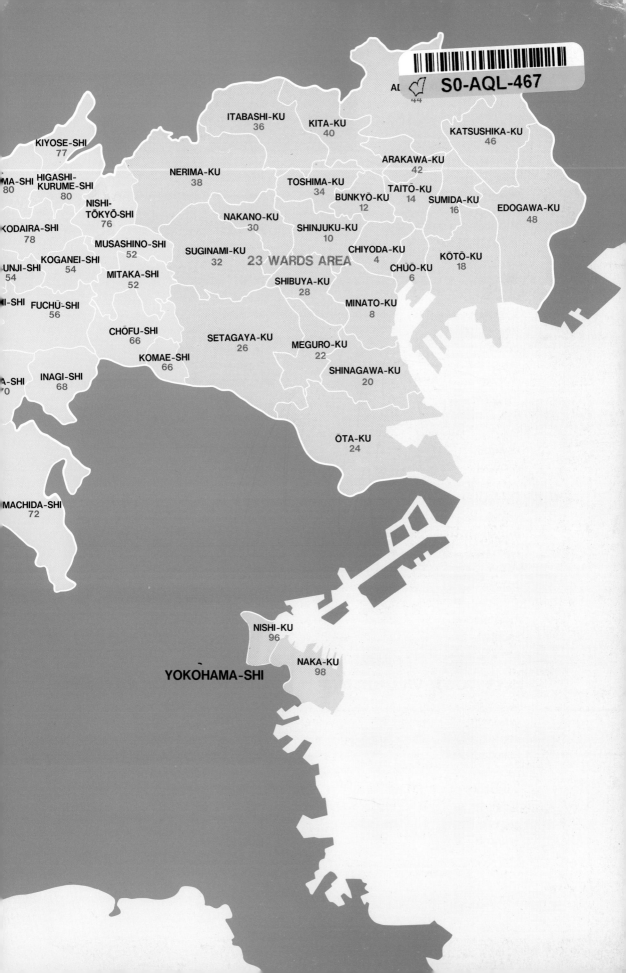

CONTENTS

Key to sectional maps ·················Inside front cover
Subway map ··2
Railway map ·························Inside back cover

WARD MAP

CHIYODA-KU ················ 千代田区 ········· 4
CHŪŌ-KU ···················· 中央区 ············ 6
MINATO-KU················· 港区 ··················8
SHINJUKU-KU············· 新宿区 ············10
BUNKYŌ-KU··············· 文京区 ············12
TAITŌ-KU···················· 台東区 ············14
SUMIDA-KU················· 墨田区 ············16
KŌTŌ-KU ···················· 江東区 ············18
SHINAGAWA-KU········· 品川区 ············20
MEGURO-KU················ 目黒区 ············22
ŌTA-KU ······················· 大田区 ············24
SETAGAYA-KU············ 世田谷区 ········26
SHIBUYA-KU··············· 渋谷区 ············28
NAKANO-KU················ 中野区 ············30
SUGINAMI-KU············· 杉並区 ············32
TOSHIMA-KU··············· 豊島区 ············34
ITABASHI-KU··············· 板橋区 ············36
NERIMA-KU·················· 練馬区 ············38
KITA-KU······················· 北区 ················40
ARAKAWA-KU············· 荒川区 ············42
ADACHI-KU·················· 足立区 ············44
KATSUSHIKA-KU········· 葛飾区 ············46
EDOGAWA-KU············· 江戸川区 ········48
BAY SHORE AREA············· 湾岸地区 ········50

CITY·TOWN·VILLAGE MAP

MUSASHINO-SHI ············ 武蔵野市 ········52
MITAKA-SHI ················· 三鷹市 ············52
KOGANEI-SHI ··············· 小金井市 ········54
KOKUBUNJI-SHI ··········· 国分寺市 ········54
FUCHŪ-SHI··················· 府中市 ············56
KUNITACHI-SHI············· 国立市 ············56
TACHIKAWA-SHI··········· 立川市 ············58
AKISHIMA-SHI ············· 昭島市 ············58
HINO-SHI ····················· 日野市 ············60

HACHIŌJI-SHI················ 八王子市·········62
CHŌFU-SHI·················· 調布市············66
KOMAE-SHI·················· 狛江市············66
INAGI-SHI ··················· 稲城市············68
TAMA-SHI ··················· 多摩市············70
MACHIDA-SHI··············· 町田市············72
NISHI-TŌKYŌ-SHI········· 西東京市·········76
KIYOSE-SHI·················· 清瀬市············77
KODAIRA-SHI··············· 小平市············78
HIGASHI-KURUME-SHI······ 東久留米市·····80
HIGASHI-MURAYAMA-SHI··· 東村山市·········80
HIGASHI-YAMATO-SHI···· 東大和市·········82
MUSASHI-MURAYAMA-SHI·· 武蔵村山市·····82
FUSSA-SHI··················· 福生市············84
AKIRUNO-SHI················ あきる野市(I)··84
HAMURA-SHI················ 羽村市············86
MIZUHO-MACHI············· 瑞穂町············86
ŌME-SHI······················ 青梅市············88
AKIRUNO-SHI················ あきる野市(II)·84
HINODE-MACHI·············· 日の出町·········90
OKUTAMA-MACHI··········· 奥多摩町·········92
HINOHARA-MURA··········· 檜原村············92
HACHIŌJI-SHI·MACHIDA-SHI······ 八王子市·町田市······94

YOKOHAMA·TSUKUBA

NISHI-KU(YOKOHAMA-SHI)····· 西区(横浜市)····96
NAKA-KU(YOKOHAMA-SHI)···· 中区(横浜市)····98
TSUKUBA-SHI················ つくば市·········100

TŌKYŌ AND ITS ENVIRONS

METROPOLITAN EXPRESSWAY ·················102
TŌKYŌ AREA ROAD MAP (I)·············104
TŌKYŌ AREA ROAD MAP (II)············106
TŌKYŌ AREA ROAD MAP (III)···········108
TŌKYŌ AREA ROAD MAP (IV)···········110

INDEX ·················112

LEGEND

BOUNDARIES

—·—·—·—·—·—·—·—·—·— Prefectural boundary

—··—··—··—··—··—··— City and ward boundary

————————————— Town and village boundary

—·—·—·—·—·—·—·—·—·— Section and chō boundary

··· Chōme boundary

RAILWAYS·STEAMER LANES

Tunnel   Station   Plan

Railway

Above ground

Subway

Monorail

Aerial ropeway

Steamer lanes

ROADS

Tunnel   Plan

Interchange

Toll road

Main road

Sub-main road

General road

Premise road

MAP SYMBOLS

Ⓜ Prefectural office

◉ City and ward office

○ Town and village office

○ Branch office

⊠ Police station

⊗ Police box

🏣 General post office

⊖ Post office

⊠ Fire station

◑ Fire sub-station

♂ Other Gov. and public office

🏛 University and college

🏫 Senior high school

🏫 Junior high school

⊗ Elementary school

🏥 Hospital

🏨 Hotel

☏ NTT office

⛩ Shrine

卍 Temple

✝ Church

⊥ Cemetery

⊖ Factory

⚡ Power station

✦ Transformer station

▫ Embassy

⚐ Golf course

   Address and block number

▭ Interchange name

▭ Intersection name

  Park and garden

Nishi-takashimadaira
Shin-takashimadaira
Takashimadaira
Nishidai
Hasune
Shimurasanchōme
Shimurasakaue
Moto-hasunuma
Itabashihonchō
Itabashikuyakushomae

AKA

Itabashi
Shin-itabash
Ni

WAKŌSHI

Direct Connection to TŌBU TŌJŌ Line (to Shinrinkōen)

KOTAKE-MUKAIHARA

Senkawa
Kanamechō

Eidan-narimasu
Eidan-akatsuka
Heiwadai
Hikawadai
Shin-sakuradai

IKEBUKURO

SUG

Ōtsuka
Sengoku
Myōgadani
Hakusan

Hikarigaoka
Nerima-kasugachō
Toshimaen

Shin-Ōtsuka
Mejiro
Higashi-ikebukuro
Gokokuji
Edogawabashi

KŌRAKUEN

KAS

NERIMA

Direct Connection to SEIBU IKEBUKURO Line (to Hannō)

Shin-egota
Ochiai-minami-nagasaki

TAKADANOBABA

Kagurazaka

NAKAI

Ochiai

SEIBU SHINJUKU Line

Shin-ōkubo

Waseda

IIDABASHI

SUID

Direct Connection to Chūō Line (to Mitaka)

OGIKUBO   **NAKANO**   **HIGASHI-NAKANO**

Seibu-shinjuku

Higashi-shinjuku
Wakamatsu-kawada
Ushigome-yanagichō
Ushigome-kagurazaka

Minami-asagaya

SHINJUKU-NISHIGUCHI

Nishi-shinjuku

SUIDŌ

Shin-kōenji

NAKANO-SAKAUE

SHINJUKU

TOCHŌMAE

Akebonobashi

ICHIGAYA

KUDANSHITA

JINBŌCHŌ

Higashi-kōenji
Shin-nakano

SHINJUKU-SANCHŌME

Hōnanchō
Nakanofujimichō
Nakanoshimbashi
Nishi-shinjuku-gochōme
Hatsudai

Shinjukugyoenmae

Hanzōmon
Kōjimachi

Hatagaya

Yotsuyasanchōme

YOTSUYA

Takebashi

YOYOGI

Shinjukugyoenmae

NAGATACHŌ

Sasazuka

Shinanomachi

Direct Connection to KEIŌ Line (to Hashimoto)

Sendagaya

Kokuritsukyōgijō

Sakuradamon

HARAJUKU

MEIJIJINGŪMAE

Direct Connection to ODAKYŪ Line (to Hon-atsugi)

YOYOGI-UEHARA

Yoyogikōen

AOYAMA-ITCHŌME

AKASAKAMITSUKE

Direct Connection to DEN-ENTOSHI Line (to Chūō-rinkan)

INOKASHIRA Line

OMOTESANDO

Gaienmae

Futakotamagawa
Yōga
Sakurashinmachi
Komazawadaigaku
Sangenjaya
Ikejiriōhashi

SHIBUYA

Nogizaka
Akasaka

KOKKAI-GIJIDŌ-MAE

KASUMIGASEKI

HIBI

TAMEIKE-SANNŌ

Roppongi-itchōme

Direct Connection to TŌYOKO Line to Kikuna)

NAKA-MEGURO

EBISU

Hiroo

ROPPONGI

Kamiyachō

Toranomon

Uchisaiwaichō

SHIROKANEDAI

SHIROKANE-TAKANAWA

Direct Connection to MEGURO Line (to Musashi Kosugi)

MEGURO

AZABUJŪBAN

Onarimon

Akabanebashi

SHINBASHI

IKEGAMI Line

Shibakōen

ŌIMACHI Line

GOTANDA

Nishi-magome
Magome
Nakanobu
Toposhi

SENGAKUJI

Takanawadai

MITA

DAIMON

Ōsaki

SHINAGAWA

Ōimachi

Tamachi

Hamamatsucho

Direct Connection to KEIHIN KYŪKŌ Railway (to Misakiguchi)

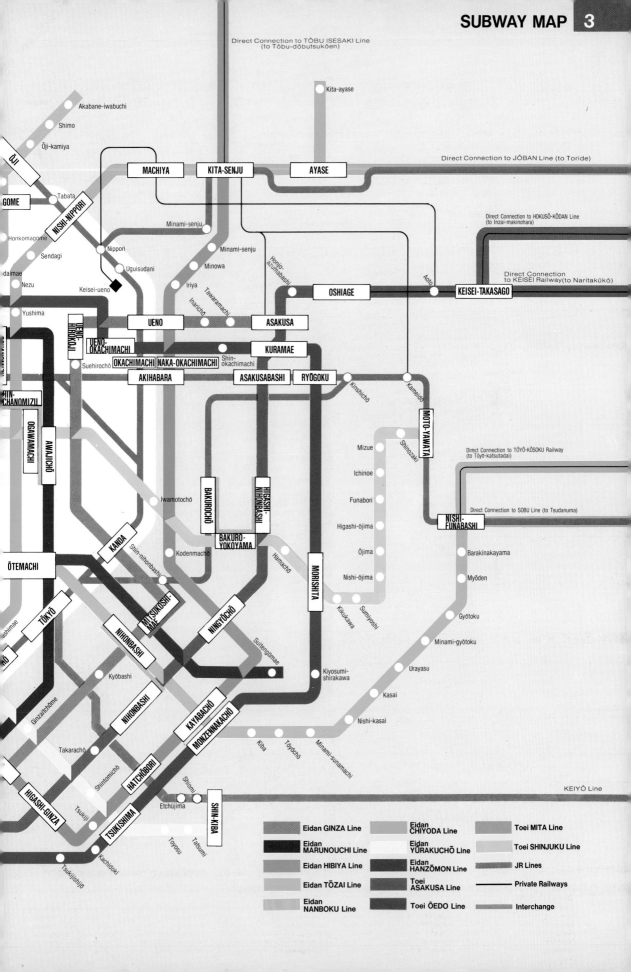

1:18,000

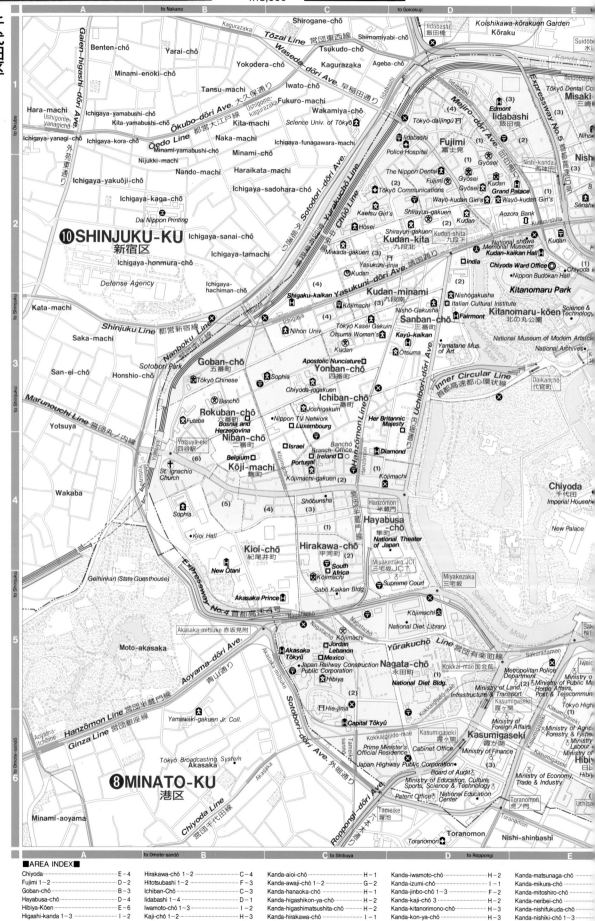

■AREA INDEX ■

Chiyoda E-4	Hirakawa-chō 1~2 .... C-4	Kanda-aioi-chō H-1	Kanda-iwamoto-chō H-2	Kanda-matsunaga-chō
Fujimi 1~2 .... D-2	Hitotsubashi 1~2 .... F-3	Kanda-awaji-chō 1~2 .... G-2	Kanda-izumi-chō I-1	Kanda-mikura-chō
Goban-chō B-3	Ichiban-chō C-3	Kanda-hanaoka-chō H-2	Kanda-jinbō-chō 1~3 .... F-2	Kanda-mitoshiro-chō
Hayabusa-chō D-4	Iidabashi 1~4 .... D-1	Kanda-higashikon-ya-chō ... H-2	Kanda-kaji-chō 3 .... H-2	Kanda-neribei-chō
Hibiya-Kōen E-6	Iwamoto-chō 1~3 .... I-2	Kanda-higashimatsushita-chō .. H-2	Kanda-kitanorimono-chō H-3	Kanda-nishifukuda-chō
Higashi-kanda 1~3 ... I-2	Kaji-chō 1~2 .... H-3	Kanda-hirakawa-chō I-1	Kanda-kon-ya-chō H-3	Kanda-nishiki-chō

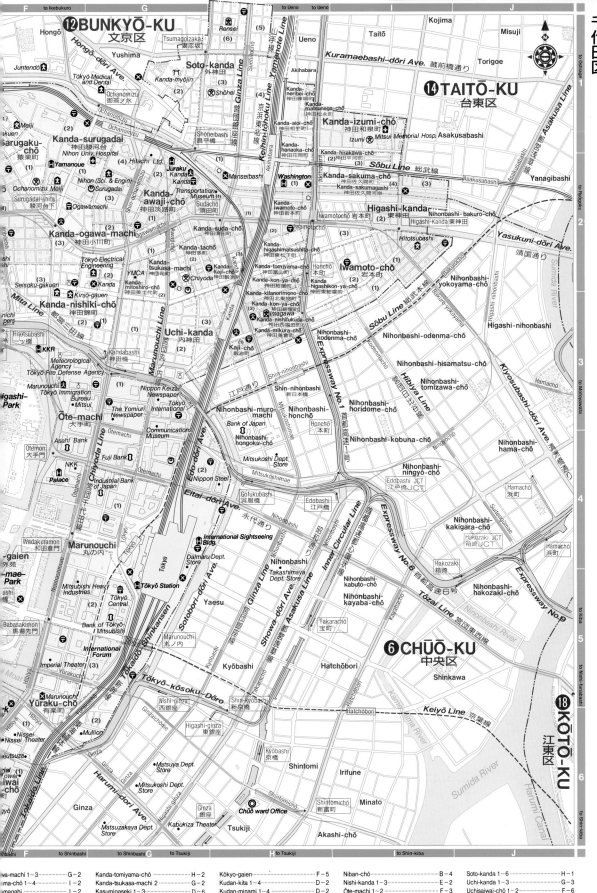

wa-machi 1–3	G–2	Kanda-tomiyama-chō	H–2	Kōkyo-gaien	F–5	Niban-chō	B–4	Soto-kanda 1–6	H–1
ma-chō 1–4	I–2	Kanda-tsukasa-machi 2	G–2	Kudan-kita 1–4	D–2	Nishi-kanda 1–3	E–2	Uchi-kanda 1–3	G–3
-chō 1–2	H–2	Kasumigaseki 1–3	D–6	Kudan-minami 1–4	D–2	Ōte-machi 1–2	F–3	Uchisaiwai-chō 1–2	F–6
gadai 1–4	F–1	Kioi-chō	B–4	Marunouchi 1–3	G–4	Rokuban-chō	B–3	Yonban-chō	C–3
	G–2	Kitanomaru-Kōen	E–3	Misaki-chō 1–3	E–1	Sanban-chō	D–3	Yūraku-chō 1–2	F–6
		Kōji-machi 1–6	C–4	Nagata-chō 1–2	D–5	Sarugaku-chō 1–2	F–1		

中央区

1:18,000

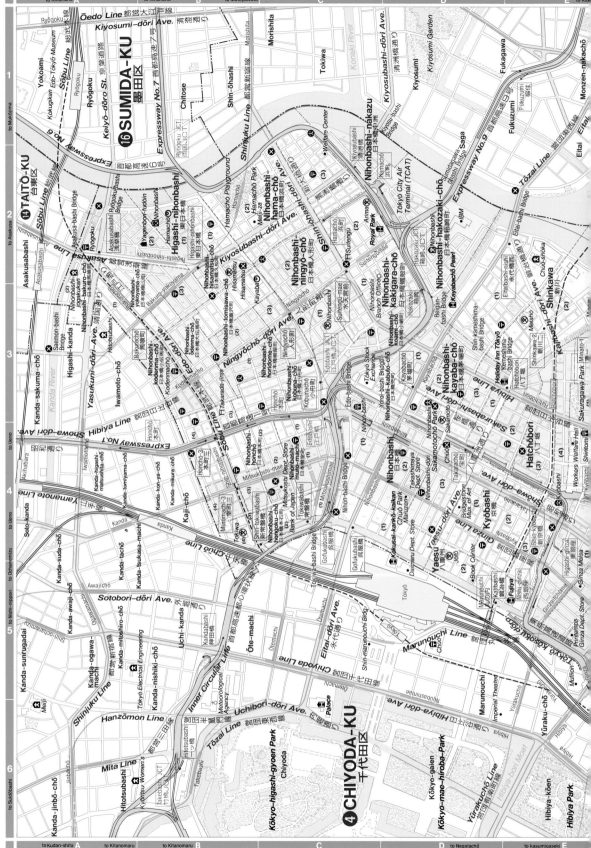

■AREA INDEX■

Akashi-chō ···· F–3	Irifune 1~3 ···· E–3	Nihonbashi-hakozaki-chō ···· D–2	Nihonbashi-kabuto-chō ···· D–3	Nihonbashi-muro-machi 1~4 ···· C–3
Ginza 1~8 ···· F–5	Kachidoki 1~6 ···· H–4	Nihonbashi-hama-chō 1~3 ···· C–2	Nihonbashi-kakigara-chō 1~2 ···· D–2	Nihonbashi-nakazu
Hamarikyū-teien ···· H–5	Kyōbashi 1~3 ···· D–4	Nihonbashi-hisamatsu-chō ···· C–3	Nihonbashi-kakaya-chō 1~3 ···· D–3	Nihonbashi-ningyō-chō 1~3 ···· C–2
Harumi 1~5 ···· I–3	Minato 1~3 ···· F–5	Nihonbashi-honchō 1~4 ···· B–4	Nihonbashi-koami-chō ···· D–3	Nihonbashi-tomizawa-chō
Hatchōbori 1~4 ···· E–4	Nihonbashi 1~3 ···· D–4	Nihonbashi-hongoku-cho 1~4 ···· C–4	Nihonbashi-kobuna-chō ···· C–3	Nihonbashi-yokoyama-chō
Higashi-nihonbashi 1~3 ···· B–2	Nihonbashi-bakuro-chō 1~2 ···· A–3	Nihonbashi-horidome-chō 1~2 ···· B–3	Nihonbashi-kodenma-chō ···· B–3	Nihonbashi-Ōdenma-chō

中央区

KŌTŌ-KU 江東区

⑱ Tōkyō univ. of Mercantile Marine

Furuishiba

Etchūjima

Harumi Canal

Yūrakuchō Line

Ishikawajima-Harima Heavy Industries

Ishikawajima-Harima Heavy Industries

Toyosu Park

Toyosu

New Tōkyō Steam-Power Plant

Tōkyō Gas

Toyosu Pier

Morishita Bridge

Kiyosumi-dōri Ave.

Tsukuda

Tsukudajima

Tsukuda

Sumiyoshi-jinja

Ōkawabata River City 21

Tsukuda Shinkawa Green Park

Asashio-ōhashi Bridge

Tsukishima Branch Office

Tsukishima-3

Tōkyō Metropolitan JC. Coll.

Harumi-bashi Bridge

New Tsukishima Park

Harumi-sōgō

Taiheiyō Cement

Harumibashi

Urashima

Harumi-daisan

Tsukishima-daichi

Harumi Houses

Harumi Pier

Hatsumi

Tōkyō Port Management Office

Customhouse Branch Office

Tsuki shima

Ōedo Line

St. Luke's Tower

New Hankyū

Akashi-chō

Akashi

Sumida River

Tsukudajima Park

Tsukishima-daini

Kachidoki-2

Reimei-bashi Bridge

Harumi-3

The Furniture Museum

Harumi Grand

Harumi

Mariners Court

Harumi Pier

St. Luke's International Hospital

Infunebashi

Akashi

Chūō Health Center

Akatsuki Park

Tsukijigawa Park

Tsukishima-dōri

Kachidoki-bashi Bridge

Kachidoki

Niijima-bashi Bridge

Hatsuzuki

Asashio Canal

Harumi-dōri Ave.

Tsukiji-6

Tsukiji-hongami

Hamanae-bashi Bridge

Rinkō

Sumida-kōgyo

Tsukishima Branch Sch.

Toyomi

Tsukishima

Tsukishima Pier

Toyomi Playground

Harumi Playground

Harumi-futō Park

Ginza

Tsukiji

New Hankyū

Shin-Ōhashi-dōri Ave.

Chūōshi-mae

Namiyoke-jinja

Central Wholesale Market

Tsukishima-jinja

Toyomi-chō

Asashio Pier

Suisan Pier

Tōkyō Port

Kyōbashi

Tōkyō

National Cancer Center

Kabukiza Theater

Tōgeki Theater

Shinbashi Enbujō Theater

Ginza

Matsuzakaya Dept. Store

Mihara-bashi

Ginza Daiichi

Gas Hall / Yamaha Hall

Maritime Safety Agency; Hydrographic Dept.; Asahi Newspaper

Shuddone

Hamarikyū-teien

Hamarikyū Garden

Nikkō

Mitsui Urban

Hakuhinkan

Tōbu Theater

Hakuhinkan

Dōbashi

Ginza Line

Dōbashi

Shinbashi

MINATO-KU 港区

⑧

Uchisaiwai

Daiichi Keihin Highway

Yokosuka Line

Yamanote Line

Tōkaidō Shinkansen

Shinbashi

Higashi-shinbashi

Hamamatsu-chō

Kaigan

Kaigan-dōri Ave.

Kyū-Shibarikyū Garden

Daimon

World Trade Center Bldg.

Inter Circulear Line

Takeshiba Pier

Hamazakibashi JCT

Hinode

Tōkyō Rinkai Shin-Kōtsū

Hinode Pier

Tōkyō Monorail

Expressway No.1

to Haneda

to Shinagawa

ia 1~2 .... E-3
1~2 .... E-4
hō I-4
~7 .... G-4
ina 1~4 .... G-3
1~3 .... F-2
Yaesu 1~2 .... D-4

1:25,000

0 250 500 750m

■AREA INDEX

Akasaka 1–9	C-3	Daiba	※	Kōnan 1–5	H-4	Nishi-azabu 1–4	D-5	Shinbashi 1–6	D-2
Atago 1–2	D-2	Hamamatsu-chō 1–2	E-2	Minami-aoyama 1–7	C-5	Nishi-shinbashi 1–3	D-2	Shirokane 1–6	
Azabu-jūban 1–4	E-4	Higashi-azabu 1–3	E-3	Minami-azabu 1–5	E-4	Roppongi 1–7	D-3	Shirokanedai 1–4	
Azabu-mamiana-chō	D-3	Higashi-shinbashi 1–2	E-1	Mita 1–5	F-4	Shiba 1–5	F-3	Siba-daimon 1–2	
Azabudai 1–3	D-3	Kaigan 1–3	G-2	Moto-akasaka 1–2	B-3	Shiba-kōen 1–4	E-2	Takanawa 1–4	
Azabu-nagasaka-chō	D-3	Kita-aoyama 1–3	B-4	Moto-azabu 1–3	E-4	Shibaura 1–4	G-3	Toranomon 1–5	

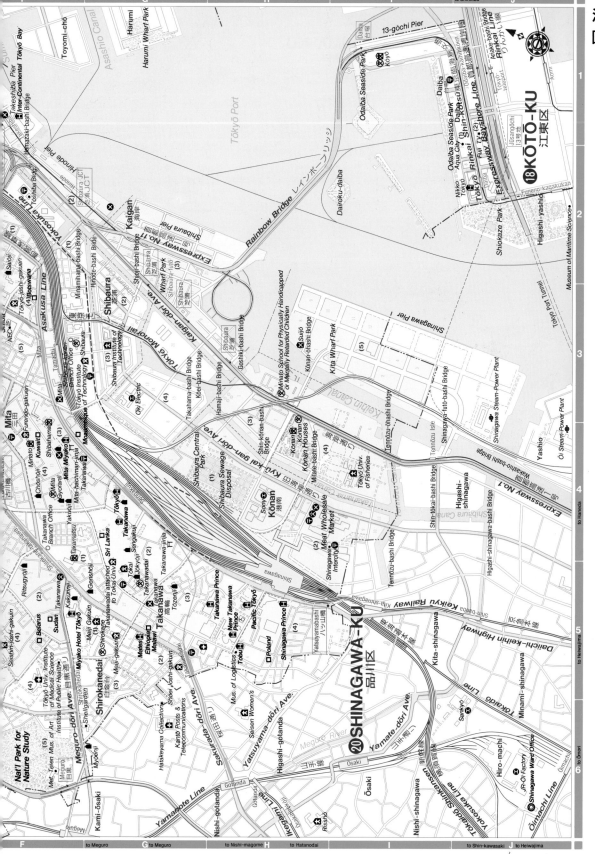

新宿区

1:22,000

0　250　500m

34 TOSHIMA-KU 豊島区

30 NAKANO-KU 中野区

32 SUGINAMI-KU 杉並区

to Hōya · to Ikebukuro · to Ikebukuro · to Mejiro
to Tanashi · to Ogikubo · to Ogikubo · to Hōnancho

Seibu Ikebukuro Line 西武池袋線
Mejiro-dōri Ave. 目白通り
Nakano-dōri Ave. 中野通り
Shin-ōme-kaidō Ave. 新青梅街道
Shin-mejiro-dōri Ave. 新目白通り
Saikyō Line 埼京線
Yamanote Line 山手線
Yamate-dōri Ave. 山手通り
Seibu Shinjuku Line 西武新宿線
Tōzai Line 東西線
Chūō Line 中央線
Ōkubo-dōri Ave. 大久保通り
Marunouchi Line 営団丸ノ内線
Ōme-kaidō Ave. 青梅街道
Ōedo Line 都営大江戸線
Seibu Shinjuku Line 西武新宿線
Kanda River

Minami-nagasaki
Minami-nagasaki-1 南長崎一
Shimo-ochiai 下落合(2)
Seibo Women's Jr. College
Otomeyama Park
Ochiai
Ochiai-daiyon
Ochiai-dairoku (4)
Nishi-Ochiai-1 西落合一
Naka-ochiai 中落合
Ochiai-daiichi
Yakuōin
Ochiai 1st Branch Office
Fuji Jr. College
Shinjuku Central Library
Shin-ōme-kaidō Ave.
Nishi-ochiai 西落合(1)
Ochiai-daini
Ochiai-daisan
Naka-ochiai-2 中落合二
Totsuka-daisan
Takadanobaba 高田馬場
Tetsugakudō Park
Mejiro-gakuen
Fudoson-hondō
Ochiai 2nd Branch Office
Nakai 中井
Ochiai-daigo
Seseraginosato Park
Ochiai Sewage Disposal
Ochiai Central Park
Nishitoyama-daini
Nishitoyama Park
Matsugaoka
Ochiai-daini
Kami-ochiai 上落合
Otakibashi 小滝橋
Nishitoyama
Toyama Houses
Shinjuku
The Globe Theater
Social Insurance Chūō Hosp.
Hyakunin-chō 百人町
Ochiai Park
Kami-ochiai-2 上落合二
Araiyakushi-mae
Kamitakada
Arai-yakushi
Yodobashi-daiyon
Hotel Kaiyō
Kita-shinjuku 北新宿
Shinjuku
Arai
Higashi-nakano
Kashiwagi
Kitashinjuku-hyakuninchō 北新宿百人町
Broadway Center
Higashi-nakano
Shinjuku
Nakano Sun Plaza Hall
Kashiwagi Branch Office
Nishi-shinjuku
Nakano Ward Office
Miyashita 宮下
Naruko-Tenjinsha
Star Hotel
Nakano
Nishi-shinjuku
Shinjukusho-mae 新宿署前
Chūō
Nakanosakaue
Yododashinichū-mae 淀橋二丁目
Tōkyō Medical Coll. Hosp.
Land Tower Asahi Center Bl
Hon-chō
Mitsui Bldg.
Nishi-shinjuku 西新宿
Kōenji-minami
Tōkyō Hilton
Sumitomo Bldg.
Higashi-kōenji
Century Hyatt
Tōkyō Metropolitan Government Office
Keiō P
Kumano-jinja
Shinjuku Central Park
NS Bldg.
Washington
Shinjuku New City
Shinjuku 新宿
School for Physically Handicapped or Mentally Retarded Children
Tsunohazu Branch Office
Nishi-shinjuku
Park Hyatt
Yayoi-cho
Honchō
Opera City
NTT Bldg.
New National Theater, Tokyo
Ehara-chō
Egota

■AREA INDEX■

Ageba-chō ·········· J–1	Enoki-chō ·········· H–2	Hyakunin-chō 1–4 ·········· E–3	Ichigaya-sadohara-chō 1~3 ·········· J–2	Iwato-chō ·········· I–2	Kawada-chō ·········· I–3
Aizumi-chō ·········· J–4	Fukuro-machi ·········· I–2	Ichigaya-chōenji-machi ·········· I–3	Ichigaya-sanai-chō ·········· I–3	Kabuki-chō 1·2 ·········· F–4	Kikui-chō ·········· I–1
Akagi-moto-machi ·········· I–1	Funa-machi ·········· H–4	Ichigaya-funagawara-machi ·········· I–2	Ichigaya-takajō-machi ·········· I–3	Kaguragashi ·········· I–2	Kita-machi ·········· I–1
Akagi-shita-machi ·········· I–1	Hara-machi 1–3 ·········· H–3	Ichigaya-hachiman-chō ·········· I–3	Ichigaya-tamachi 1~3 ·········· H–3	Kagurazaka 1~6 ·········· I–2	Kita-shinjuku 1~4 ·········· E–3
Araki-chō ·········· H–4	Haraikata-machi ·········· I–2	Ichigaya-honmura-chō ·········· I–2	Ichigaya-yakuōji-machi ·········· I–3	Kaitai-chō ·········· I–1	Kita-yamabushi-chō ·········· I–2
Babashita-chō ·········· G–2	Higashi-enoki-chō ·········· I–2	Ichigaya-kaga-chō 1·2 ·········· H–2	Ichigaya-yamabushi-chō ·········· I–2	Kami-ochiai 1~3 ·········· C–3	Minami-chō ·········· I–3
Benten-chō ·········· H–2	Higashi-goken-chō ·········· I–1	Ichigaya-kōra-chō ·········· I–3	Ichigaya-yanagi-chō ·········· H–3	Kasumigaoka-machi ·········· H–6	Minami-enoki-chō ·········· I–2
Daikyō-chō ·········· D–5	Honshio-chō ·········· I–4	Ichigaya-nakanochō ·········· H–3	Ichigayadai-machi ·········· H–4	Kata-machi ·········· H–4	Minami-motomachi ··········

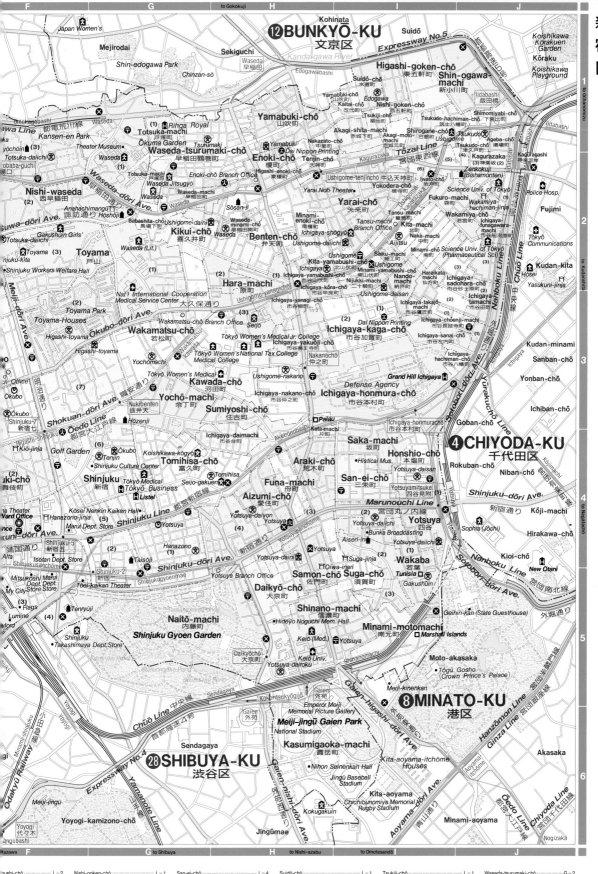

...oushi-chō ... I–2	Nishi-goken-chō ... I–1	San-ei-chō ... I–4	Suidō-chō ... I–1	Tsukiji-chō ... I–1	Waseda-tsurumaki-chō ... G–2
... G–5	Nishi-ochiai 1–4 ... B–2	Shimo-ochiai 1–4 ... D–1	Sumiyoshi-chō ... H–3	Tsukudo-chō ... J–1	Yamabuki-chō ... H–1
... I–2	Nishi-shinjuku 1–8 ... E–5	Shimomiyabi-chō ... J–1	Takadanobaba 1–4 ... E–2	Tsukudo-hachiman-chō ... J–1	Yarai-chō ... H–2
...4 ... C–1	Nishi-shinjuku 1–8 ...	Shin-ogawa-machi ... J–1	Tansu-machi ... I–2	Wakaba 1–3 ... I–4	Yochō-machi ... G–3
... B–2	Nishi-waseda 1–3 ... F–2	Shinano-machi ... H–5	Tenjin-chō ... H–1	Wakamatsu-chō ... G–3	Yokodera-chō ... H–2
... H–1	Ōkubo 1–3 ... F–3	Shinjuku 1–7 ... G–4	Tomihisa-chō ... G–4	Wakamiya-chō ... J–2	Yotsuya 1–4 ... I–4
... I–2	Saiku-machi ... I–2	Shirogane-chō ... I–1	Totsuka-machi 1 ... G–2	Waseda-machi ... G–2	
... I–2	Samon-chō ... H–5	Suga-chō ... I–5	Toyama 1–3 ... G–2	Waseda-minami-chō ... H–2	

文
京
区

1:18,000

| 0 | 250 | 500m |

to Itabashihonchō　A　to Ōji　B　to Ōji　C　to Nishi-takashimadaira　D　E

Kami-ikebukuro

34 TOSHIMA-KU
豊島区

Sugamo-shinden

to ikebukuro

Kita-ōtsuka

Sugamo

Komagome

Meiji-dōri Ave.

Toshima Ward Office
首都高速5号

Expressway No.5

Kasuga-dōri Ave. 春日通り

Ōtsuka

Ōtsukaekimae

Yamanote Line 山手線

Nakasendō Ave. 中山道

Sugamo-1 巣鴨一

Bunkyō-josh

to ikebukuro

Higashi-ikebukuro
東池袋

Sunshine 60
Sunshine City

Higashi-ikebukuro

Mukōhara

Minami-ōtsuka

Tōyō Girl's

(4)

Sengoku-1 千石一

Kag

Sengoku
千石

Sanbyakunir

Mint Bureau

Marunouchi Line 営団丸ノ内線

Shi-Otsuka

(3)

Ōhara Branch Office

Sengokue
千

Minami-ikebukuro

Higashi-ikebukuro
Zōshigaya

Yūrakuchō Line

Higashi-ikebukuroyonchōme

(6)

Ōtsuka Park

Ōtsuka

(4)

Ōtsuka

Hayashichō

Ichi

(3)

Daijū

营团有楽町線

Zōshigaya Cemetery

Toshimagaoka Cemetery

(5)

Tōhō Music Jr. Coll.

Nittō

(4)

Tsukuba

Daijū

Zōshigaya

Aoyagi

Gokokuji

Ōtsuka

Ōtsuka-3
大塚三

Kubomachi-higashi Park
Sports Center

Koishika
Botanical G

to Mejiro

Kishibojinmae

Buzan attached to Nihon Univ.

Ōtsuka
大塚

Tsukuba

H.S.

Kyōiku-no-mori Park

Shinobazu-dōri Ave. 不忍通り

Koishikawa

Gokokuji-nishi 護国寺西

Gokokuji-nishi 護国寺

Kōdansha

Jr. H. S.

H. S.
E. S.

Univ. of the Air

Senkawa-dōri Ave.

School for the blind attached
to Univ. of Tsukuba

(2)

Ochanomizu Women's

Ōtsuka Branch Office

Daiichi

Koishi

Mejirodai-2
目白台二

Japan Women's

Mejirodai
目白台

Otowa
Branch Office

Ōtsuka

Dainana

(1)

Atomi-gakuen

(5)

Daiichi

Takehaya Park

Takada

Hōmei attached to
Japan Women's

Mejiro-dōri Ave. 目白通り

Otowa-dōri Ave.

Tsukuba

Atomi Gakuen Jr. Coll.

(3)

Teisei-gakuen

Takushoku

Koishikawa-5
小石川五

Koish

Government official
Mutualaid Playground

Tōkyō Music

St. Mary's Cathedral

(3)

Otowa
音羽

Kohinata
小日向

Shinkōji

Takehaya at
Tōkyō Gaki

(4)

Koishikawa
to Tōkyō Gaki

Shin-edogawa
Park

Chinzansō

Dokkyō

Sekiguchi
関口

Kohinatadaimachi

Takushoku

Meidai

Bashōan

Arakawa Line
都電荒川線

Four Seasons

Kanda River

Sekiguchidaimachi

Otowa-1 音羽一

(1)

Shōmyōji

Kanatomi

(2)

Waseda

Shin-mejiro-dōri Ave. 新目白通り

Edogawa Park

Waseda 早稲田

Daigo

Kohinata-jinja

Suidō
水道

Nishi-waseda

Waseda

Daigo

Expressway No.5 首都高速5号

Ōmagari
大曲

Toppan Printing

And

Totsuka-machi

Edogawabashi
江戸川橋

Edogawabashi

Yūrakuchō Line 営団有楽町線

(1)

Waseda-tsurumaki-chō

Yamabuki-chō

Suidō-chō

Shin-ogawa-machi

Waseda-machi

Waseda

Kaitai-chō

Nishi-goken-chō

Tsukiji-chō

Iidabashi
飯田橋

Babashita-chō

Enoki-chō

Nakazato-chō

Akagi-shita-machi

Waseda-minami-chō

Higashi-enoki-chō

Akagi-moto-machi

Tsukudo-hachiman-chō

10 SHINJUKU-KU
新宿区

Kikui-chō

Benten-chō

Waseda-dōri Ave. 早稲田通り

Tōzai Line 営団東西線

Shirogane-chō

Welfare Pension

Toyama

Gaien-higashi-dōri Ave. 外苑東通り

Tenjin-chō

Minami-enoki-chō

Yarai-chō

Yokodera-chō

Kagurazaka

Tsukudo-chō

Ageba-chō

Kagurazaka

Wakamatsu-chō

Hara-machi

Tansu-machi

Ushigome-
kagurazaka

Iwato-chō

Fukuro-machi

Kuraga̲gashi

to Ichigaya

■AREA INDEX■

Hakusan 1~5 ········· F-3	Kōraku 1~2 ········· F-6	Ōtsuka 1~6 ········· D-3	Yushima 1~4 ········· I-6
Hon-komagome 1~6 ········· F-2	Mejirodai 1~3 ········· B-4	Sekiguchi 1~3 ········· C-5	
Hongō 1~7 ········· H-5	Mukōgaoka 1~2 ········· G-3	Sendagi 1~5 ········· H-3	
Kasuga 1~2 ········· F-5	Nezu 1~2 ········· H-3	Sengoku 1~5 ········· E-2	
Kohinata 1~4 ········· D-4	Nishikata 1~2 ········· G-4	Suidō 1~2 ········· D-5	
Koishikawa 1~5 ········· E-4	Otowa 1~2 ········· C-4	Yayoi 1~2 ········· H-4	

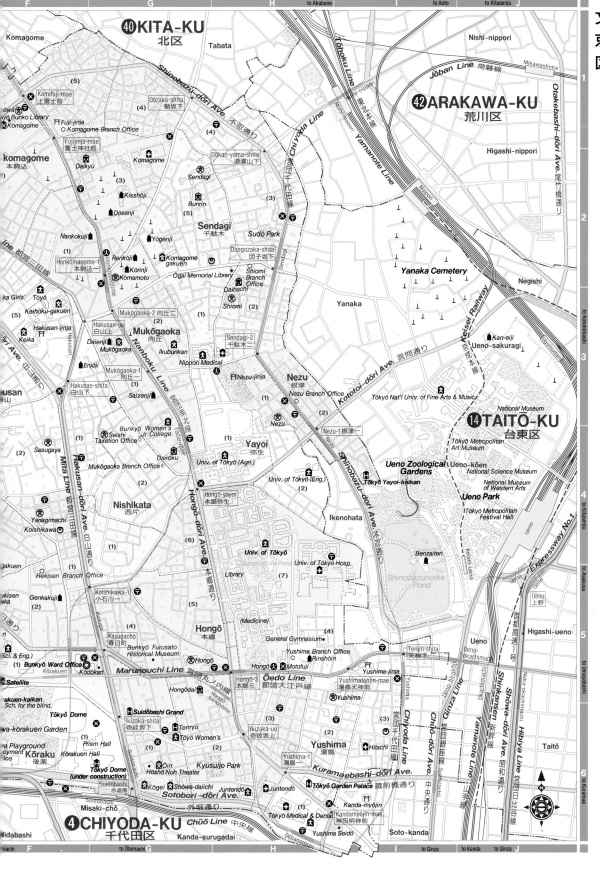

文京区

F · G · H · to Akabane · I · to Aoto · J · to Kitasenju

40 KITA-KU
北区

Komagome   Tabata   Nishi-nippori

Shinobazu-dōri Ave. 不忍通り   Jōban Line 常磐線   Mikawashima

Kamifuji-mae 上富士前   **42 ARAKAWA-KU**
...o Bunko Library   荒川区
× Komagome
Fuji-jinja   Dōzaka-shita 動坂下
× Fujijinja-mae   Higashi-nippori
富士神社前   Komagome Branch Office
komagome
本駒込   Dōkan-yama-shita 道灌山下
Daikyū   Dōzaka-shita

Komagome   Komagome

Sendagi   Dōkan-yama-shita 道灌山下
Kisshōji   × Bunrin
Dōsenji
Nankokuji   Yōgenji   **Sendagi** 千駄木   Sudō Park

Honkomagome-1   Komagome   Dangozaka-shita 団子坂下
本駒込   gakuen 駒込学園
Renkōji   Ōgai Memorial Library   Shiomi Branch Office   **Yanaka Cemetery**
Kōrinji   Shiomi Branch Office 塩見
Komamoto   Daihachi
...ka Girls'   Mukōgaoka-2 向丘二   Shiomi   Yanaka
Tōyō   塩見
Keihoku-gakuen   Sendagi-2 千駄木二   **Yanaka**
Hakusan-jinja 白山神社   Ikubunkan
Keika   **Mukōgaoka** 向丘   Nippon Medical   Kan-eiji
Daienji   Mukōgaoka-1 向丘一   Nezu-jinja 根津神社   Ueno-sakuragi
...usan   Enjōji   Hakusan-shita 白山下   Nezu Branch Office   Keisei Railway
...san   Saizenji   **Nezu** 根津   Tōkyō Nat'l Univ. of Fine Arts & Music   Negishi
Nezu
Bunkyō Women's   Nezu-1 根津一   National Museum
Seishi   Jr. College   **14 TAITŌ-KU**   台東区
Taxation Office   Dairoku   **Yayoi** 弥生   Tōkyō Metropolitan
Sasugaya   Mukōgaoka Branch Office   Univ. of Tōkyō (Agri.)   Art Museum
Univ. of Tōkyō (Eng.)   **Ueno Zoological**   National Science Museum
Nishikata 西片   Hongō-yayoi   Gardens Ueno-kōen
本郷弥生   Tōkyō Yayoi-kaikan   National Museum
Yanagimachi   of Western Arts
Koishikawa   **Ikenohata**   **Ueno Park**
Tōkyō Metropolitan
Rekisen Branch Office   Univ. of Tōkyō   Festival Hall
Koishikawa-1   Benzaiten   Ueno 上野
小石川一
Genkakuji   Univ. of Tōkyō Hosp.   **Shinobazunoike**   Higashi-ueno
Library   **Pond**
Kasuga   **Hongō** 本郷   Ueno
(Medicine)   Ueno-okachimachi
Kasugachō   General Gymnasium   Ueno-okachimachi
春日町   Yushima Branch Office
Bunkyō Furusato   Rinshoin
Historical Museum   Hongō × Motofuji   Yushima-jinja
Bunkyō Ward Office   Kōdōkan   Hongō-3   Yushima-shita 天神下   Umayabashi
Kōrakuen   本郷三   Yushimatenjin-mae
Satellite   Hongō   湯島天神前
...rakuen-kaikan   Hongōdai   Hongō   × Yushima
Sch. for the blind   Hongō
Tōkyō   **Suidōbashi Grand**   sanchome   Hitachi
Dome   Ikizaka-shita
...a Playground   (under construction)   壱岐坂下   Tenryū   **Yushima** 湯島
...oyment Center   Kōrakuen Hall   Tōyō Women's   Ikizaka-ue   Taitō
Kōraku   壱岐坂上   Yushima-1
後楽   Ōin   Hōshō Noh Theater   湯島一
Prism Hall   Kōgei   Shōwa-daiichi   Juntendō
Tōkyō Dome   Kyūsuijo Park   **Tōkyō Garden Palace** 蔵前橋通り
(under construction)   Juntendō   Kur; maebashi-dōri Ave.
...a-kōrakuen Garden   Suidōbashi 水道橋   Kanda-myōjin
Misaki-chō   Sotobori-dōri Ave.   Kandamyōjin-mae   Soto-kanda
Prism Hall   外堀通り   神田明神前
...dabashi   Tōkyō Medical & Dental   Yushima Seidō
4 CHIYODA-KU   Chūō Line 中央線
千代田区   Kanda-surugadai
...machi   F · G to Ōtemachi · H to Ochanomizu · I to Ginza · to Kanda · to Ginza · J

1:18,000

0   250   500m

■AREA INDEX■

Akihabara···············D–5	Higashi-ueno 1~6···········E–4	Kiyokawa 1~2···········H–1	Minowa 1~2···········G–1	Ryūsen 1~3···········F–2
Asakusa 1~7···········G–3	Ikenohata 1~4···········C–3	Kojima 1~2···········E–5	Misuji 1~2···········F–5	Senzoku 1~4···········G–2
Asakusabashi 1~5···········E–6	Imado 1~2···········H–2	Komagata 1~2···········G–5	Moto-asakusa 1~4···········E–4	Shitaya 1~3···········F–3
Hanakawado 1~2···········H–4	Iriya 1~2···········F–2	Kotobuki 1~4···········F–4	Negishi 1~5···········E–2	Taitō 1~4···········F–4
Hashiba 1~2···········I–1	Kaminarimon 1~2···········G–4	Kuramae 1~4···········F–5	Nihonzutsumi 1~2···········G–1	Torigoe 1~2···········F–5
Higashi-asakusa 1~2···········H–2	Kita-ueno 1~2···········E–3	Matsugaya 1~4···········F–3	Nishi-asakusa 1~3···········F–4	Ueno 1~7···········E–3

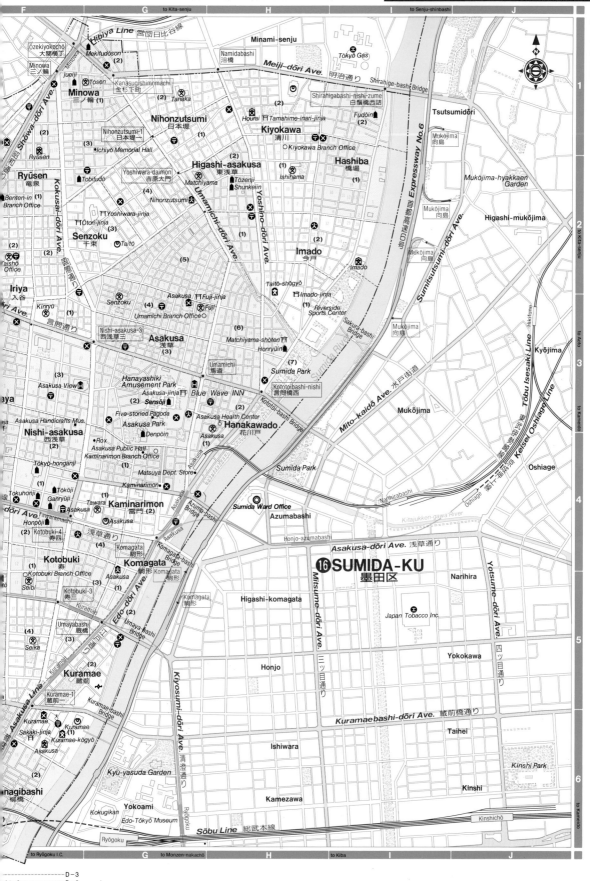

台東区

Hibiya Line 営団日比谷線

Minami-senju

Tōkyō Gas

Namidabashi
泪橋

Meiji-dōri Ave. 明治通り

Shirahige-bashi Bridge

Tsutsumidōri

Ōzekiyokochō
大関横丁

Minowa
三ノ輪

Mekifudōson

Kanasugishimomachi
金杉下町

Shirahigabashi-nishi-zume
白鬚橋西詰

Mukōjima
向島

Jueiji

Tōsen

Tanaka

Fudōin

Mukōjima-hyakkaen
Garden

Minowa
三ノ輪 (1)

Nihonzutsumi
日本堤

Hōrai

Tamahime-inari-jinja

Kiyokawa
清川

Mukōjima
向島

Nihonzutsumi-1
日本堤一 (3)

Ichiyō Memorial Hall

Higashi-asakusa
東浅草

Kiyokawa Branch Office

Hashiba
橋場

Mukōjima
向島

Higashi-mukōjima

Ryūsen
竜泉

Tobifudō

Yoshiwara-daimon
吉原大門

Matchiyama

Tōzenji

Shunkeiin

Ishihama

Benten-in
Branch Office

Yoshiwara-jinja

Nihonzutsumi

Imado
今戸

Sumifitsutsumi-dōri Ave.

Ōtori-jinja

Imado

Senzoku
千束

Taitō

Taitō-shōgyō

Imado-jinja

Mukōjima
向島

Higashi-mukōjima

Taishō
Office

Iriya
入谷

Kinryū

Senzoku

Asakusa

Fuji-jinja

Fuji

Riverside
Sports Center

Mukōjima
向島

Kyōjima

Umamichi Branch Office

Sakura-bashi
Bridge

Nishi-asakusa-3
西浅草三

Matchiyama-shōten

Honryūin

Asakusa
浅草

Umamichi
馬道

Sumida Park

Mukōjima

Asakusa View

Hanayashiki
Amusement Park

Kototoibashi-nishi
言問橋西

Asakusa Handicrafts Mus.

Asakusa-jinja

Blue Wave INN

Sensōji

Nishi-asakusa
西浅草

Five-storied Pagoda

Asakusa Park

Asakusa Health Center

Oshiage

Rox

Denpōin

Asakusa

Hanakawado
花川戸

Narihirabashi

Asakusa Public Hall
Kaminarimon Branch Office

Tokuhonji

Matsuya Dept. Store

Tōkōji

Sumida Park

Kitajukken-gawa River

Ganryūji

Kaminarimon
雷門

Azumabashi

Sumida Ward Office

Honjo-azumabashi

Honpōji

Tawara
田原

Azumabashi

Asakusa-dōri Ave. 浅草通り

Narihira

Kotobuki-4
寿四 (2)

Komagata
駒形

Kotobuki
寿

Asakusa

Komagata
駒形

⑯ SUMIDA-KU
墨田区

Kotobuki Branch Office

Higashi-komagata

Seibi

Kotobuki-3
寿三

Kuramae
蔵前

Komagata
駒形

Japan Tobacco Inc.

Umayabashi
厩橋

Umaya-bashi
Bridge

Mitsume-dōri Ave. 三ツ目通り

Yotsume-dōri Ave. 四ツ通り

Seika

Honjo

Yokokawa

Kuramae
蔵前

Kuramae-1
蔵前一

Kuramae-bashi
Bridge

Kuramae
蔵前

Kuramaebashi-dōri Ave. 蔵前橋通り

Sakaki-jinja

Kuramae-kōgyō

Taihei

Asakusa

Kinshi Park

Yanagibashi
柳橋

Ishiwara

Kamezawa

Kinshi

Kyū-yasuda Garden

Yokoami

Kokugikan

Edo-Tōkyō Museum

Sōbu Line 総武本線

Kinshichō

Ryōgoku

.... D–3
gi 1–2 .... D–2
1–2 .... F–6
.... C–2

墨田区

1:20,000

0 200 400 600m

Ward & area labels

46 KATSUSHIKA-KU 葛飾区

48 EDOGAWA-KU 江戸川区

44 ADACHI-KU 足立区

42 ARAKAWA-KU 荒川区

14 TAITŌ-KU 台東区

Arakawa River
Sumida River
Ayase River

to Aoto
to Kosuge
to Aoto
to Matsudo / to Takenotsuka
to Ueno
to Ueno

Central Circular Line
Keisei Oshiage Line
Keisei Railway
Tōbu Isesaki Line
Hibiya Line
Jōban Line
Route 6
Mito-kaidō Ave.
Meiji-dōri Ave.
Heiwabashi-dōri Ave.
Kanegafuchi-dōri Ave.
Sumida-dōri Ave.
Hikifune-dōri Ave.
Nakaibori-dōri Ave.
San-ya-dōri Ave.
Tsutsumidōri

Place names
Tateishi, Horikiri, Horikiri-shobuen Garden, Yotsugi, Higashi-tateishi, Higashi-yotsugi, Nishi-shinkoiwa, Higashi-sumida, Yahiro, Daiyo-azuma, Kyōjima, Mukōjima, Higashi-mukōjima, Higashi-sumida Playground, Sumida, Sumida Playground, Yotsugibashi Green Park, Kaneboko, Tamonji, Kanegafuchi, Minami-senju, Senju-akebono-chō, Senju-azuma, Senju-sekiya, Senju-sekiya-chō, Senju-nakachō, Yanagihara, Hashiba, Kiyokawa, Imado, Higashi-asakusa, Nikonzutsumi, Senzoku, Ōkawabata, Asahi Breweries, Tōkyō Gas, Met. Aeronautics Coll.

■AREA INDEX■

Azumabashi 1~3 ········· G−5	Honjo 1~4 ········· H−5	Kyōjima 1~3 ········· E−3
Bunka 1~3 ········· F−3	Ishiwara 1~4 ········· H−5	Midori 1~4 ········· I−5
Chitose 1~3 ········· J−5	Kamezawa 1~5 ········· I−5	Mukōjima 1~5 ········· F−4
Higashi-komagata 1~4 ········· G−5	Kikukawa 1~3 ········· J−4	Narihira 1~5 ········· G−4
Higashi-mukōjima 1~6 ········· D−4	Kinshi 1~4 ········· H−3	Oshiage 1~3 ········· F−4
Higashi-sumida 1~3 ········· D−2	Kōtōbashi 1~5 ········· I−3	Ryōgoku 1~4 ········· J−6

Sumida 1~5 ········· B−4	Yokoami 1~2 ·········
Tachibana 1~6 ········· F−1	Yokokawa 1~5 ·········
Taihei 1~4 ········· H−4	
Tatekawa 1~4 ········· J−4	
Tsutsumidōri 1~2 ········· C−5	
Yahiro 1~6 ········· D−3	

江東区

1:35,000

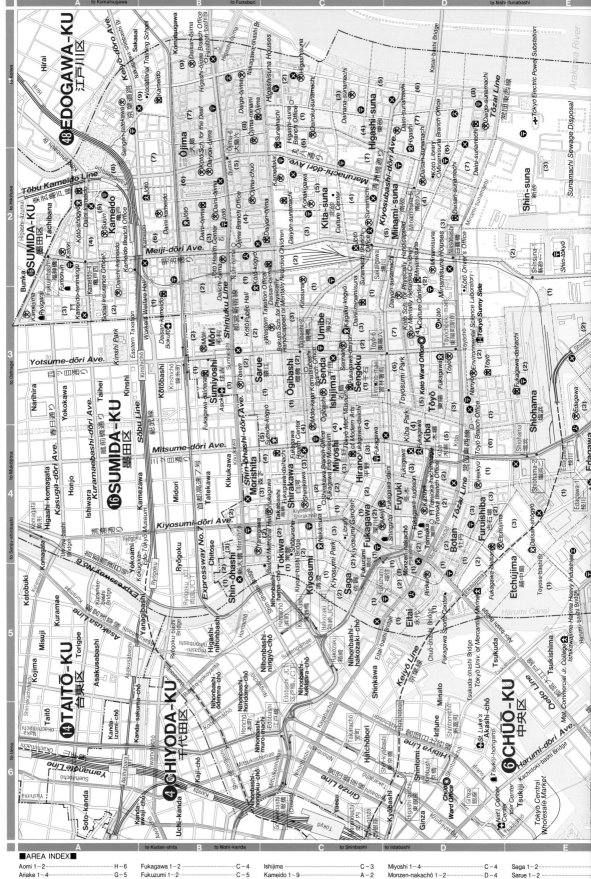

■AREA INDEX■

Aomi 1~2	H-6	Fukagawa 1~2	C-4	Ishijima	C-3	Miyoshi 1~4	C-4	Saga 1~2	C-5
Ariake 1~4	G-5	Fukuzumi 1~2	C-5	Kameido 1~9	A-2	Monzen-nakachō 1~2	D-4	Sarue 1~2
Botan 1~3	D-4	Furuishiba 1~3	D-4	Kiba 1~6	D-4	Mōri 1~3	B-3	Senda
Edagawa 1~3	E-4	Fuyuki	D-4	Kita-suna 1~7	C-2	Morishita 1~5	C-3	Sengoku 1~3
Eitai 1~2	D-5	Higashi-suna 1~8	C-1	Kiyosumi 1~3	C-5	Ōgibashi 1~3	C-4	Shin-kiba 1~4
Etchūjima 1~3	D-5	Hirano 1~4	C-4	Minami-suna 1~7	D-2	Ōjima 1~9	B-2	Shin-ōhashi 1~3

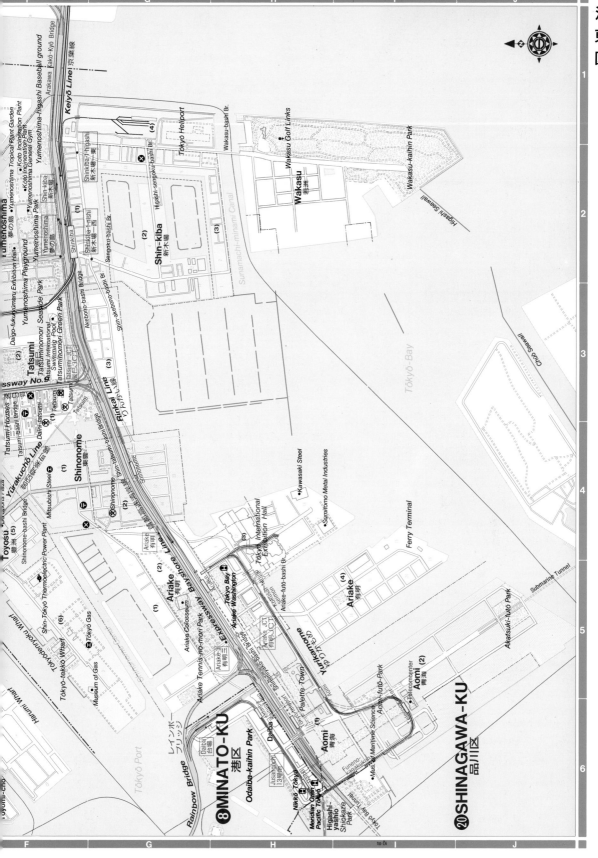

~3	E–2	Takahashi	C–4	Umibe	C–3
1~2	G–4	Tatsumi 1~3	F–3	Wakasu	H–2
~3	E–3	Tokiwa 1~2	D–4	Yumenoshima	F–2
~4	E–3	Tomioka 1~2	D–4		
~4	C–4	Tōyō 1~7	D–3		
~3	B–3	Toyosu 1~6	F–5		

品川区

1:25,000

0　250　500　750m

■AREA INDEX■

Ebara 1~7 ·············· B-4	Higashi-shinagawa 1~5 ·········· G-3	Kita-shinagawa 1~6 ·········· E-2	Nishi-gotanda 1~8 ·········· C-3	Togoshi 1~6 ·········· D-3
Futaba 1~4 ·············· E-5	Higashi-yashio ·············· I-1	Koyama 1~7 ·········· B-4	Nishi-nakanobu 1~3 ·········· C-5	Yashio 1~5 ··········
Hatanodai 1~6 ·············· B-5	Hiratsuka 1~3 ·········· C-4	Koyamadai 1~2 ·········· B-3	Nishi-ōi 1~6 ·········· E-5	Yutaka-chō 1~6 ··········
Higashi-gotanda 1~5 ·········· D-2	Hiro-machi 1~2 ·········· E-4	Minami-ōi 1~6 ·········· F-5	Nishi-shinagawa 1~3 ·········· D-4	
Higashi-nakanobu 1~2 ·········· C-4	Kami-ōsaki 1~4 ·········· C-1	Minami-shinagawa 1~6 ·········· F-3	Ōi 1~7 ·········· E-5	
Higashi-ōi 1~6 ·········· F-4	Katsushima 1~3 ·········· G-5	Nakanobu 1~6 ·········· C-5	Ōsaki 1~5 ·········· D-3	

F | G | H | I | J

to Hamamatsuchō | to Shin-kiba

18 KŌTŌ-KU
江東区

Jūsangōchi
13号地

Daiba

Kōnan-ōhashi Bridge

Ariake

Aomi

Tōkyō Custom House

Shiokaze Park

Aomi-futō Park

Higashi-yashio
東八潮

Funeno-kagakukan

Tōkyō Univ.
of Fisheries

Shinagawa Wharf

Mus. of Maritime Science

Tennōzu-ōhashi
Bridge

Telecomcenter

Daiba

Kōnan

Keihin Canal

Konan-dōri Ave.

Tōkyō Monorail 東京モノレール

Expressway No.1 首都高速1号

(5)

Shinagawafutō-iriguchi
品川埠頭入口

Tennōzu Isle

Shinagawa Thermoelectric Power Plant

Tokyo Bay Tunnel

Tōkyō Port

Shin-tōkai-bashi Bridge

Shin-tōkaibashi
新東海橋

Tennōzu Baseball Ground

Wakashio-bashi Bridge

(2)

Shinagawa
General Hosp.

Higashi-shinagawa-bashi
Bridge

Ōi Thermoelectric
Power Plant

Open-air
Baseball Ground

Daiba

fukuji
ōzenji

(1)

(2)

a-jinja

Ebara-jinja

Higashi-shinagawa-3
東品川三

Library

Jōnan-daini

Higashi-
shinagawa
東品川

Yashio-kita Park

Ōi
大井

Vocational Training School

Ōi JCT
大井JCT

Ōi Wharf

1st Area Center

Shinagawa

Minami-shinagawa-4
南品川四

Tōkai

Ōikito futō
bashi Bridge

Shinagawa

Jōnan

Yashio

Ōi Incineration Plant

Yashio-bashi Bridge

Ōi JCT
大井JCT

Gangyōji

Myōkokuji

Matsushita Electric

(4)

Higashi-shinagawa-4
東品川四

Ōi Wharf

Games Slope

Shinagawa 2nd Area Center

Welfare Center

Aomono
Yokochō
青物横丁

Shinagawa-dera

Kaiunji

(3)

Metropolitan Technical Coll.
Samezu-kōgyo

Shinagawa Etoile
Girl's

Kaiunji

Minami-
shinagawa-3
南品川三

Yashio-kita
八潮

Ōi-minami
大井南

(2)

Tonan

Automobile Taxation Office

Thames-sakaue

(1)

Examination Room of Driver Licence

Expressway Bayshore Line 首都高速湾岸線

minkaikan Hall

(4)

Tachiai

Yashio
八潮

Yashio
八潮

Shinagawa

Yashio

Bayshore
Green Park

(5)

Higashi-ōi
東大井

Samezu-bashi Bridge

Yashio Area Center

Dalei Store

Yashio Park Town

Route 357 国道357号

Minatogaoka-futō Park

Raifukuji

Samehama

Yashio-minami

(3)

Toshiba

(1)

Yashio-minami

Ōi-chūō Tikkyō

Customhouse Branch Office

Hamakawa

Chūō-kaihinkōen-mae
中央海浜公園前

Hamakawa

Katsushima
勝島

Katsushima-bashi Bridge

Sports Park

Minami-ōi
南大井

(5)

Ōi-minami
大井南

Tōkai

1st Area Center

Ward Park

(2)

(5)

Suzugamori
鈴ヶ森

Suzugamori

Katsushima
勝島

**Ōi Wharf Central
Marine Park**

Ōi-minami
大井南

Hamakawa-jinja
鈴ヶ森

Daikyōji

Ōi Race Course

Ōi-minami-rikkyō
大井南陸橋

Minami-ōi
南大井

Suzugamori
鈴ヶ森

Katsushima-2
勝島二

Tōkyō Freight Terminal

Suzugamori
鈴ヶ森

Minami-ōi-3
南大井三

Tōkai

(6)

(3)

Shin-heiwa-bashi Bridge

Tōkai Playground

Seiyū Store

Shinagawa Aquarium

Keihin Truck Terminal

Kannana-ōifutō
環七大井埠頭

Ōmori-honchō

Heiwajima

Ōta Wholesale Market

Jōnanjima

Ōmori-kita

F | G | H | I | J

to Yokohama | to Yokohama | to Haneda | to Haneda

1:22,000

目黒区

■AREA INDEX■

Aobadai 1~4 ········ B-4	Himon-ya 1~6 ········ G-3	Meguro-honchō 1~6 ········ F-2	Nakane 1~2 ········ H-4	Takaban 1~3 ········ H-4
Chūō-chō 1~2 ········ E-3	Jiyūgaoka 1~3 ········ I-5	Midorigaoka 1~3 ········ I-4	Ōhashi 1~2 ········ B-5	Yakumo 1~5 ········ H-4
Gohongi 1~3 ········ E-4	Kakinokizaka 1~3 ········ G-5	Minami 1~3 ········ H-3	Ōokayama 1~2 ········ I-3	Yūtenji 1~2 ········ F-3
Hara-machi 1~2 ········ G-2	Kami-meguro 1~5 ········ C-3	Mita 1~2 ········ C-2	Senzoku 1~2 ········ H-2	
Higashigaoka 1~2 ········ G-6	Komaba 1~4 ········ A-5	Naka-chō 1~2 ········ E-3	Shimo-meguro 1~6 ········ E-2	
Higashiyama 1~3 ········ C-4	Meguro 1~4 ········ D-2	Naka-meguro 1~5 ········ D-2	Taira-machi 1~2 ········ H-4	

目黒区

F G H I J

Hoshi

㉒SHINAGAWA-KU 品川区

Nakahara-kaidō Ave. 中原街道

Ebara

Nishi-nakanobu

Meguro-honchō 5

Koyama

目黒本町五

Shōwa

Musashi-koyama

Hatanodai

Kamiikedai

Nakahara

1

Meguro-honchō 目黒本町 (5)

Koyama

Nishi-koyama

Koyama-7 小山七

Minami-senzoku

Higashi-yukigaya

(6)

Mukaihara

Hara-machi 原町

Senzoku 洗足

Kita-senzoku

Senzokuike Park

Senzoku-ike Pond

2

Gekkōhara

Daikei

Kita-senzoku

Tokyo Institute of Technology

㉔ŌTA-KU 大田区

Ishibumi

Haramachikōban-mae 原町交番前

Tōkyū Ōimachi Line

Kita-senzoku

Ishikawa-machi

Dainana

En-yūji

Meguro-seibi-gakuen

Senzoku-gakuen-daiichi

Senzoku-gakuen-daiichi

Haratachi

Minami 南

Salesio Church

Tōkyū

3

Daiei Store

Tokiwamatsu-gakuen

Uganda

Himon-ya-hachimangū

Kannana-dōri Ave. 環七通り

Ōkayama 大岡山

Ōkayamachō-mae 大岡山町

Ōokayama

Daiichi

Himon-ya Health Center

Welfare Center

Himon-ya 碑文谷

Dafeichi

Ōokayama

Midorigaoka

Kazakhstan

Kakinokizakanikyo 柿ノ木坂教会

Taira-machi 平町

Nakane 中根

Midorigaoka- 緑が丘

4

Himon-ya Park

Nakane 中根

Midorigaoka 緑が丘

Okusawa

Komazawa-rikkyō 駒沢聖教

Ōtsusdaigaku

Tokyo Tōyoko Line

Nakane

Tōkyū Store

Nakane

Nozawa 野沢

Kakinokizaka 柿の木坂

Tōritsudai-zaka 都立大坂

Site of Tokyo

Metropolitan Univ.

Tōritsudaigakueki-mae 都立大学駅前

Yakumo

Nakane 中根

Jiyūgaoka 自由が丘

5

Higashigaoka 東が丘

Joenji

Tokyo Metropolitan

Yakumo 八雲

Hikawa-jinja 氷川神社

Yakumo

Yakumo-gakuen

Jiyugaoka-gakuen

Jiyū-dōri Ave. 自由通り

Nakane

Miyamae

Kenya

Jiyugaoka-gakuen

Jōshinji

Higashigaoka

Komazawa-dōri Ave. 駒沢通り

North Tokyo

Medical Service Center

Daiu

Hokuritsubyōin-mae 都立病院前

Komazawa

Sports Stadium

Komazawa Olympic Park

Jiyū-dōri Ave.

Sanma

Kunihonbutsu

Komazawa-kōen

Fukasawa

Todoroki

Tōkyū Ōimachi Line 東急大井町線

Ōyamadai

6

0   500   1000m

to Shibuya · to Meguro · to Gotanda · to Gotanda

㉒ MEGURO-KU 目黒区

㉖ SETAGAYA-KU 世田谷区

NAKAHARA-KU 中原区

KŌHOKU-KU 港北区

KANAGAWA KAWASAKI-SHI 川崎市

SAIWAI-KU 幸区

to Yōga · to Futakotamagawa · to Noborito · to Yokohama · to Hiyoshi · to Shin-yokohama

to Yokohama · to Kawasaki · to Yokohama · to Kawasaki

■AREA INDEX■

Chidori 1–3	D–4	
Chūō 1–8	E–2	
Den-enchōfu 1–5	B–2	
Den-enchōfu-honchō	B–3	
Den-enchōfu-minami	B–3	
Haginaka 1–3	F–5	
Haneda 1–6	G–6	
Haneda-asahi-cho	G–5	
Haneda-kūkō 1–3	H–5	
Heiwajima 1–6	G–3	
Heiwanomori-Kōen	F–5	
Higashi-kamata 1–2	F–5	
Higashi-kōjiya 1–6	G–5	
Higashi-magome 1–2	E–2	
Higashi-mine-machi	C–3	
Higashi-rokugō 1–3	E–5	
Higashi-yaguchi 1–3	D–4	
Higashi-yukigaya 1–5	C–2	
Hon-haneda 1–3	F–6	
Ikegami 1–8	D–4	
Jōnanjima 1·2·4–6	I–3	
Kamata 1–4	E–4	
Kamata-honchō 1–2	E–5	
Kamiikedai 1–5	C–1	
Keihinjima 1–3		
Kita-kōjiya 1–3		
Kita-magome 1–2		
Kita-mine-machi 1–3		
Kita-senzoku		

大田区

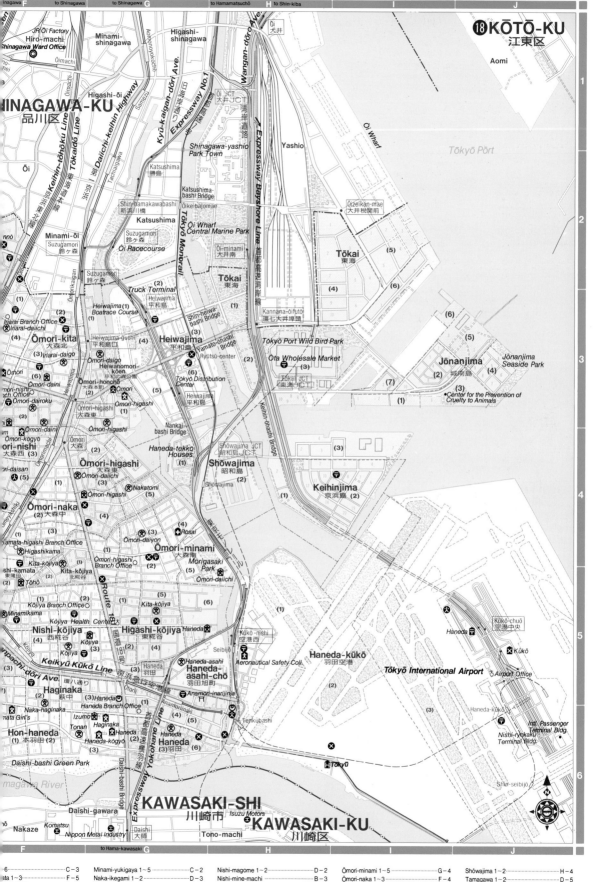

…6	C–3	
…ata 1~3	F–5	
…hara 1~2	C–1	
…ome 1~6	E–3	
…roku 1~3	E–6	
Minami-yukigaya 1~5	C–2	
Naka-ikegami 1~2	D–3	
Naka-magome 1~3	D–2	
Naka-rokugō 1~4	E–5	
Nishi-kamata 1~8	E–4	
Nishi-kōjiya 1~4	F–5	
Nishi-magome 1~2	D–2	
Nishi-mine-machi	B–3	
Nishi-rokugō 1~4	D–6	
Ōmori-higashi 1~5	G–4	
Ōmori-honchō 1~2	F–3	
Ōmori-kita 1~6	F–3	
Ōmori-minami 1~5	G–4	
Ōmori-naka 1~3	F–4	
Ōmori-nishi 1~7	F–3	
Sannō 1~4	F–3	
Shimomaruko 1~4	E–5	
Shin-kamata 1~3	E–5	
Shōwajima 1~2	H–4	
Tamagawa 1~2	D–5	
Tōkai 1~6	H–3	
Unoki 1~3	B–3	
Yaguchi 1~3	C–4	
Yukigaya-Ōtsuka-machi	B–2	

世田谷区

1 : 38,000

0　500　1000m

到 ② SUGINAMI-KU 杉並区

⑤② MITAKA-SHI 三鷹市

⑤② MITAKA-SHI 三鷹市

⑥⑥ CHŌFU-SHI 調布市

⑥⑥ KOMAE-SHI 狛江市

KANAG

Wadabori Park
Ōmiya
Izumi
Takachiho Univ. of Commerce
Ogikubo
Narita-nishi
Nishiogi-minami
Miyamae
Itsukaichi-kaidō Ave. 五日市街道
Inokashira-dōri Ave. 井の頭通り
Shōan
京王井の頭線
Nishi-eifuku
Eifukuchō
Eifuku
Matsub
Meiji
Hamadayama
Hamadayama
Keiō Inokashira Line
Takaido-nishi
Takaido-higashi
Shimo-takaido 下高井戸
Shimotakaidoeki-Iriguchi 下高井戸駅入口
Nikaidō attached to Japan Women's Col. of Physical Education
Mats
Takaido
Kugayama
Fujimigaoka
Mitakadai
Kami-takaido
Chūō Expressway 中央自動車道
Takaido I.C. 高井戸IC
Kami-takaido 上高井戸
Takaido 高井戸
Expressway No.4 首都高速4号
京王線 Keiō Line
Sakurajōsui
Matsuzawa
Matsuzawa Branch Office
Matsubara
Nihon Univ. (Hum. & Sci.)
Matsubara
Akatsutsumi 赤堤
Nichidai-sakuragaoka
Midorigaoka
Sakurajōsui 桜上水
Akatsutsumi
Kyōdō
Inokashira
Kami-kitazawa
Kami-kitazawa
Kami-kitazawa Branch Office
Kami-kitazawa 上北沢
Hachiman-yama 八幡山
Hachiman-yama
Kibōgaoka
Odakyū OX Store
Keisen-jogakuen
Kyōdō
Kyōdō 経堂
Kita-karasuyama 北烏山
Musashigaoka
Kōgen-in
Karasuyama-kita
Minami-karasuyama 南烏山
Karasuyama
Roka
Roka
Kasuya 粕谷
Roka Park
Roka-kōshun-en
Chitosedai 千歳台
Kibōgaoka
Daitō-gakuen
Funabashi
Funabashi 船橋
Funabashi Branch Office
Chitosegaoka
Chitose
Chitosedai
Chitose
Kōen-in
Karasuyama Hosp. attached to Shōwa Univ.
Karasuyama Branch Office
Karasuyama Sōgō Branch Office
Kōsei-gakuen Girls'
Kyūden 給田
Kyūden
Kyūden
Midorigaoka
Shirayuri Women's
Kitano
Kitano
Aoyama Gakuin
Chitose
Tsukado
Seijō
Kanpachi-funabashi 環八船橋
Sakuragaoka
Sakuragaoka
Tōkyō
Chitosedai 千歳台
Tōkyō Univ. of Agricul
Sakuragaoka 桜丘
Kami-soshigaya 上祖師谷
Kami-soshigaya
Kami-soshigaya Branch Office
Shinkawa
Sengawa-chō
Shiseikai 2nd
Soshigaya 祖師谷
Yamano
Sasahara
Kanto Yōga
Ka
Nakahara
Tōhō Gakuen Sch. of Music
Setagaya-kōgyō
Soshigaya
Soshigaya Branch Office
Kinuta-2
Kinuta
Kinuta 砧
Wakaba-chō
Seijō
Seijō-gakuen
Seijō-gakuen
Kanpachi-setagaya-dōri
Kanpachi-setagaya-dōri 環八世田谷通
Incineration Plant
NHKgiken-mae NHK 技研前
Nishi-tsutsujigaoka
Higashi-tsutsujigaoka
Irima-chō
Seijō
Seijō-gakuen
Seijō Branch Office
Kinuta Sōgō Branch Office
NHK Science & Technical Research Laboratories
Kinuta Branch Office
Meguro-seibi-gakuen
Kinuta 砧
Kinuta Park
Kiunji
Tōkyō Media City
Nihon Univ. (Comm.)
Nat'l Ōkura
Welfare Pension Sports Center
Art Gallery
Kikunodai
Seijō 成城
Seijō
Seijō Ogikurimae
Kinuta
Meisei
Musashi Institute of Technology
Toyoko-gakuen
Kagakugijutsu-gakuen
Toyoko Kinuta
Ōkura 大蔵
Okamoto 岡本
Seikadō Librar
St. Domini
Nishi-nogawa
Higashi-nogawa
Kunimoto-soshigaen
Kunimoto-soshigaen
Kitami 喜多見
Kitami Branch Office
Tenjinmori-bashi 天神森橋
Kinuta-minami
Kinuta-minami
Kokuryō-chō
Izumi-honchō
Iwado-kita
Iwado-minami
Kitami
Unane 宇奈根
Eianji
Seikadō
Komae City Office
Naka-izumi
Nishi-izumi
Higashi-izumi
Kitami
Kinuta-minami
Futako-tama
Komazawa Univ. Tamagawa College
Moto-izumi
Inogata
Komai-machi
Kinuta-kami Purification Plant
Kinuta-kami Purification Plant

to Yahara
to Kichijōji
to Chōfu
to Noborito

■AREA INDEX■

Akatsutsumi 1~5	E-2	Hanegi 1~2	J-6	Kami-yōga 1~6	E-4	Komazawa-kōen	
Chitosedai 1~6	D-4	Higashi-tamagawa 1~2	J-6	Kasuya 1~4	C-3	Kyōdō 1~5	
Daita 1~6	F-2	Ikejiri 1~4	H-2	Kinuta 1~8	D-4	Kyūden 1~5	
Daizawa 1~6	G-2	Kamata 1~4		Kinuta-kōen	E-5	Matsubara 1~5	
Fukasawa 1~8	G-5	Kami-kitazawa 1~5	D-2	Kita-karasuyama 1~9	A-2	Minami-karasuyama 1~6	
Funabashi 1~7	D-3	Kami-noge 1~4		Kitami 1~9	D-5	Mishuku 1~2	
Gōtokuji 1~2	F-3	Kami-soshigaya 1~7	B-4	Kitazawa 1~5	G-1	Miyasaka 1~3	
Hachiman-yama 1~3	C-3	Kami-uma 1~5	G-3	Komazawa 1~5	G-4	Naka-machi 1~5	

Komazawa-kōen
Kyōdō 1~5
Kyūden 1~5
Matsubara 1~5
Minami-karasuyama 1~6
Mishuku 1~2
Miyasaka 1~3
Naka-machi 1~5

G−6	Sakura-shinmachi 1−2	F−4
H−3	Sakuragaoka 1−5	E−4
F−1	Sakurajōsui 1−5	D−3
E−5	Sangenjaya 1−2	H−3
D−5	Seijō 1−9	C−5
H−6	Seta 1−5	F−5
F−4	Setagaya 1−4	G−3
	Shimo-uma 1−6	H−3

Shin-machi 1−3	G−4	Tsurumaki 1−5	H−4
Soshigaya 1−5	C−4	Umegaoka 1−3	F−3
Taishidō 1−5	G−2	Unane 1−3	D−6
Tamagawa 1−4	F−6	Wakabayashi 1−5	G−3
Tamagawa-den-enchōfu 1−2	I−6	Yōga 1−4	H−5
Tamagawadai 1	H−6		
Tamazutsumi 1−2	H−6		
Todoroki 1−8	H−5		

渋谷区

1:20,000

■AREA INDEX■

Daikan-yama-chō············ H–6	Hatagaya 1~3··············· B–4	Jinnan 1~2··············· F–4	Ōyama-chō··············· C–5	Shinsen-chō
Dōgenzaka 1~2············· F–5	Hatsudai 1~2··············· C–3	Kamiyama-chō··········· E–5	Sakuragaoka-chō········ G–5	Shōtō 1~2
Ebisu 1~4················· J–6	Higashi 1~4················ H–5	Maruyama-chō·········· F–5	Sarugaku-chō············ G–6	Tomigaya 1~3
Ebisu-minami 1~3········· I–6	Hiroo 1~5·················· I–5	Motoyoyogi-chō·········· D–4	Sasazuka 1~3··········· A–5	Udagawa-chō
Ebisu-nishi 1~2··········· H–6	Hon-machi 1~6············· B–3	Nanpeidai-chō··········· G–6	Sendagaya 1~6·········· F–2	Uehara 1~3
Hachiyama-chō············ G–6	Jingūmae 1~6·············· G–3	Nishihara 1~3··········· C–4	Shibuya 1~4············· G–4	Uguisudani-chō

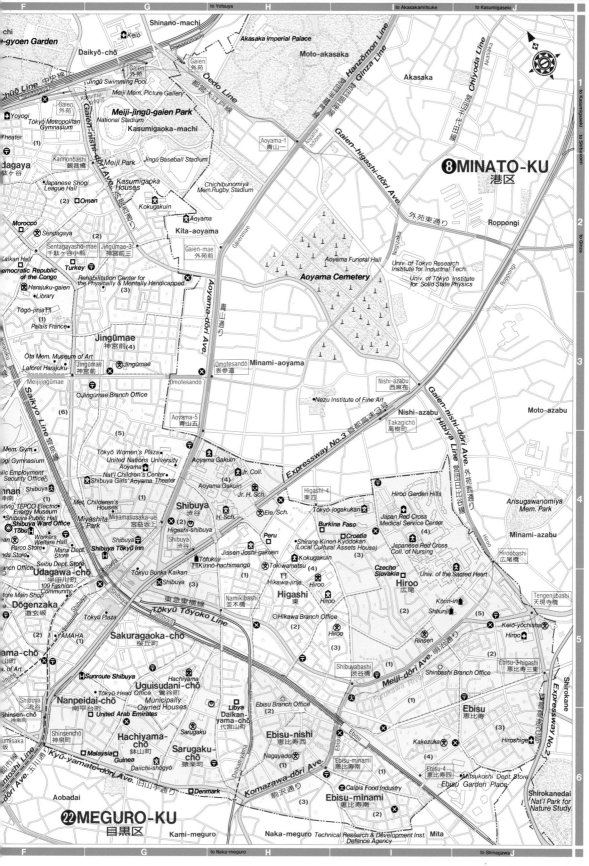

中野区

1:22,000

0　250　500　750m

to Ikebukuro

to Ikebukuro

TOSHIMA-KU 豊島区

NERIMA-KU 練馬区 ③⑧

Yūrakuchō Line

Seibu Yūrakuchō Line

Seibu Ikebukuro Line

Ōedo Line

Dōedo Line

Seibu Toshima Line

Mejiro-dōri Ave.

Senkawa-dōri Ave.

Kannana-dōri Ave.

Nakasugi-dōri Ave.

Shin-ōme-kaidō Ave.

Senkawa-dōri Ave.

Waseda-dōri Ave.

Seibu Shinjuku Line

Nerima Ward Office

Toshimaen (Amusement Park)

Nihon Univ. (Art)

Sakuradai

Hazawa

Kotake-chō

Sakae-chō

Asahigaoka

Ekoda

Ehara-chō 江原町

Egota United Houses

Ebaracho 江原町

Rengeji

Matsugaoka 松が丘

Tetsugakudō Park

Egota Park

Kita-egota

Musashino-kōen

Egota 江古田

Historical Folklore Collection

Dainana

Hikawa-jinja

Nakano-Kita Health Center

Numabukuro 沼袋

Numabukuro Area Center

Heiwanomori Park

Nogata 野方

Nakano-Kōgyō

Toyotama-kami

Toyotama-kita

Toyotama-naka

Toyotama-minami

Maruyama 丸山

Maruyama-rikkyo 丸山陸橋

Wakamiya 若宮

Yamato-chō 大和町

Nakamura-kita

Nakamura

Nakamura-minami

Nogata Area Center

Nerima

Nukui

Kōyama

Fujimidai

Hachinari Park

Kami-saginomiya 上鷺宮

Saginomiya 鷺宮

Shirasagi 白鷺

Saginomiya Houses

Saginomiya-nishi Houses

Saginomiya-dainana Houses

Saginomiya Area Center

Health Clinic

Center for the aged

Daihachi

Senzōin

Toritsukasei

Musashigaoka

Kita-nakadō

Nakamurabashi

Nishi-nakano

Shimo-igusa

Igusa

Fujimidai

to Kami-igusa

to Hōya

to Tanashi

to Tanashi

to Zenpukuji

to Asagaya

■AREA INDEX■

Arai 1~5	E-3	Kami-saginomiya 1~5	A-5	Nogata 1~6	D-4	Yayoi-chō 1~6	I-4
Chūō 1~5	H-3	Kamitakada 1~5	F-2	Numabukuro 1~4	D-3		
Egota 1~4	D-2	Maruyama 1~2	D-4	Saginomiya 1~6	B-5		
Ehara-chō 1~3	D-1	Matsugaoka 1~2	E-2	Shirasagi 1~3	C-6		
Higashi-nakano 1~5	H-2	Minamidai 1~5	J-5	Wakamiya 1~3	D-5		
Hon-chō 1~6	I-4	Nakano 1~6	G-3	Yamato-chō 1~4	E-5		

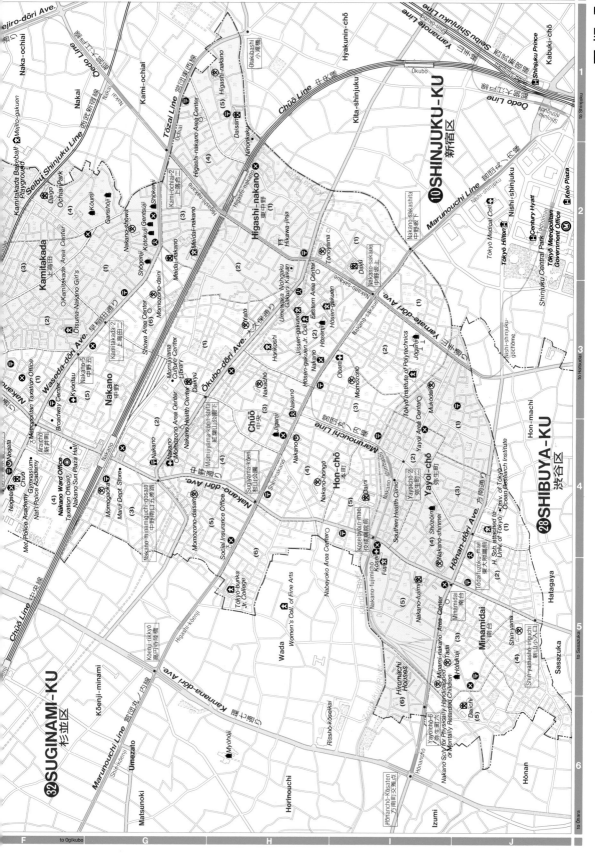

中野区

F to Kanamechō to Edogawabashi to Takadanobaba G to Takadanobaba H to Takadanobaba J

Mejiro-dōri Ave.

Naka-ochiai

Nakai

Kami-ochiai

Meijiro-gakuen

Seibu Shinjuku Line

Kamitakada Baseball Playground

Daigo

Ochiai Park

Kourii

Ganshōji

Shōkenji

Shōgenji

Kōtokuji Gentsūji

Kami-ochiai-2

Ochiai

Higashi-nakano Area Center

Daisan

Nihonkaku

Chūō Line

Kita-shinjuku

Ōkubo

Hyakunin-chō

Otakibashi

Higashi-nakano

Hikawa-jinja

SHINJUKU-KU
新宿区

Yamanote Line

Seibu Shinjuku Line

Shin Shinjuku Line

Ōedo Line

Shinjuku Prince

Kabuki-chō

to Shinjuku

Keiō Plaza

Nishi-shinjuku

Century Hyatt

Tōkyō Medical Coll.

Tōkyō Hilton

Shinjuku Central Park

Tōkyō Metropolitan Government Office

Nishi-shinjuku-gochōme

to Hatsudai

Kamitakada

Ōkamitakada Area Center

Ōtsuma-Nakano Girl's

Showa Area Center

Momozono-dai

Dakyu

Daiku

Kyōdai

Broadway Center

Nakano-shōwa

Momiyama Culture Center Library

Momozono Area Center

Nakano Health Center

Nogata

Chūō

Araiichi

Met Police Academy

Nakano Ward Office

Taxation Office

Gymnasium

Nat'l Police Academy

Nakano Sun Plaza Hall

Momogaoka

Marui Dept. Stores

Nakano-minamiguchi-gosato

Nakano

Waseda-dōri Ave.

Metropolitan Taxation Office

Kamitakada-2

Sugiyama-kōen

Horikoshi

Nakano

Nakano

Chūō

Jiganji

Nakano-koen

Shin-nakano

Marunouchi Line

Umeyama Nongaku

Eastern Area Center

Hōsen-gakuen Jr. Coll.

Jissen-gakuen Gakuin Kaikan

Nakano

Hōsenji

Obari

Momozono

Nakano-sakaue

Nakano-sakaue

Nakano-dōri Ave.

Yamate-dōri Ave.

Tōyama

Dairō

Tōkyō Institute of Polytechnics

Jōgakuin

Mukōdai

Hon-chō

Nakano-hongo

Yayoi Area Center

Yayoichō-2

Yayoi-chō

Shōzōin

SHIBUYA-KU
渋谷区

Hon-machi

Southern Health Clinic

Kōsetyoun-mae

Kōsetsu

Hōnan-dōri Ave.

Univ. of Tokyo Ocean Research Institute

H. Sch. attached to Univ. of Tokyo

Tōdaifuzoku-mae

Hōdaifuzoku-mae

Nakano-shimmei

Nakano-fujimi-mae

Nakano-fujimi-mae

Minamidai

Minamidai

Shinyama

Shin-yamashō-iriguchi

Hatagaya

Sasazuka

to Sasazuka

Nogata

Chūō Line

Chūō Line

SUGINAMI-KU
杉並区

Kōenji-minami

Umezato

Matsunoki

Shin-Kōenji

Koenji-rikkyo

Higashi-Kōenji

Marunouchi Line

Social Insurance Office

Tōkyō-bunka Jr. College

Women's Coll. of Fine Arts

Wada

Kanana-dōri Ave.

Myōhōji

Atsushō-kōseikai

Nakano-minamiguchi-gosau

Nabeyoko Area Center

Nakano Area Center

Minami-nakano Area Center

Tada

Hokutoii

Hiromachi Houses

Hōhanchō-Kōsaten

Yayoichō-6

Honanchō

Horinouchi

Izumi

Honan

Daiichi

Shin-yamashō-iriguchi

to Ōnara

F to Ogikubo G to Ogikubo H I J

杉並区

1:30,000

500 1000m

to Tanashi

| | A | B | C | D |

㊳NERIMA-KU 練馬区

Musashi-seki
Seibu Shinjuku Line 西武新宿線
Kami-shakujii
Kami-shakujii
Shimo-shakujii
Sekimachi-kita
Sekimachi-higashi
Ōme-kaidō Ave. 青梅街道
Kami-igusa
Igusa 井草
Hachinarishō-mae 八成小前
Ikuei College
Hachinari
Iogi
Shimo-igusa Branch Office
Mitsui Taiyo K
Sekimachi-minami
Kami-shakujii-minamichō
Kami-igusa Ground
Kami-igusa 上井草
Momoi-daigo
Shim
Tateno-chō
Zenpukuji 善福寺
Igusa
Shinomiya
Iogi
Shimizu-3 清水三
Nakase
Zenpukuji
Momoi-daiyon
Igusa-hachimangū
Mitsuya
Suginami-kōgyō
Nōgei (Agricu Iture)
Kansenji
Myōshōji Park
Shimizu 清水
Shimizu
Myōshōji
Seikei
Zenpukuji Park
Zenpukuji 善福寺
Imagawa 今川
Chūō-suginami Health Center
Kami-igusa Branch Office
Branch Office of Regional Legal Affairs Bureau
Hon-a
Kichijōji-kita-machi
Seikei
Ogikubo
Momoi-4 桃井四
Iogi
Nissan Motor
Momoi 桃井
Ogikubo
Momoi-daiichi
Seitōnakadōri Branch Office
Aman
Tōkyō Women's Christian
Ogikubo
Ogikubo-hachiman
Kami-ogikubo Branch Office
Ogikubo Taxation Office
Amanuma
Wakasugi
Tōkyō Adventist
㊷MUSASHINO-SHI 武蔵野市
Joshidai-dōri Ave. 女子大通
Jizōzaka 地蔵坂
Kamiogi 上荻
Shimendō 四面道
Suginami Public Hall
Kichijōji-honchō
Kichijōji-higashi-chō
Nishiogi-kita 西荻北
Momoi-daisan
Town Seven
Ogikubo
Chūō Line 中央線
Ogikubo
Goten-yama
Kichijōji
Nishiogikubo
Minami-ogikubo 南荻窪
Ogikubo
Momoi-daini
Nishi He (Under I)
Natural Culture Park
Inokashira Park
Kichijōji-minami-chō
Shōanshō-mae 松庵小前
Nishiogi-minami 西荻南
Shinmei
Ogikubo Branch Office
Ogikubo-2 荻窪二
Ogikub
Shōan
Shōan-1 松庵一
Shōan 松庵
Shōan-2 松庵二
Takaido-daiyon
Ogikubo
Shōke
Miyamae-5 宮前五
Miyamae 宮前
Inokashira Park
Rikkyō-jogakuin
Itsukaichi-kaidō Ave. 五日市街道
Miyamae Branch Office
Nishimiya
Miyamae
Kasuga-jinja-mae 春日神社前
Kanpachi-shinmeidōri 環八神明通り
Tōkyō Women's Christian
Inokashira
Mitakadai
Keio Inokashira Line 京王井の頭線
Takaido-daini
Nishi 西
Miyamae-4 宮前四
Takaido
Kanpachi-itsukaichi 環八五日市
Kugayama 久我山
Takaido-daini
Yamazaki
Kanpachi-inokashira 環八井の頭
Mure
Hitomi-kaidō Ave. 人見街道
Fujimigaokaeki-iriguchi 富士見ヶ丘駅入口
Kugayama
Takaido-nishi 高井戸西
㊷MITAKA-SHI 三鷹市
Kugayama attached to Kokugakuin Univ.
Iwatsu Electric
Fujimigaoka
Takaido Branch Office
Takaido
Takaido Ward Center
Suginami Incinera
Kitano
Kugayama Sch. for the blind
Kugayama
NHK Ground
Yokufūkai
Yokufuen
Takaido I.C 高井戸I.C
Takaido-higashi 高井戸東
Takaido-hi
Shinkawa
Fujimigaoka
Fujimigaoka
Kami-takaido 上高井戸
Takaido 高井戸
Sakura
Tsuku
Kita-karasuyama
Japan Women's Coll. of Physical Education
Chūō Expressway 中央自動車道
㉖SETAGAYA-KU 世田谷区
Kōshū-kaidō Ave. 甲州街道
Kami-kitazawa
Mitaka Tollgate
Kyūden
Minami-karasuyama
Kami-takaido-1 上高井戸一
Hachiyama
Shimo-taka
㊳CHŌFU-SHI 調布市
Rokaōen
to Chōfu
to Yōga

■AREA INDEX■

Amanuma 1–3 .... E–3	Hōnan 1–2 .... I–6	Kami-takaido 1–3 .... D–6
Asagaya-kita 1–6 .... G–3	Horinouchi 1–3 .... H–4	Kamiogi 1–4 .... D–3
Asagaya-minami 1–3 .... G–3	Igusa 1–5 .... E–1	Kami-igusa 1–4 .... D–1
Eifuku 1–4 .... G–6	Imagawa 1–4 .... D–2	Kōenji-kita 1–4 .... H–3
Hamadayama 1–4 .... F–5	Izumi 1–4 .... H–6	Kōenji-minami 1–5 .... H–3
Hon-amanuma 1–3 .... E–2	Kami-igusa 1–4 .... D–1	Kugayama 1–5 .... C–5

Matsunoki 1–3 .... G–4		
Minami-ogikubo 1–4 .... D–3	Nishiogi-minami 1–4 .... D–4	
Miyamae 1–5 .... D–4	Ogikubo 1–5 .... D–3	
Momoi 1–4 .... D–2	Ōmiya 1–2	
Narita-higashi 1–5 .... F–4	Shimizu 1–3	
Narita-nishi 1–4 .... F–4	Shimo-igusa 1–5	
Nishiogi-kita 1–5	Shimo-takaido 1–5	

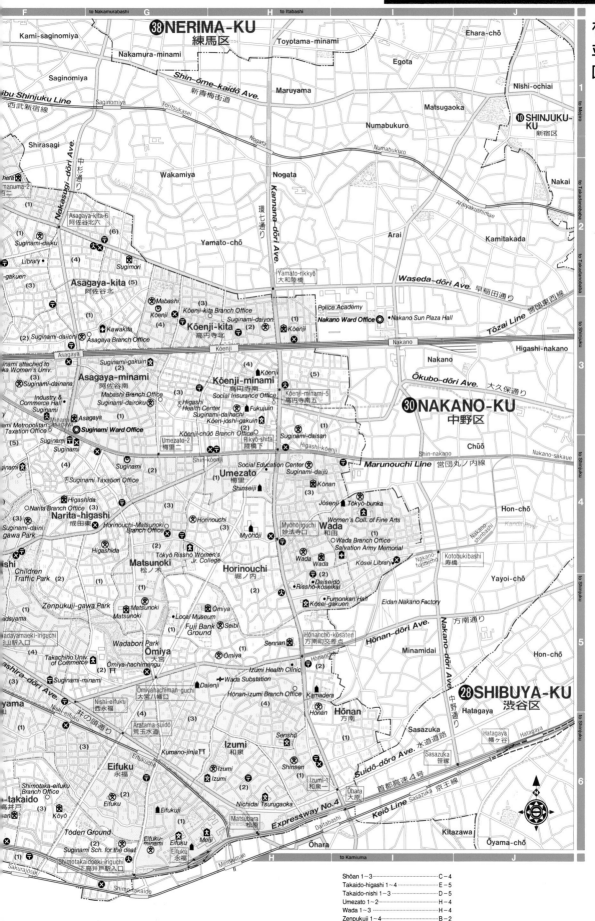

Shōan 1～3 ·················· C-4
Takaido-higashi 1～4 ········ E-5
Takaido-nishi 1～3 ········· D-5
Umezato 1～2 ·············· H-4
Wada 1～3 ················· H-4
Zenpukuji 1～4 ············· B-2

豊島区

1:20,000

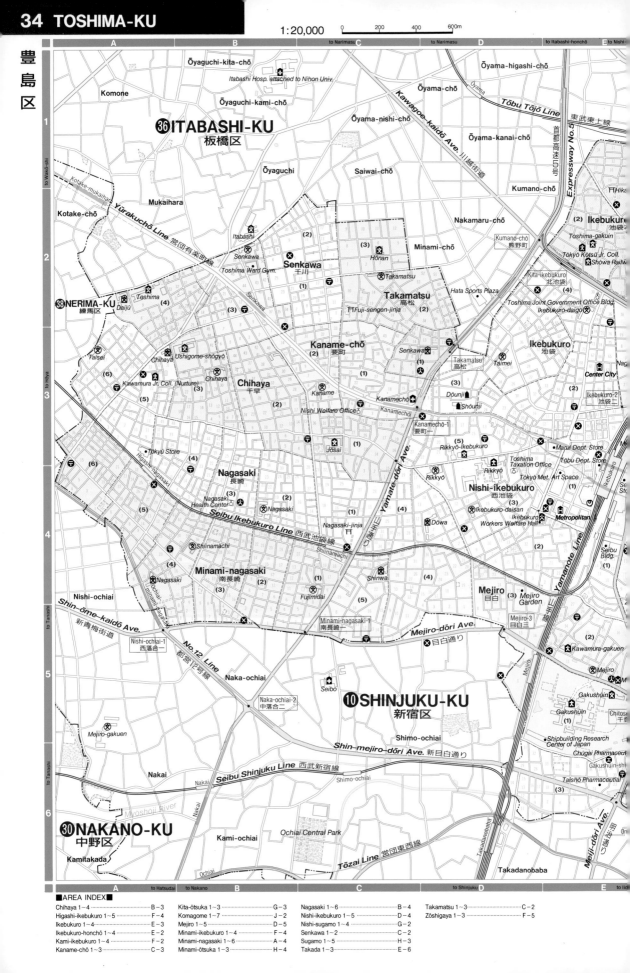

Komone

Ōyaguchi-kita-chō

Itabashi Hosp. attached to Nihon Univ.

Ōyama-higashi-chō

Ōyaguchi-kami-chō

Ōyama-chō

Tōbu Tōjō Line 東武東上線

㊱ ITABASHI-KU
板橋区

Ōyama-nishi-chō

Kotake-mukaihara

Yūrakuchō Line 営団有楽町線

Mukaihara

Ōyaguchi

Saiwai-chō

Ōyama-kanai-chō

Nakamaru-chō

Kumano-chō

Kotake-chō

Itabashi

Senkawa

Kumano-chō
熊野町

Ikebukuro
池袋

Toshima-gakuin

Toshima Ward Gym.

Senkawa
千川

(2)

Hōnan

Minami-chō

Tōkyō Kōtsū Jr. Coll.

Shōwa Railw

Kita-ikebukuro
北池袋

Toshima

Daijū

(3)

Takamatsu

Hata Sports Plaza

Toshima Joint Government Office Bldg.
Ikebukuro-daigo

㊳ NERIMA-KU
練馬区

Chihaya

Ushigome-shōgyō

Takamatsu
高松

Kaname-chō
要町

Senkawa

Ikebukuro
池袋

Taisei

Kawamura Jr. Coll. (Nurture)

Chihaya
千早

Chihaya

(2)

Takamatsu
高松

Taimei

Center City

Ikebukuro-2
池袋二

Higashi-nagasaki

Kaname

Dōunji

Shōunji

Nishi Welfare Office

Kanamechō

Kanamechō-1
要町一

Rikkyō-ikebukuro

Marui Dept. Store

Tōkyū Store

Jōsai

(1)

Toshima
Taxation Office

Tōbu Dept. Store

Tōkyō Met. Art Space

Nagasaki
長崎

Rikkyō

Rikkyō

Nishi-ikebukuro
西池袋

Nagasaki
Health Center

Nagasaki

Ikebukuro-daisan

Metropolitan

Shiinamachi

Nagasaki-jinja

Dōwa

Ikebukuro
Workers Welfare Hall

Seibu
Bldg.

Minami-nagasaki
南長崎

Nagasaki

Shiinamachi

Shinwa

(4)

Seibu Ikebukuro Line 西武池袋線

Fujimidai

Mejiro
目白

Mejiro
Garden

Nishi-ochiai
西落合

Nishi-ochiai-1
西落合一

Shin-ōme-kaidō Ave.
新青梅街道

Minami-nagasaki-1
南長崎一

Mejiro-dōri Ave. 目白通り

Mejiro-3
目白三

Kawamura-gakuen

No. 12 Line
新営12号線

Naka-ochiai

Seibō

⑩ SHINJUKU-KU
新宿区

Mejiro

Gakushūin

Mejiro-gakuen

Naka-ochiai-2
中落合二

Shimo-ochiai

Gakushūin

Chitose

Nakai

Shin-mejiro-dōri Ave. 新目白通り

Shipbuilding Research
Center of Japan

Chūgai Pharmaceutical

Seibu Shinjuku Line 西武新宿線

Shimo-ochiai

Gakushūin-shi

Nakai

Taishō Pharmaceutical

Myoshoji River

㉚ NAKANO-KU
中野区

Kami-ochiai

Ochiai Central Park

Kamitakada

Tōzai Line 営団東西線

Takadanobaba

Meiji-dōri Ave. 明治通り

■AREA INDEX■

Chihaya 1~4 ················ B–3	Kita-ōtsuka 1~3 ················ G–3	Nagasaki 1~6 ················ B–4	Takamatsu 1~3 ················ C–2
Higashi-ikebukuro 1~5 ········ F–4	Komagome 1~7 ················ J–2	Minami-ikebukuro 1~5 ········ D–4	Zōshigaya 1~3 ················ F–5
Ikebukuro 1~4 ················ E–3	Mejiro 1~5 ················ D–5	Nishi-sugamo 1~4 ················ G–2	
Ikebukuro-honchō 1~4 ········ E–2	Minami-ikebukuro 1~4 ········ F–4	Senkawa 1~2 ················ C–2	
Kami-ikebukuro 1~4 ········ F–2	Minami-nagasaki 1~6 ········ A–4	Sugamo 1~5 ················ H–3	
Kaname-chō 1~3 ················ C–3	Minami-ōtsuka 1~3 ················ H–4	Takada 1~3 ················ E–6	

豊島区

F G to Ōji to Ōji H J

Shin-itabashi
Nakasendō Ave. 中三柳
Takinogawa
Meiji-dori Ave. 明治通り
Arakawa Line
Takinogawa
Asukayama Park
Tōhoku Line Shōwa-machi
Kami-nakazato
Tōhoku Jōetsu Shinkansen
Keihintōhoku Line

1

to Ueno
to Tabata

⓪ KITA-KU
北区
Factory of Printing Bureau Kami-nakazato

Japan Food Warehouse

Nishigahara

Nanboku Line

Ryōkanji Nishigaharayonchome
Asahi
Zenyōji
Saihōji Myōkōji
Taishō
Seiunji
Nishi-sugamo
Ōtsuka
Hakusenji
Shin-kōshinzuka
Shukutoku-sugamo (3)
Tōkyō Univ. of Foreign Studies
Former Furukawa Garden

Ikebukuro-daiichi
Asahi
Nakazato

Library
(4)
(3)
Nishi-sugamo
西巣鴨
Kōshinzuka
Jiganji (5)
Honmyōji
Shōrinji (7)
(6)
Saifukuji
Kagawa Nutrition Coll.
Komagome (2)
Komagome 駒込
Komagome Library

2

to Tabata

Kami-Ikebukuro
上池袋
Kami-ikebukuro
Nishi-sugamo
Toshima Wholesale Market
Tōkyō Swimming Center
Somei Cemetery (5)
Komagome

Shima Central (2)
Cancer Institute
Sugamo (1)
Ōtsuka Sch. for the deaf
Gyōkō
Hongō
Komagome (3)
(4)

Sugamo (1)
Bunkyō
Sugamoshinden
Seiwa
Togenuki-jizō
Mitsubishi Gymnasium
Sōkagakkai Toda Memorial Hall

Housei
Kita-ōtsuka-3 北大塚三
Sugamo
巣鴨
Shinshō-ji
(3)
Seiyū Store

3

to Komagome
to Ikenohata

Ikebukuro-mutsumatarikkyō
池袋六ツ又陸橋
Kita-ōtsuka
北大塚 (2)
R&B
Ōtsuka
Jūmonji (1)
Sugamoeki-mae
巣鴨駅前 (1)
Rikugien Garden

Public Employment Security Office
Ikebukuro (2)
Ōtsukaekimae
Sugamo
Yamanote Line 山手線
Mita Line 都営三田線
Hon-komagome

Amlux (3)
Prince
Sunshine 60
Tenso-jinja (3)
Higashi Welfare Office
Sugamo (1)
Sengoku-1 千石一

4

to Hongō
to Suidōbashi

Mitsukoshi Dept. Store
Sunshine City
Toshima
Toshima
Ōtsukadai
Mūkōhara
Nishi-sugamo
Sugamo
Sengoku

Ancient Orient Mus.
Mint Bureau (4)
Higashi-ikebukuro
東池袋
Library
Minami-ōtsuka
南大塚 (2)
Kyū-hakusan-dōri Ave.
Hakusan-dōri Ave.

Higashi-Ikebukuro
東池袋 (5)
Shin-ōtsuka
Shinobazu-dōri Ave. 不忍通り
Tōyō

Hinode
Honkyōji
Ōtsuka
Sengoku
Sengoku-3 千石三

Ikebukuro
Higashi ikebukuro yonchome

Zōshigaya

5

to Suidōbashi

Zōshigaya Cemetery (4)
Koishikawa Botanical Garden
Hakusan

Zōshigaya
雑司が谷 (1)
Gokokuji
Ōtsuka

Kada
Dormitory of Japan Women's Univ.
Gokokuji 護国寺
Ochanomizu Women's
⑫ BUNKYŌ-KU
文京区
Koishikawa

Hosp. in affailiation, the Univ. of Tōkyō
Atomi-gakuen
Kasuga-dōri Ave.
Myogadani
Marunouchi Line 都営丸ノ内線

jirodai-2
白台三
Japan Women's
Mejirodai
Yūrakuchō Line
Expressway No.5 首都高速5号
Takushoku

6

to Suidōbashi

ric (1)
Shin-edogawa Park
Kohinata
Koishikawa

Waseda
Sekiguchi
Kasuga

eda
to Iidabashi
to Ochanomizu

F G H I J

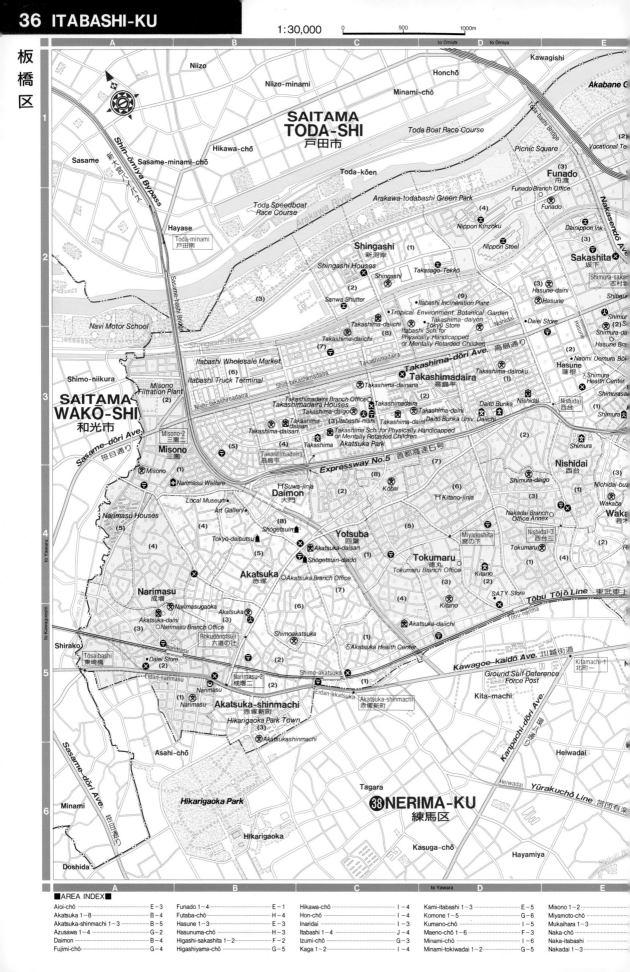

1:30,000

板橋区

■AREA INDEX■

Aioi-chō ⋯⋯⋯ E-3	Hikawa-chō ⋯⋯⋯ I-4	Misono 1~2 ⋯⋯⋯
Akatsuka 1~8 ⋯⋯⋯ B-4	Funado 1~4 ⋯⋯⋯ E-1	Hon-chō ⋯⋯⋯ I-4	Miyamoto-chō ⋯⋯⋯
Akatsuka-shinmachi 1~3 ⋯⋯⋯ B-5	Futaba-chō ⋯⋯⋯ H-4	Inaridai ⋯⋯⋯ I-3	Mukaihara 1~3 ⋯⋯⋯
Azusawa 1~4 ⋯⋯⋯ G-2	Hasune 1~3 ⋯⋯⋯ E-3	Itabashi 1~4 ⋯⋯⋯ J-4	Naka-chō ⋯⋯⋯
Daimon ⋯⋯⋯ B-4	Hasunuma-chō ⋯⋯⋯ H-3	Izumi-chō ⋯⋯⋯ G-3	Naka-itabashi ⋯⋯⋯
Fujimi-chō ⋯⋯⋯ G-4	Higashi-sakashita 1~2 ⋯⋯⋯ F-2	Kaga 1~2 ⋯⋯⋯ I-4	Nakadai 1~3 ⋯⋯⋯
	Higashiyama-chō ⋯⋯⋯ G-5	Kami-itabashi 1~3 ⋯⋯⋯ E-5	
		Komone 1~5 ⋯⋯⋯ G-6	
		Kumano-chō ⋯⋯⋯ I-5	
		Maeno-chō 1~6 ⋯⋯⋯ F-3	
		Minami ⋯⋯⋯ A-6	
		Minami-tokiwadai 1~2 ⋯⋯⋯ G-5	

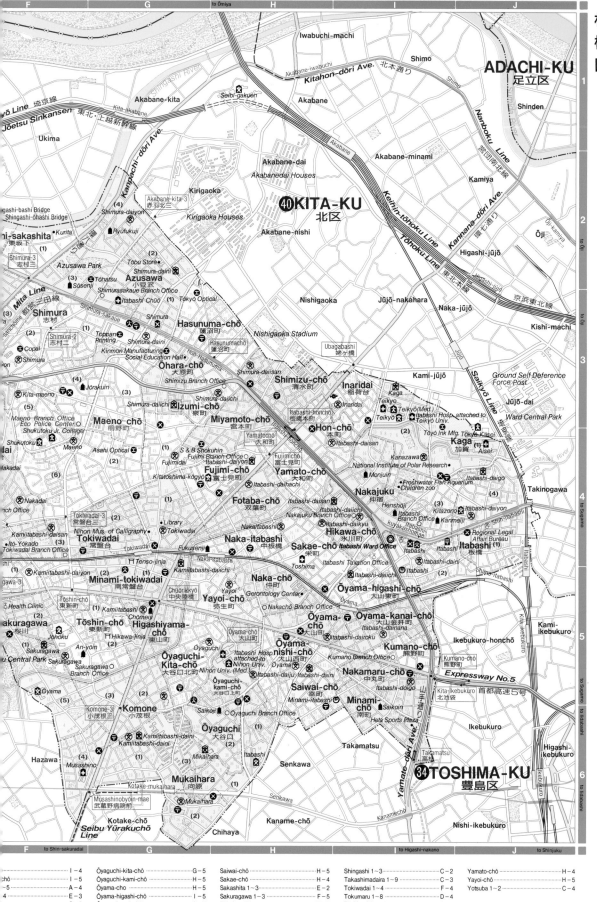

I – 4	Ōyaguchi-kita-chō G–5	Saiwai-chō H–5	Shingashi 1–3 C–2	Yamato-chō H–4
I – 5	Ōyaguchi-kami-chō H–5	Sakae-chō H–4	Takashimadaira 1–9 C–3	Yayoi-chō H–5
A – 4	Ōyama-cho H–5	Sakashita 1–3 E–2	Tokiwadai 1–4 F–4	Yotsuba 1–2 C–4
E – 3	Ōyama-higashi-chō I–5	Sakuragawa 1–3 F–5	Tokumaru 1–8 D–4	
G – 3	Ōyama-kanai-chō I–5	Shimizu-chō H–3	Tōshin-chō 1–2 G–5	
H – 6	Ōyama-nishi-chō H–5	Shimura 1–3 F–3	Wakagi 1–3 E–4	

練馬区

1:32,000

0　　　500　　　1000m

to Kawagoe

SAITAMA NIIZA-SHI
新座市

SAITAMA WAKŌ-SHI
和光市

Baba
Kurume River
Sakae
Hirosawa
Dōjō
Ikeda
Katayama

Ōizumi-gakuen
Ōizumi-gakuen-sakura
Ōizumi-gakuen-sakura
Ōizumi Sch. of Physically Handicapped or Mentally Retarded Children
Ōizumi-kōseien
Ōizumi Central Park
(9)

Ōizumi-gakuen-chō
大泉学園町

Health Clinic
Ōizumi-gakuen-midori
Ōizumi-kita Branch Office
Ōizumi-gakuen
Ōizumi-daiichi
Ōizumi-machi
大泉町
5th Branch Office
Doshida-dōri
土支田通り
Dosida
土支田
Hōki

Nishi-Ōizumi-machi
西大泉町
Ōizumi-nishi
Ōizumi-gakuen
Zen-yaku-kōgyō
Ōizumi I.C.
大泉IC
Ōizumi-kita
Shakujii Sch. for the deaf
Takan

Nishi-ōizumi
西大泉
Ōizumi-daisan
Ōizumi-daisanshō-mae
大泉第三小前
Kitazono
北園
Ōizumi-kita
Ōizumi-kita
Bikuni
比丘尼
Nerima I.C.
練馬I.C.
Incineration Plant
Sangendera
三軒寺
Yahara
Kitahara
Yahara
谷原

Kita-machi
Maruyamanishibashi
丸山西橋
Ōizumi-daiyon
Miharadai
Senshin
Miharadai
三原台
Miharadai-1
三原台一
Yahara

Shimo-hōya
Ōizumi-dairoku
Myōfukuji
Ōizumi-nishi Branch Office
Ōizumi Traffic Park
Ōizumigakueneki-mae
大泉学園駅前
Tōei Movie Studio
Livin OZ Store
Tōei Animation
Myōenji
Higashi-ōizumi
東大泉
Maehara
前原
Nerima Social Insurance Office
Yahara-5
谷原五
Synthet

Seibu Ikebukuro Line　西武池袋線
Workers Welfare Hall
Tax Office
Higashi-ōizumi
東大泉
Ōizumi-higashi
Shakujii-machi
石神井町
Kōwa
Takanodai
高野台

Minami-ōizumi
南大泉
Makino Memorial Garden
Ōizumi attached to Tōkyō Gakugei Univ.
Ōizumi-daini
Tōkyō Gakugei
Ōizumi attached to Tokyo Gakugei Univ.
Shakujii Health Center
Shakujii-chōshamae
石神井町
Shakujii
Shakujii-shōbōshomae
石神井消防署前

Higashi-chō
Ōizumi-daini
Ōizumi-minami
Met. Nurse College
Shakujiichū-mae
石神井中前
Shakujii Government office Bldg.
Yahara Branch Office
Shak

NISHI-TŌKYŌ-SHI
西東京市
Ōizumi-dainishō-minami
大泉第二小南
Asahide Sch. for Physically Handicapped or Mentally Retarded Children
Shakujii
Shakujiigakuen-mae
石神井公園前
Shakujii
Shakujii Park
Minami-tanaka Houses
Minami-tanaka
南田中
Minami-tanaka
南田中

Naka-machi
Fuji-kaidō Ave. 富士街道
Outdoor Concert Hall
Dōjōji
Sanpoji
Library
Shakujii-shō-mae
石神井小前
Shakujii

Takatsuka
高塚
Shakujii Sch. for Physically Handicapped or Mentally Retarded Children
Shakujiidai-8
石神井台八
Shakujiidai
Kami-shakujii-kita
Shakujiidai
石神井台
Shimo-shakujii
下石神井
Minamigaoka

Shakujiiko-mae
石神井高前
Sekimachi-kita
Shakujii-koen Houses
Shimo-shakujii
下石神井
Shimo-shakujii
Minami-tanaka

Fujimi-chō
Shakujii
Tōkyō-jogakuin
Shin-ōme-kaidō Ave. 新青梅街道
Kami-Shakujii Houses
Sodai-gakuin
Shakujiishōbōsho-mae
石神井消防署前
Shimo-shakujii-4
下石神井四
Shakujii-minami
Hachinaribashi
八成橋

Higashi-fushimi
Waseda Univ. Ground Musashiseki Park
Catholic Teological Sch.
Ministry of Labor Government office
Kami-shakujii
上石神井
Shakujii
Chihiro Iwasaki Memorial Gallery
Senkawa-dōri
千川通り

Sekimachi-kita
関町北
Honryūji
Musashi-seki
Sophia (Teology) Sekimachi
Kami-shakujii
Shimo-shakujii
Shakujii
Shakujii-minami

Seibu-Shinjuku Line 西武新宿線
Health Clinic
Sekimachikita-1
関町北一
Kami-shakujii
Igusa
Igusa-4
井草四
Igusa-3
井草三
Igus

Higashi-fushimi
Sekimachi-higashi
関町東
Kami-shakujii Branch Office
Kami-shakujii-minamichō
上石神井南町
togi

Kitaura
北裏
Sekimachi-4
関町四
Sekimachi-3
関町三
Sekimachi-nishi
関町二
Sekimachi-2
関町二
Sekimachi-1
関町一
Tatenobashi
立野橋
Kami-igusa
上石神井
③②SUGINAMI-KU
杉並区

Green Town
Sekimachi
青梅街道
Seki Branch Office
Sekimachi-nishi
関町二
Kami-igusa-2
上草二

Midori-chō
Sekimachi-minami
関町南
Sekimachi-minami
関町南
Tateno
Shakujiinishichū-mae
石神井西中前
Tokyo-sah-iku
Kami-igusa-4
上草四
Waseda-dōri Ave.
早稲田通り
Shimizu

Musashino City Office
Kichijōji-kita-machi
吉祥寺北町
Tateno
Zenpukuji
Imagawa-3
今川三
Imagawa
今川

⑤②MUSASHINO-SHI
武蔵野市
Tateno-chō
立野町
Seikei
Zenpukuji Park
Zenpukuji-ike Pond

to Shinjuku
to Takaido

■AREA INDEX■

Asahi-chō 1~3 .... F-1
Asahigaoka 1~2 .... J-5
Doshida 1~4 .... E-2
Fujimidai 1~4 .... F-4
Hayamiya 1~4 .... H-3
Hazawa 1~3 .... J-4

Heiwadai 1~4 .... I-2
Higashi-ōizumi 1~7 .... B-3
Hikarigaoka 1~7 .... F-2
Hikawadai 1~4 .... I-3
Kami-shakujii 1~4 .... C-5
Kami-shakujii-minamichō H-6

Kasuga-chō 1~6 ....
Kita-machi 1~8 ....
Kotake-chō 1~4 .... E-2
Kōyama 1~4 ....
Miharadai 1~3 ....
Minami-ōizumi 1~6 ....

練馬区

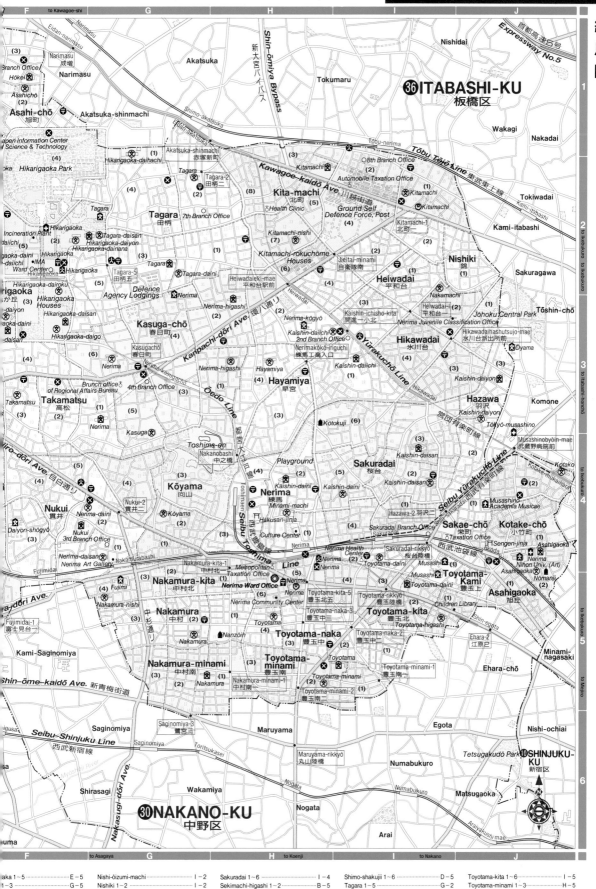

...aka 1–5	E–5	Nishi-ōizumi-machi I–2	Sakuradai 1–6 I–4	Shimo-shakujii 1–6 D–5	Toyotama-kita 1–6 I–5
...1–3	G–5	Nishiki 1–2 I–2	Sekimachi-higashi 1–2 B–5	Tagara 1–5 G–2	Toyotama-minami 1–3 H–5
...kita 1–5	G–5	Nukui 1–5 F–4	Sekimachi-kita 1–5 A–5	Takamatsu 1–3 F–3	Toyotama-naka 1–4 H–5
...minami 1–3	G–5	Ōizumi-gakuen-chō 1–9 C–2	Sekimachi-minami 1–4 B–6	Takanodai 1–5 E–4	Yahara 1–6 E–3
...chō 1–4	H–4	Ōizumi-machi 1–6 D–2	Shakujii-machi 1–8 D–4	Tateno-chō B–6	
...1–6	A–2	Sakae-chō J–4	Shakujiidai 1–8 B–4	Toyotama-kami 1–2 H–4	

1:27,000

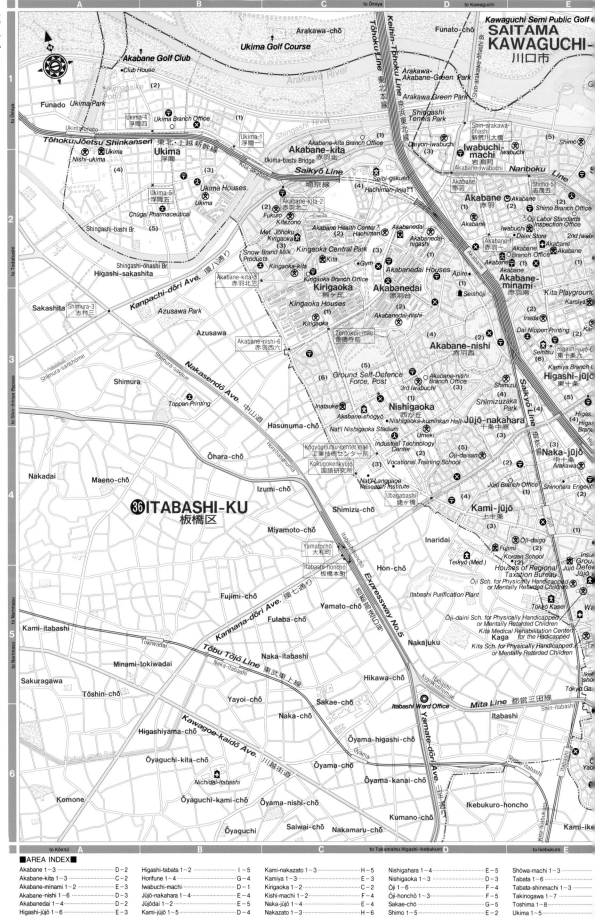

■AREA INDEX■

Akabane 1~3 ·········· D-2	Higashi-tabata 1~2 ·········· I-5	Kami-nakazato 1~3 ·········· H-5	Nishigahara 1~4 ·········· E-5	Shōwa-machi 1~3 ·········· F-5
Akabane-kita 1~3 ·········· C-2	Horifune 1~4 ·········· G-4	Kamiya 1~3 ·········· E-3	Nishigaoka 1~3 ·········· D-3	Tabata 1~6 ·········· I-6
Akabane-minami 1~2 ·········· E-3	Iwabuchi-machi ·········· D-1	Kirigaoka 1~3 ·········· F-2	Ōji 1~6 ·········· F-4	Tabata-shinmachi 1~3 ·········· I-5
Akabane-nishi 1~6 ·········· D-3	Jūjō-nakahara 1~4 ·········· E-4	Kishi-machi 1~2 ·········· F-4	Ōji-honchō 1~3 ·········· F-5	Takinogawa 1~7 ·········· H-6
Akabanedai 1~4 ·········· E-2	Jūjōdai 1~2 ·········· E-5	Naka-jūjō 1~4 ·········· E-4	Sakae-chō ·········· G-5	Toshima 1~8 ·········· G-5
Higashi-jūjō 1~6 ·········· E-3	Kami-jūjō 1~5 ·········· D-4	Nakazato 1~3 ·········· H-6	Shimo 1~5 ·········· E-2	Ukima 1~5 ·········· C-2

北区

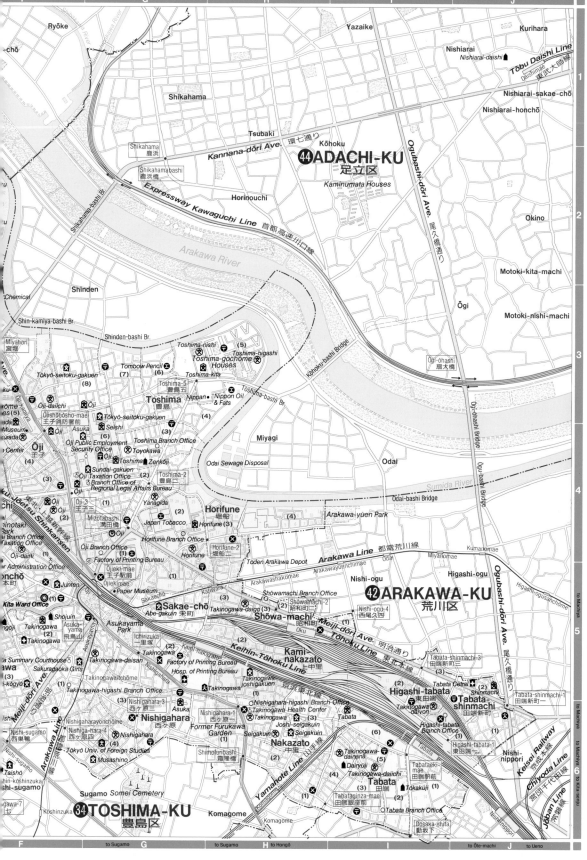

荒川区

1:18,000

0　　250　　500m

to Kōhoku-rikkyō

| A | B | C | D | E |

Miyagi

Odai

Citizen Ground

Arakawa River

Horifune

Sumida River

Ogu-bashi Bridge

Ogubashi-dōri Ave.

1

Arakawa-yūen Park

Odaibashi

Ogu-hachiman

Higashi-ogu Sewage Disposal (Under Construction)

Ogunohara Kōen

Har

(8)

Ogu-dairoku

Ogu-dairokushō-mae　尾久第六小前

(6)

(3)

Ogu

College of Health Sciences

(7)

Twin City

Sports Center Ground

Arakawashakomae

Nishi-ogu-7　西尾久七

Arakawayūenchōmae

Ogu Branch Office

Ogu

尾久橋通り

Kitatoshima

Daimon

(7)

Ogu-nishi

Nishi-ogu 西尾久

Odai

Miyanomae

Arakawa Line

Higashi-ogu-oguhonmachi-dōri

(6)

Jōchi Public Welfare

Shōwa-machi

(5)

Sato

Kumanomae

(5)

Arakawa Social Insurance Office

Tōkyō Women's Med. Coll.

(2)

Ogu

Ogu-miyamae

Tōden Electric Supply Sta.

Higashi-oguhonmachi-dōri　東尾久本町通

Machiyachōme

Higashi-ogu 東尾久

Daiyori

Machiya Branch Office

(2)

Mac

2

to Ōji

to Akabane

Okuki-mae　尾久駅前

Oku

Dainana

(4)

(1)

Nishi-ogu-1

(5)

(9)

(3)

Higashi-ogusanchōme

(6)

Machiyachōme

(2)

Daiyon

(4)

Kami-nakazato

Tōhoku-Jōetsu Shinkansen

Tōhoku Line

Health Clinic 西尾久一

Akado

(2)

Daikyū

Daikyū-haketa

Daiyon

(2)

3

to Ōji

Keihin-tōhoku Line

Tabata-shinmachi-3　田端新町三

Meiji-dōri Ave. 明治通り

Nakazato

Higashi-tabata

Tabata-shinmachi

(1)

Arakawa-5 荒川五

(5)

Hananoh 花の木本

Ar

(4)

4

to Sugamo

Yamanote Line 山手線

Tabata

Tabataeki-mae　田端駅前

Tabata

⑩KITA-KU 北区

㉞TOSHIMA-KU 豊島区

Arakawa Taxation Office

(6)

Keisei Railway 京成本線

Dairoku-nippori

(4)

Miyaji 宮地

Araka

Haketa

Meiji-

明治

(5)

(1)

Nishi-nippori 西日暮里

Chiyoda Line 営団千代田線

Dōkanyama

Nishi-nippori-5　日暮里五

Mikawashima

Higashi Br

東日暮

Otakebashi-dōri Ave.

Higashi 東日暮

5

Shinobazu-dōri Ave. 不忍通り

Dōzaka-shita　動坂下

Kaisei

Kaisei

(4)

(5)

Marushin Felt

(2)

Higurashi

Nishi-nippori-2　西日暮里二

(6)

Suwadai

Nipporieki-mae　日暮里駅前

Nippori Branch Office

Daini-nippori

Nippori

日暮里

Hon-komagome

Dōkan-yamashita　道灌山下

Seiunji

Suwa-jinja

Daiichi-nippori

Jōkōji

Shūsei-in

(3)

Zenpukuji

Nansenji

Nippori Sunny Hall

Zenshōji

(5)

Inageya Store

Takenodai

Nanboku-Line

Hongō-dōri Ave. 本郷通り

Enmei-in

Hongyōji

Takenodaikōkō-mae　竹台高校前

6

Mita Line

Tōyō

Hakusan

Mukōgaoka

Honkomagome

⑫BUNKYŌ-KU 文京区

Sendagi

Sendagi

Yanaka

Yanaka Cemetery

Ueno-sakuragi

Kan-eiji

Negishi

Yamanote Railway 山手線

Keisei Railway

Tōhoku Line 東北本線

Uguisudani 鶯谷

Uguisudani

| A | B | C | D | E |
| | to Ōtemachi | to Kōhoku | to Keisei-ueno | to Ueno |

■AREA INDEX■

Arakawa 1~8	F-4
Higashi-nippori 1~6	E-5
Higashi-ogu 1~6	D-2
Machiya 1~8	F-2
Minami-senju 1~8	H-4
Nishi-nippori 1~6	D-4

Nishi-ogu 1~8	B-2

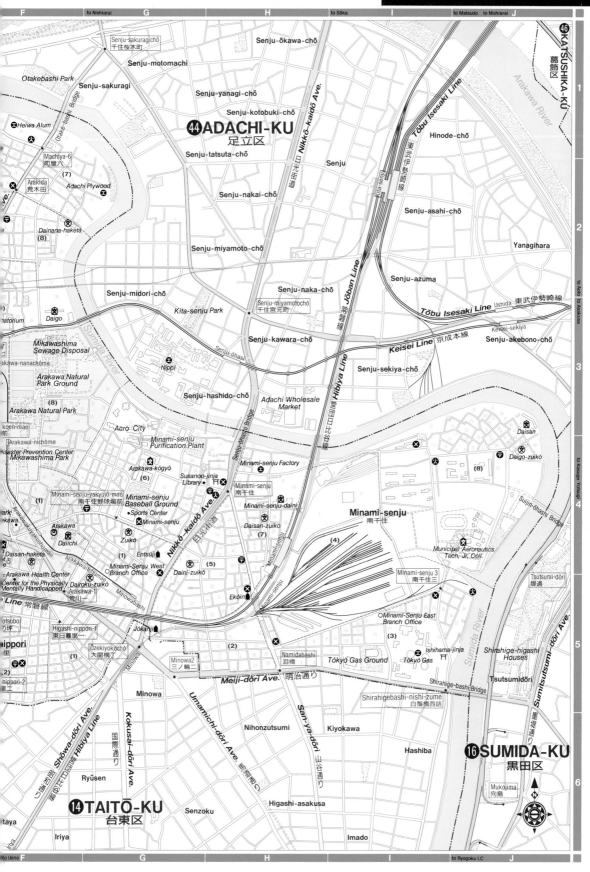

荒川区

㊻KATSUSHIKA-KU 葛飾区

Arakawa River

to Nishiarai
to Sōka
to Matsudo   to Nishiarai

Senju-sakuragichō 千住桜木町

Senju-ōkawa-chō

Senju-motomachi

Otakebashi Park

Senju-sakuragi

Senju-yanagi-chō

Otake-bashi Bridge

Senju-kotobuki-chō

Hinode-chō

✚Heiwa Alum

㊹ADACHI-KU 足立区

Senju-tatsuta-chō

Senju

Machiya-6 町屋六
(7)

Tōbu Isesaki Line 東武伊勢崎線

Arakida 荒木田

Adachi Plywood

Senju-nakai-chō

Senju-asahi-chō

Kita-senju

Dainana-haketa (8)

Senju-miyamoto-chō

Yanagihara

Jōban Line

Senju-naka-chō

Senju-azuma

Senju-midori-chō

Kita-senju Park

Senju-miyamotochō 千住宮元町

Tōbu Isesaki Line Ushida 東武伊勢崎線

Daigo

Senju-kawara-chō

Keisei Line 京成本線

Senju-akebono-chō

Keisei-sekiya

Mikawashima Sewage Disposal

Sumida River

Senju-ōhashi

Senju-sekiya-chō

akawa-nanachōme

Nippi

Arakawa Natural Park Ground

Senju-hashido-chō

Adachi Wholesale Market

Arakawa Natural Park

Daisan

koen-mae

Acro City

Daigo-zuikō

Arakawa-nichōme

Minami-senju Purification Plant

(8)

Disaster Prevention Center Mikawashima Park

Minami-senju Factory

Arakawa-kōgyō (6)

Susanoo-jinja Library

Minami-senju 南千住

Minami-senju-yakyūjō-mae 南住野球場前

Minami-senju Baseball Ground

Minami-senju-daini

Minami-senju

Daisan-zuikō (7)

• Sports Center
✕Minami-senju

Daisan-zuikō

Municipal Aeronautics Tech. Jr. Coll.

Arakawa Daiichi

Zuikō

(4)

Entsūji

(1)

Daini-zuikō

(5)

Minami-senju 3 南千住三

Daisan-haketa

Minami-Senju West Branch Office

Dairoku-zuikō

Daini-zuikō

Ekōin

Arakawa Health Center
Center for the Physically Mentally Handicapped

Arakawa-1 荒川一

Minowabashi

Minami-Senju East Branch Office

Shirahige-higashi Houses

Higashi-nippori-1 東日暮里一

Jōkanji

Tsutsumi-dōri 堤通

(3)

 nippori

Ōzekiyokochō 大関横丁

(1)

Minowa2 三ノ輪二

(2)

Namidabashi 泪橋

Tōkyō Gas Ground

Ishihama-jinja

Tōkyō Gas

Tsutsumidōri

nippori-2

Meiji-dōri Ave. 明治通り

Shirahige-bashi Bridge

Minowa

Shirahigebashi-nishi-zume 白髭橋西詰

Shōwa-dōri Ave.

Hibiya Line

Kokusai-dōri Ave.

Umamichi-dōri Ave.

San-ya-dōri Ave.

Nihonzutsumi

Kiyokawa

Hashiba

⑯SUMIDA-KU 黒田区

Ryūsen

Sumitsutsumi-dōri Ave.

Mukōjima 向島

⑭TAITŌ-KU 台東区

Senzoku

Higashi-asakusa

itaya

Iriya

Imado

to Ueno
to Ryogoku I.C

足立区

HATOGAYA-SHI 鳩ヶ谷市

SAITAMA KAWAGUCHI-SHI 川口市

SAITAMA SŌKA 草加

Minami · Mitsuwa · Toneri-daiichi · Hikawa-jinja · Niisato-chō · Ryōshinden-Higashi-chō

Asahi · Iriya · Toneri 舎人 · Ryōshinden-Nishi-chō · Yatsuka-kamichō · Yatsuka

Aoki · Suehiro · Iriya · Toneri-1 舎人一 · Kojiya · Higashi-ikō 東伊興 · Adachi Incinerat Ikōmachi-hazama

Sakae-machi · Arai-chō · Yahei · Tonerishō-nishi 舎人小西 · Toneri · Toneri Branch Office · Higashi-ikō · Iko-honchō 伊興本町

Hon-chō · Adachi-iriya 足立入谷 · Iriya-minami · Kojiya-honchō 古千谷本町 · Ikō 伊興 · Iko-honchō

Motogō · Iriya-minami · Iriya 入谷 · Adachi Distribution Center · Kojiya 古千谷 Toneri Park · Adachi Health Center

Higashi-ryōke · Kaga 加賀 · Kita-adachi Market · Adachi Truck Terminal 舎人公園 · Ikōmachi-maenuma 伊興町前沼 · Nishi-ikō 西伊興

Ryōke · Ryutsu-center-minami 流通センター南 · Saranuma 皿沼 · Nishi-Ikōmachi 西伊興町 · Ikō 伊興 · Daijuyon · Nishi-Iko · Iko Branch Office · Nishi-takenotsuka 西竹の塚

Funato-chō · Kaga 加賀 · Saranumakyō-mae 皿沼農区前 · Nishiarai-daini · Nishiarai-daisan Houses · Kurihara-kita · Takene · Shimane

Kawara-chō · Higashi-ryōke 東領家 · Yazaike 谷在家 · Adachi-Kōgyō · Nishiarai 西新井 · Kurihara-kita · Entenji

Rengō · Kita-shikahama · Shikahama · Shikahama-daiichi · Nishiarai-1 西新井一 · Nishiarai-Ōuchi · Nishiarai-daiichi · Kurihara 栗原

Shimō · Shikahama 鹿浜 · Shikahama Branch Office · Nishiarai · Nishiarai-daishi · Daishi Line · Cult

Nanboku Line · Shikahama-nishi · Shikahama 鹿浜 · Tsubaki 椿 · Kaminumata-chō 上沼田町 · Kaminumata · Kōhoku-rikkyō 江北陸橋 · Nishiarai Branch Office · Daigo · Taxation Office

Shikahamabashi · Shikahamabashi Green Park · Horinouchi 堀之内 · Kōhoku 江北 · Kaminumata · Adachi-nishi · Kōya · Nishiarai-honchō 西新井本町 · Nishiarai-sakae-chō 西新井栄町

Shinden · Shikahamabashi Green Park · Kōhoku Branch Office · Health Center · Ayame · Nishiarai · Dainana

Shinden-1 新田一 · Keijin · Kōhoku · Okimoto · Adachi-nishi · Dainana · Kam

Branch Office Annexe · Ōgi · Okimoto · Sekihara · Sekibara 関原

Shin-kamiya-bashi Bridge · Adachi-shinden 足立新田 · Citizen Golf Course · Kōhoku-2 江北 · Okino 興野 · Okimoto Branch Office · Motoki-higashi-machi · Motoki 本木

Kamiya · Miyahori 宮堀 · Ōgi 扇 · Motoki-kita-machi 本木北町

Higashi-jūjō · Ōji-kamiya · Toshima · Kōhoku-bashi Bridge · Dairokū 大六 · Motoki-minami-machi · Motoki-higashi

Higashi-jūjō · Kitahon-dōri Ave. · Toshima-bashi Bridge · Kōhokubashi Green Park · Teraji · Motoki-nishi-machi 本木西町

Ōji · Miyagi 宮城 · Miyagi · Expressway Kawagu

KITA-KU 北区 · Odai Sewage Disposal Branch Office Annexe · Nishiarai-bashi Bridge

Kishi-machi · Kōnan · Odai 小台 · Ōgi-ohashi 扇大橋 · Ōgi-ohashi Bridge · Senju-sakuragichō 千住桜木町 · Senju-m

Naka-jūjō · Japan Tobacco · Arakawa-shōgyō · Ōgi-ohashi-minami 扇大橋南 · Senju-sakuragi 千住桜木 · Motojuk

Ōji-honchō · Horifune · Arakawa Park · Odai-bashi Bridge · Ogu-bashi Bridge · Otake-bashi Bridge

Kita Ward Office · Ōji · Miyanomae · Met. Medical Technology Jr. Coll.

Asukayama · Sakaechō · Arakawa Line · Nishi-ogu · Machiya · Chiyoda Line

Takinogawa · Takinogawa Park · Mejii-dōri Ave. · Higashi-ogu · Summa

Nishigahara · Tōhoku Jōetsu Shinkansen · Keihin-tōhoku Line 京浜東北線 · Tōhoku Line 東北本線 · **ARAKAWA-KU** 荒川区 · Mikawashima Sewage Disposal

Tōkyō Univ. of Foreign Studies · Nishigahara · Tabata-shinmachi · Arakawa

Koshinzuka · Nakazato · Tabata

to Ōtsuka · to Nippori · to Ueno · to Ōtemachi · to Minowabashi

■AREA INDEX■

Adachi 1–4 ········ F–5	Higashi-ikō ········ E–2	Ikō 1–5 ········ E–2	Kaga 1–2 ········ C–2	Minami-hanahata 1–5 ········ G–2	Nakagawa 1–5
Aoi 1–6 ········ G–4	Higashi-rokugatsu-chō ········ F–3	Ikō-honchō ········ E–2	Kahei 1–3 ········ H–3	Miyagi 1–2 ········ B–5	Nishi-ayase 1–4
Ayase 1–7 ········ G–4	Hinode-chō ········ F–6	Ikōmachi-hazama ········ E–1	Kita-kahei-chō ········ H–3	Motoki 1–2 ········ E–4	Nishi-hokima 1–4
Chūō-honchō 1–5 ········ G–4	Hirano 1–3 ········ F–3	Ikōmachi-maenuma ········ E–1	Kōdō 1–2 ········ C–4	Motoki-higashi-machi ········ D–4	Nishi-ikō 1–4
Hanahata 1–8 ········ G–1	Hitotsuya 1–5 ········ G–3	Ikōmachi-shirahata ········ E–1	Kōhoku 1–7 ········ C–4	Motoki-kita-machi ········ D–4	Nishi-ikō-chō
Higashi-ayase 1–3 ········ H–4	Hokima 1–4 ········ G–1	Ikōmachi-tanishita ········ E–1	Kojiya 1–2 ········ D–1	Motoki-minami-machi ········ D–5	Nishi-kahei 1–2
Higashi-hokima 1–2 ········ G–2	Horinouchi 1–2 ········ C–4	Iriya 1–9 ········ C–1	Kojiya-honchō1–4 ········ D–2	Motoki-nishi-machi ········ D–5	Nishi-takenotsuka 1–7
Higashi-ikō 1–2 ········ E–1	Hozuka-chō ········ G–3	Iriya-machi ········ C–2	Kurihara 1–4 ········ E–3	Mutsugi 1–4 ········ I–2	Nishiarai 1–6

足立区

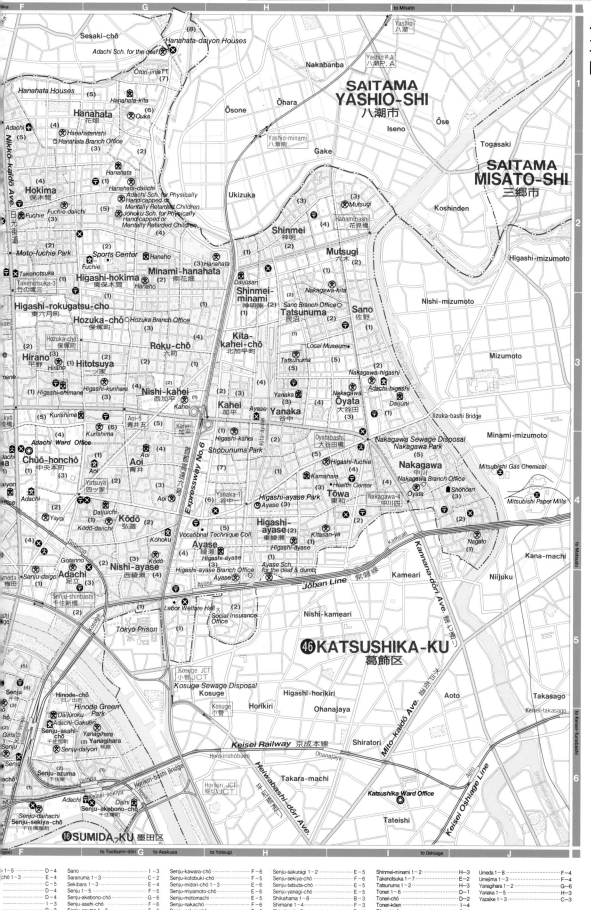

1:38,000

...1-5 — D-4	Sano — I-3	Senju-kawara-chō — F-6	Senju-sakuragi 1~2 — E-5
...chō 1~3 — E-4	Saranuma 1~3 — C-2	Senju-kotobuki-chō — F-5	Senju-sekiya-chō — F-6
... — C-5	Sekibara 1~3 — E-4	Senju-midori-chō 1~3 — E-6	Senju-tatsuta-chō — F-5
...chō — D-4	Senju 1~5 — D-4	Senju-miyamoto-chō — E-5	Senju-yanagi-chō — F-6
... — I-3	Senju-akebono-chō — G-6	Senju-motomachi — E-5	Shikahama 1~8 — B-3
... — G-3	Senju-asahi-chō — F-6	Senju-nakachō — F-6	Shimane 1~4 — B-3
... — E-3	Senju-azuma 1-2 — F-6	Senju-nakai-chō — F-6	Shinden 1~3 — B-4
	Senju-hashido-chō — F-6	Senju-ōkawa-chō — F-5	Shinmei 1~3 — H-2

Shinmei-minami 1~2 — H-3	Umeda 1~8 — F-4
Takenotsuka 1~7 — E-2	Umejima 1~4 — F-4
Tatsunuma 1~2 — H-3	Yanagihara 1~2 — G-6
Toneri 1~6 — D-1	Yanaka 1~5 — H-3
Toneri-chō — D-2	Yazaike 1~3 — C-3
Tōwa 1~5 — C-3	
Tsubaki 1~2 — F-4	

葛飾区

1:32,000

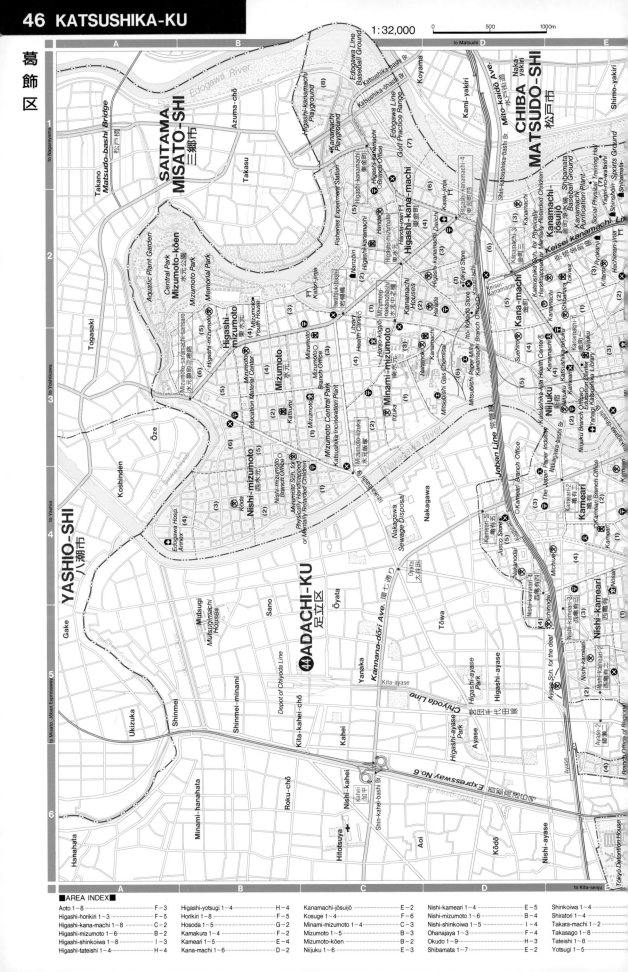

■AREA INDEX■

Aoto 1~8 ·········· F−3	Higashi-yotsugi 1~4 ·········· H−4	Kanamachi-jōsuijō ·········· E−2	Nishi-kameari 1~4 ·········· E−5	Shinkoiwa 1~4 ·········· H−4
Higashi-horikiri 1~3 ·········· F−5	Horikiri 1~8 ·········· F−5	Kosuge 1~4 ·········· F−6	Nishi-mizumoto 1~6 ·········· B−4	Shiratori 1~4 ·········· F−4
Higashi-kana-machi 1~8 ·········· C−2	Hosoda 1~5 ·········· G−2	Minami-mizumoto 1~4 ·········· C−3	Nishi-shinkoiwa 1~4 ·········· I−4	Takara-machi 1~2 ·········· H−4
Higashi-mizumoto 1~6 ·········· B−2	Kamakura 1~4 ·········· F−2	Mizumoto 1~5 ·········· B−3	Ohanajaya 1~3 ·········· F−4	Takasago 1~8 ·········· E−3
Higashi-shinkoiwa 1~8 ·········· I−3	Kameari 1~5 ·········· E−4	Mizumoto-kōen ·········· B−2	Okudo 1~9 ·········· E−3	Tateishi 1~8 ·········· G−4
Higashi-tateishi 1~4 ·········· H−4	Kana-machi 1~6 ·········· D−2	Niijuku 1~6 ·········· E−3	Shibamata 1~7 ·········· E−2	Yotsugi 1~5 ·········· G−4

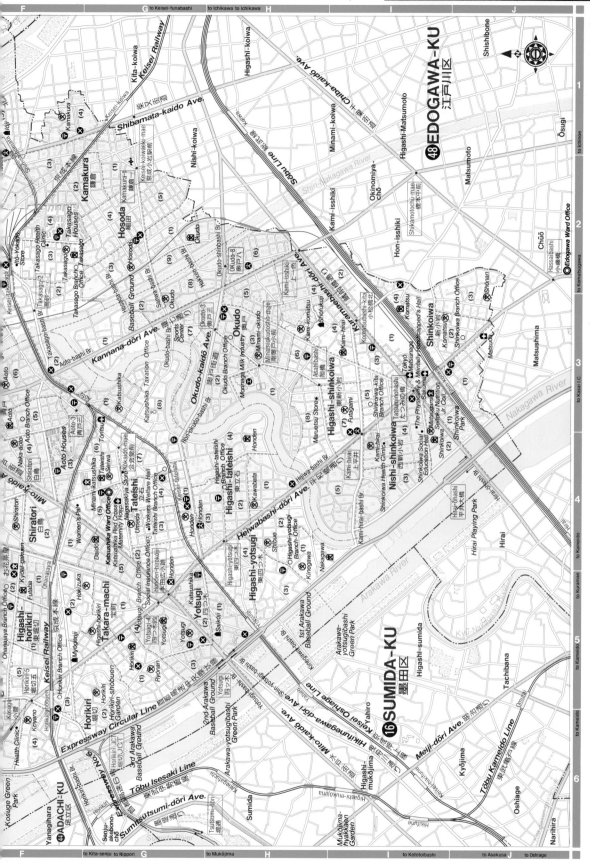

葛飾区

16 **SUMIDA-KU** 墨田区

40 **ADACHI-KU** 足立区

江戸川区

1:38,000

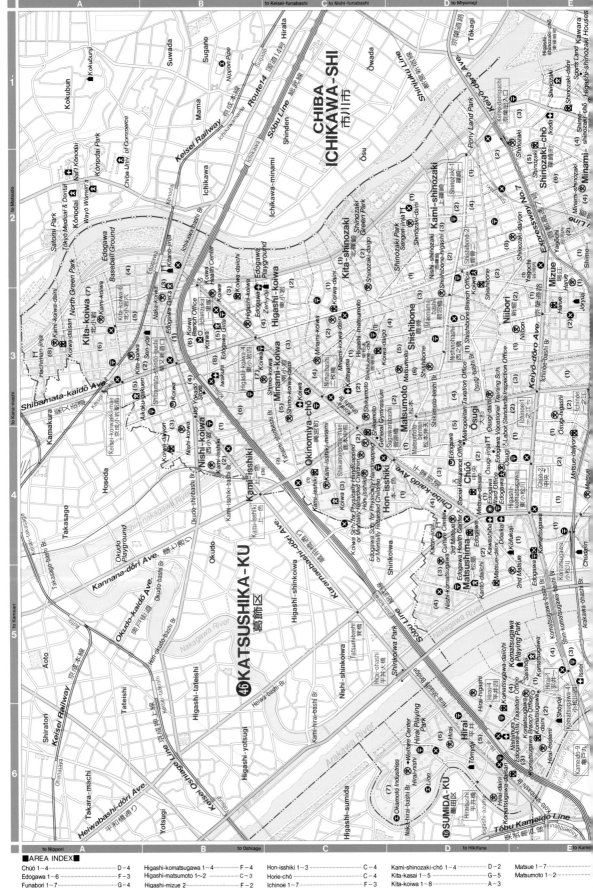

■AREA INDEX■

Chūō 1~4 ·········· D-4	Higashi-komatsugawa 1~4 ······ F-4	Hon-isshiki 1~3 ········ C-4	Kami-shinozaki-chō 1~4 ······ D-2	Matsue 1~7 ········
Edogawa 1~6 ·········· F-3	Higashi-matsumoto 1~2 ······ C-3	Horie-chō ········ G-5	Kita-kasai 1~5 ········	Matsumoto 1~2 ········
Funabori 1~7 ··········	Higashi-mizue 2 ······ F-2	Ichinoe 1~7 ········ F-3	Kita-koiwa 1~8 ········ A-3	Matsushima 1~4 ········
Harue-chō 1~5 ·········· E-3	Higashi-shinozaki 1~2 ······ E-1	Ichinoe-chō ········ F-4	Kita-shinozaki-chō ········ D-2	Minami-kasai 1~7 ········
Higashi-kasai 1~9 ·········· H-4	Higashi-shinozaki-chō ······ E-1	Kami-isshiki 1~2 ········ C-4	Kita shinozaki-cho 1~2 ········ F-5	Minami-koiwa 1~8 ········
Higashi-koiwa 1~6 ·········· C-3	Hirai 1~7 ······ D-6	Kami-shinozaki-chō ········ D-2	Komatsugawa 1~4 ········	

江戸川区

...zaki-chō 1~5 ················· E-2	Nishi-kasai 1~8 ················· H-5	Ōsugi 1~5 ················· D-3
	Nishi-koiwa 1~5 ················· B-3	Rinkai-chō 1~6 ················· J-5
...~8 ················· H-4	Nishi-komatsugawa-machi ················· E-5	Seishin-chō 1~2 ················· H-5
················· E-3	Nishi-mizue 1~5 ················· F-3	Shimo-shinozaki-chō ················· E-1
················· G-4	Nishi-shinozaki 1~2 ················· D-2	Shimokamata-chō ················· F-2
1~4 ················· G-4	Okinomiya-chō ················· C-4	Shinozaki-chō 1~7 ················· E-1

Shishibone 1~6 ················· D-3
Shishibone-chō ················· D-3
Ukita-chō ················· G-4
Yagōchi 1~2 ················· E-2

CHIBA
URAYASU-SHI
浦安市

18 KŌTŌ-KU
江東区

to Chiba

to Monzennakachō   to Ōtemachi   to Ariake

湾岸地区

1:50,000

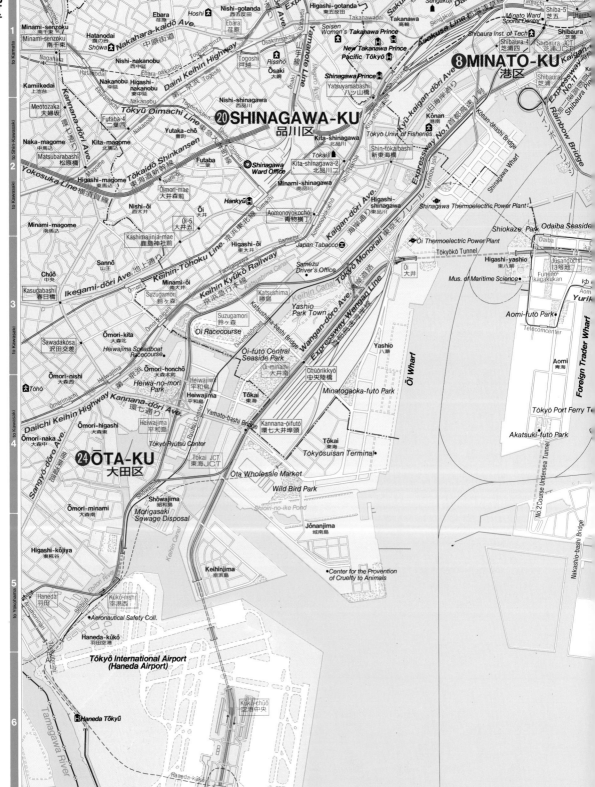

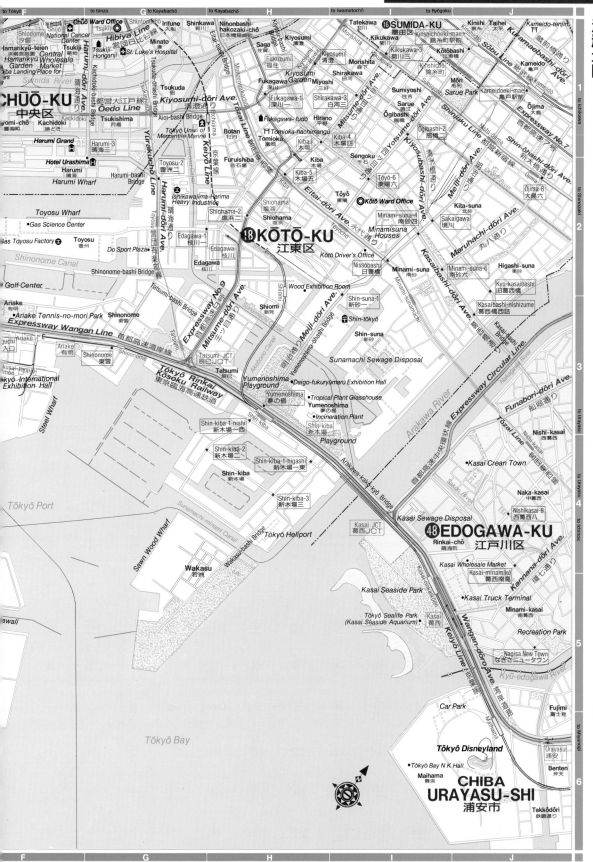

武蔵野市・三鷹市

1:30,000

0   500   1000m

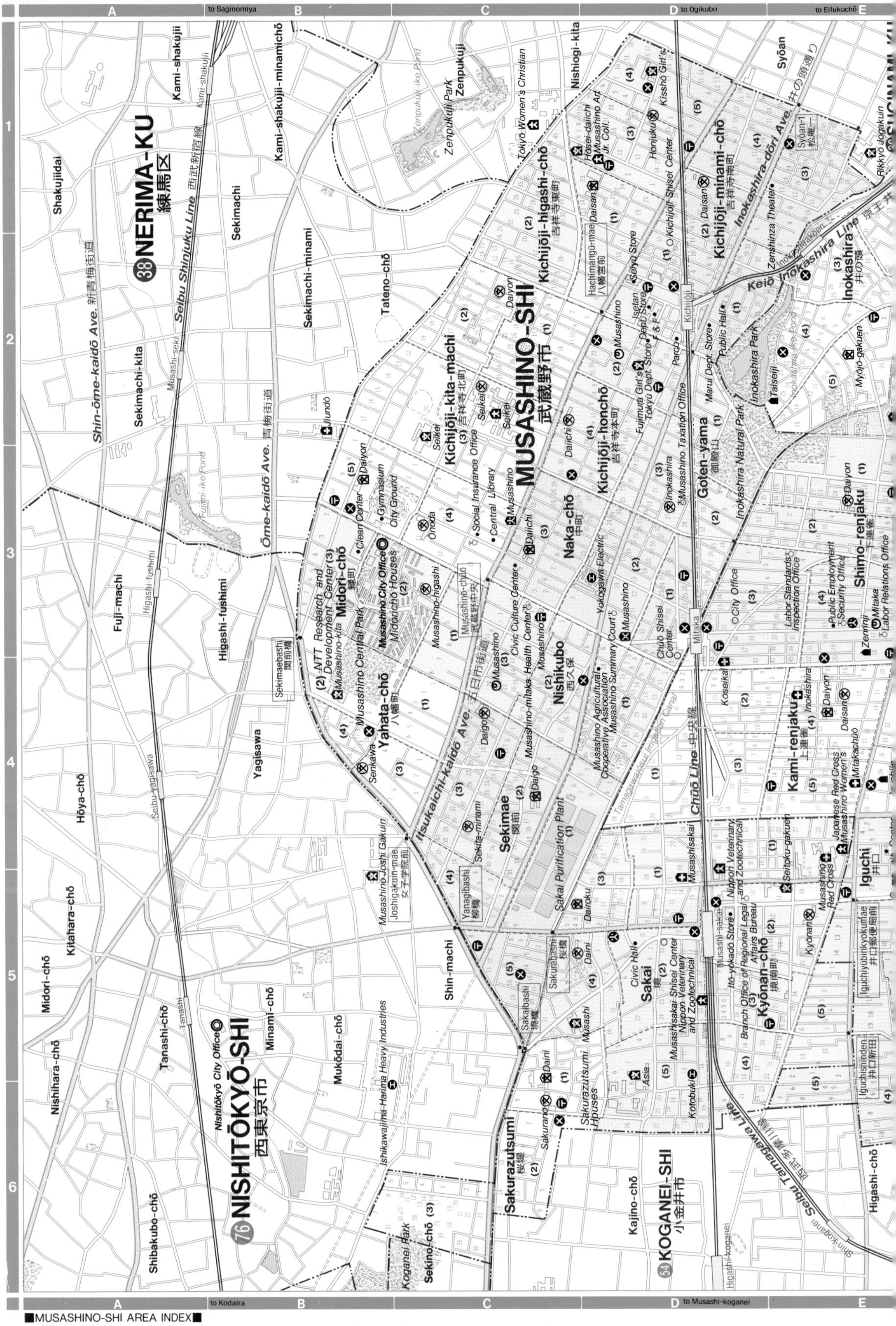

to Saginomiya　to Ogikubo　to Eifukuchō

NERIMA-KU 練馬区 38

MUSASHINO-SHI 武蔵野市

NISHITŌKYŌ-SHI 西東京市 76

KOGANEI-SHI 小金井市 64

to Kodaira　to Musashi-koganei

■MUSASHINO-SHI AREA INDEX■

Goten-yama 1～2	D-3
Kichijōji-higashi-chō 1～4	D-1
Kichijōji-honchō 1～4	D-2
Kichijōji-kita-machi 1～5	C-2
Kichijōji-minami-chō 1～5	D-1
Kyōnan-chō 1～5	D-5
Midori-chō 1～3	B-3
Naka-chō 1～3	C-3
Nishikubo 1～3	C-4
Sakai 1～5	D-5
Sakurazutsumi 1～3	C-6
Sekimae 1～5	C-4
Yahata-chō 1～4	B-4

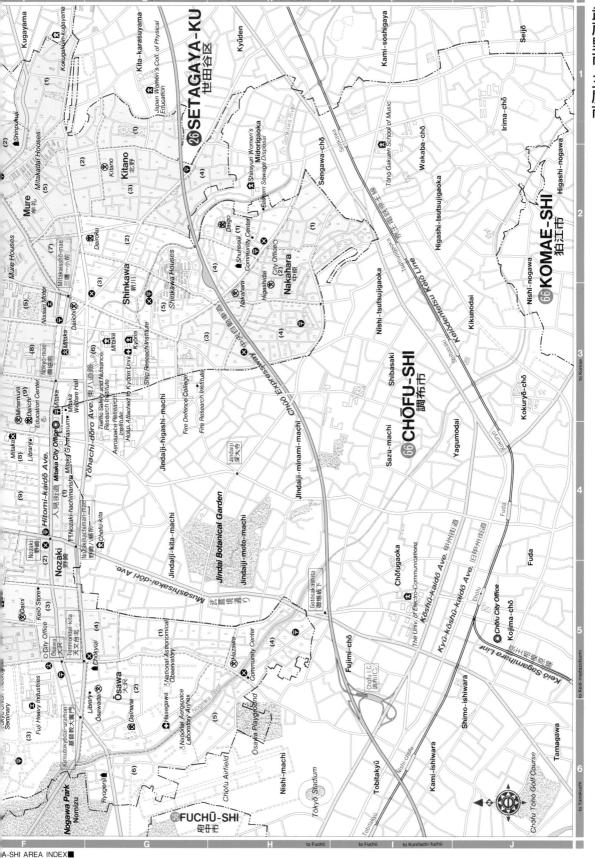

武蔵野市・三鷹市

■A-SHI AREA INDEX■

───── E-5	Nakahara 1~4 ········· H-3
~5 ········· E-2	Nozaki 1~4 ········· F-5
········· F-5	Ōsawa 1~6 ········· G-6
u 1~9 ········· E-4	Shimo-renjaku 1~9 ········· E-3
········· G-2	Shinkawa 1~6 ········· G-3
········· F-2	

小金井市・国分寺市

1:30,000

0   500   1000m

HIGASHIYAMATO-SHI 東大和市

TACHIKAWA-SHI 立川市
Nakajima-chō

Saiwai-chō

Seibu Haijima Line 西武拝島線

Ogawa-nishi-chō
Ogawa-higashi-chō
to Ogawa   to Shin-akitsu

Kodaira City Office

Ogawa-chō

Musashino Art

Jōsui-shin-machi

Takanodai

Tsuda-machi
Josuihonchō 上水本町

Gakuen-nishi-m

TACHIKAWA-SHI 立川市

Wakaba-chō

Keyakidai Houses

Daihachi

Kitamachi Park

Kita-machi 北町

Myōhōji

Tsuda

Hitotsubashi

Kokubunjikōkō-kita 国分寺高校北
Hōrin-in
Namiki-chō 並木町
Daigo
Dairoku

Higashi-tokura-1 東戸倉
Higashi-tokura 東戸倉

Jōsui-honchō

Daiichi
Koigakubo 恋ヶ窪

Takagi-chō 高木町
Daisan

Nishi-machi 西町
Sakae-chō

Shin-machi 新町
Kokubunji
Tokura-3 戸倉三
Manpukuji

Veterinary Assay Laboratory

Kokubunji City Office
Tokura 戸倉
Kokubunji

Kokubunji Agricultural Cooperative Association
Gymnasium

Itōyōkadō Store
Daisan

Kannonji

Health Center
Daini

Fujimoto 富士本
Inarijinja 稲荷神社

Daijū

Welfare Center
Daigo

KOKUBUNJI-SHI 国分寺市

Library
Daikyū

Higashi-koigakubo 東恋ヶ窪
Kokubunji

Ground Self-Defense Force
Air Self-Defense Force
Akebono-chō

Hikari-machi 光町
Bentenhachimangū-mae 弁天八幡宮前
Synthetic Technical Institute of Railway

Hiyoshichō 日吉町

Cooperative Society
Daigo

Kumano-jinja

Nishi-koigakubo 西恋ヶ窪
Hitachi Central Institute

Kita

Hiyoshi-chō 日吉町

Bureau of Sewerage Branch Office

Nishi-koigakubo

Marui

Site of National Japanese Railway Settlement Corporation
Workers We

Chūō Line 中央線
Kunitachi

Izumi Hall
Izumi-cho 泉町
Izumichō 泉町

Daisenji
Naitō 内藤

Nishi

Naka
Hitotsubashi

Higashi-2 東二

Higashi

Man-yō Botanical Garden
Kokubunji
Daiyon

Hagoromo-chō

Musashidai
Fuchū
Nishi-motomachi 西元町

Kurogane Park
Daiyon

Tōkyō Women's Coll. of Physical Education

Tōhō-gakuen

KUNITACHI-SHI 国立市

Kitayama-chō

Tokyo Police Hospital Tama Branch Hosp.

Fujimidai
Fujimi Houses

Nanbu Line 南武線

Kunitachi City Office

Yagawa

Kōshū-kaidō Ave. 甲州街道

Yaho

Fuchū Prison

Saka

Yaho

Chūō Expressway 中央自動車道

Nishifu-machi

Nishihara-machi

Toshiba Fuchū Factory

Tōshiba-chō

Honshuku-machi

Nikkō-chō

Kotobuk

Kunitachi-Fuchū I.C 国立府中I.C

Miyoshi-chō

to Chōfu I.C   to Fuchū   to Fuchū-honmachi

■KOKUBUNJI-SHI AREA INDEX

Fujimoto 1~3 ⋯⋯ C-3	Hon-chō 1~4 ⋯⋯ E-4	Namiki-chō 1~3 ⋯⋯ C-2	Tokura 1~4 ⋯⋯ C-3
Higashi-koigakubo 1~6 ⋯⋯ E-3	Honda 1~5 ⋯⋯ F-3	Nishi-koigakubo 1~4 ⋯⋯ D-4	
Higashi-motomachi 1~4 ⋯⋯ F-4	Izumi-chō 1~3 ⋯⋯ E-4	Nishi-machi 1~5 ⋯⋯ A-3	
Higashi-tokura 1~2 ⋯⋯ D-2	Kita-machi 1~5 ⋯⋯ C-2	Nishi-motomachi 1~4 ⋯⋯ E-5	
Hikari-chō 1~3 ⋯⋯ B-3	Minami-chō 1~3 ⋯⋯ F-4	Shin-machi 1~3 ⋯⋯ C-3	
Hiyoshi-chō 1~4 ⋯⋯ C-4	Naitō 1~2 ⋯⋯ C-4	Takagi-chō 1~3 ⋯⋯ B-3	

小金井市・国分寺市

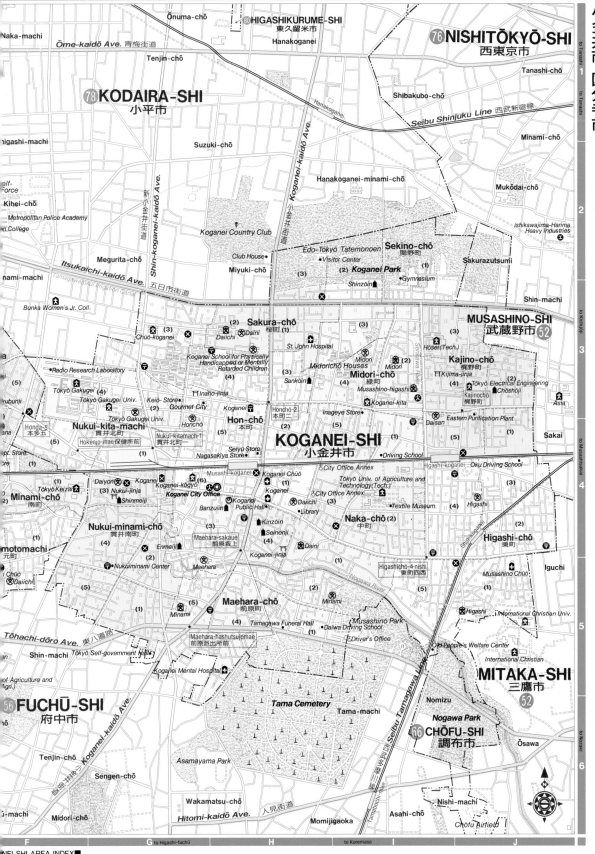

■NEI-SHI AREA INDEX■

5〜5 ·················· J−4	Nukui-kita-machi 1〜5 ·············· G−3	
〜6 ·················· H−4	Nukui-minami-chō 1〜5 ·············· G−4	
〜5 ·················· J−3	Sakura-chō 1〜3 ·················· H−3	
1〜5 ·················· H−5	Sekino-chō 1〜2 ·················· I−2	
1〜5 ·················· I−3		
−4 ·················· I−4		

府中市・国立市

54 KOKUBUNJI-SHI 国分寺市

58 TACHIKAWA-SHI 立川市

KUNITACHI-SHI 国立市

60 HINO-SHI 日野市

70 TAMA-SHI 多摩市

to Shin-akitsu · to Ok
to Shin-akitsu
to Tachikawa
to Hachiōji
to Hachiōji
to Takahatafudō
to Machida

Chūō Line 中央線
Nambu Line 南武線
Musashino Line 武
Keiōdentetsu Keiō Line 京王電鉄京王線
Kawasaki-kaidō Ave. 川崎街道
Kōshū-kaidō Ave. 甲州街道
Chūō Expressway 中央自動車道

Takamatsu-chō
Tachikawa Bicycle Racetrack
Sakae-chō
Hikari-chō
General Technical Laboratory of Railway
Fujimoto
Hiyoshi-chō
Nishi-koigakubo
Kita-tama
Nishi-machi
Automobile Taxation Office
Tachikawa Child Guidance Center
Marushige
Daiyon
Kita 北
Nishi-kokubunji
Akebono-chō
Kunitachi
Naitō
Nishi-r
Daihachi
Nishi-1 西一
Seiyū store
Kinokuniya Store
Prevention of Disasters Center
Kunitachi
Ozenji
Higashi-2 東二
Nishi-
Kunitachi Community Center
Central Clinic
Kunitachi Coll. of Music
Hagoromo-chō
Kunitachi Coll. of Music
Daini
Naka 中
Hitotsubashi
Higashi 東
Negishi
Musashidai 武蔵台
Nishiki-chō
Posts and Telecommunication Laboratory
Prevention of Disasters Center
Nishi 西
Hitotsubashi
Tōhō-gakuen
Metropolitan Fuchū
Metropolitan Neurological Hospital
Posts and Telecommunication College
Tachikawa City Office
Tachikawa Advanced Vocational Training School
Tōkyō Women's Coll. of Physical Education
Daigo-shōgyō
Tōhō-gakuen-mae 桐朋学園前
Tōkyō Kaijo Training Center
Medical Center for the Severely Handicapped
Police Hospital
Dainana
Musashidai
Yagawa Houses
Daimaru
Peacock Store
Fujimidai 富士見台
Disabled Person's Center
Kunitachi
Daiichi
Daisan
Musashidai Culture Center
Aoyagi 青柳
Daini
Kunitachi
NHK-gakuen
Dainana
Kitayama-chō 北山町
Fuchū-keimusho-ka
府中刑務所
Health Center
Health Clinic
Yagawa
Ishida
Dairoku
General Gymnasium
Daigo Central Library
Fujimidai No. 1 Houses
Nishihara-machi 西原町
Tōshiba-chō 東芝町
Tōshiba Fuchū Factory
KUNITACHI-SHI 国立市
Aoyagi-minami Houses Ishida
Kunitachi Agricultural Cooperative Association
Kunitachi City Office
Nagasakiya Store
Dainana
Aoyagi 青柳
Yagawaeki-iriguchi 矢川駅入口
Library Annex
Gourmet City
Honshuku
Nishifu-machi 西府町
Honshuku-machi 本宿町
Home for the Aged Kunitachi-en
Nan-yōji
Yaho
Yaho 谷保
Yaho-tenmangū 保
Daiju
Shimoda
Kita-tama No.2 Sewage Disposal
Kunitachi Kyōdo Bunka-kan
Yakult
Daisan
Kunitachi-Fuchū IC-iriguchi 国立府中インター入口
Honshuku-2 本宿二
Miyoshi-chō 美好町
Izumi 泉
Holiday Inn Tōkyō Kunitachi
Fruits and Vegetables market
Honshukumachi 本宿町
Yaho Green Park
Clean Center
Kunitachi-Fuchū IC 国立府中IC
Fuchū-nishi
Western Branch Office
Bubaigawara
Arai
Ishida
Nisshin-chō 日新町
Daigo
Honshuku-1 本宿
Bubai-chō 分梅町
Nisshin
NEC
60 HINO-SHI 日野市
Seiyū Distribution Center
Misawa
Ochikawa
Yotsuya Area Center
Yotsuya 四谷
Sumiyoshi-chō 住吉町
Chūjitsuya Store
Hōonji
Mogusa
Yotsuya
Daihachi
Seiyū Store
Nakagawara
Sumiyoshi-2 住吉二
Minami-machi Purification
Minami
Japanese School Attached to Tōkyō Univ. of Foreign Studies
Keijinkai
Fuchū-minamimachi Houses
Sumiyoshi
Rehabilitation Center for The Physically and Mentally Handicapped
Ichinomiya
Tamagawa Green Park
Tōkyō Tama
Tōden-gakuen
Wada
Higashiteragata
Sekido
70 TAMA-SHI 多摩市
Sakuragaoka
Seiseki sakuragaoka
Renkōji
Sakuragaoka Coun

Tamagawa River
Asakawa River
Fuchū-yotsuya-bashi Bridge
Sekido-bashi Bridge

■KUNITACHI-SHI AREA INDEX■

Aoyagi	A-3
Fujimidai 1-4	B-2
Higashi 1-4	D-2
Ishida	A-2
Izumi 1-2,4	B-4
Kita 1-3	B-1
Naka 1-3	C-2
Nishi 1-3	B-2
Yaho	B-3

■FUCHŪ-SHI AREA INDEX■

Asahi-chō 1-3	J-4	Hiyoshi-chō	G-5	Kotobuki-chō 1-3	G-5
Bubai-chō 1-5	E-5	Hon-machi 1-4	F-4	Koyanagi-chō 1-6	F-4
Fuchū-machi	G-4	Honshuku-machi 1-4	E-4	Midori-chō	
Hachiman-chō 1-3	G-4	Kata-machi 1-3	E-4	Minami-machi 1-6	
Hachimanshuku	G-4	Kitayama-chō 1-4	D-2	Miya-machi 1-3	
Harumi-chō 1-4	F-3	Koremasa 1-6	G-5	Miyanishi-chō 1-	

府中市・国立市

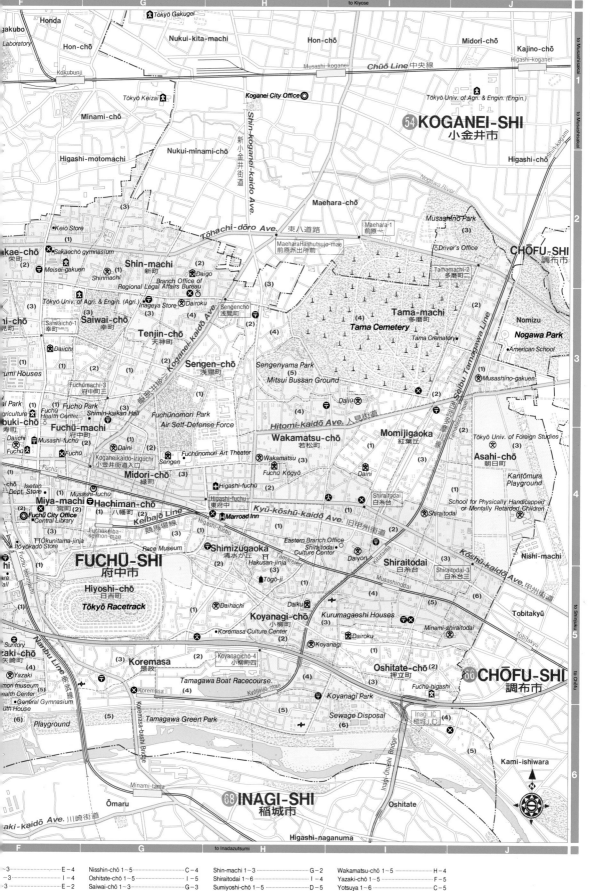

KOGANEI-SHI 小金井市 (54)

CHŌFU-SHI 調布市

FUCHŪ-SHI 府中市

CHŌFU-SHI 調布市 (66)

INAGI-SHI 稲城市 (68)

~3·············E-4
~3·············I-4
~3·············E-3
1~5·············D-3
1~4·············D-3

Nisshin-chō 1~5·············C-4
Oshitate-chō 1~5·············I-5
Saiwai-chō 1~3·············G-3
Sakae-chō 1~3·············F-2
Sengen-chō 1~4·············H-3
Shimizugaoka 1~3·············H-4

Shin-machi 1~3·············G-2
Shiraitodai 1~6·············I-4
Sumiyoshi-chō 1~5·············D-5
Tama-machi 1~4·············I-3
Tenjin-chō 1~4·············G-3
Tōshiba-chō·············E-3

Wakamatsu-chō 1~5·············H-4
Yazaki-chō 1~5·············F-5
Yotsuya 1~6·············C-5

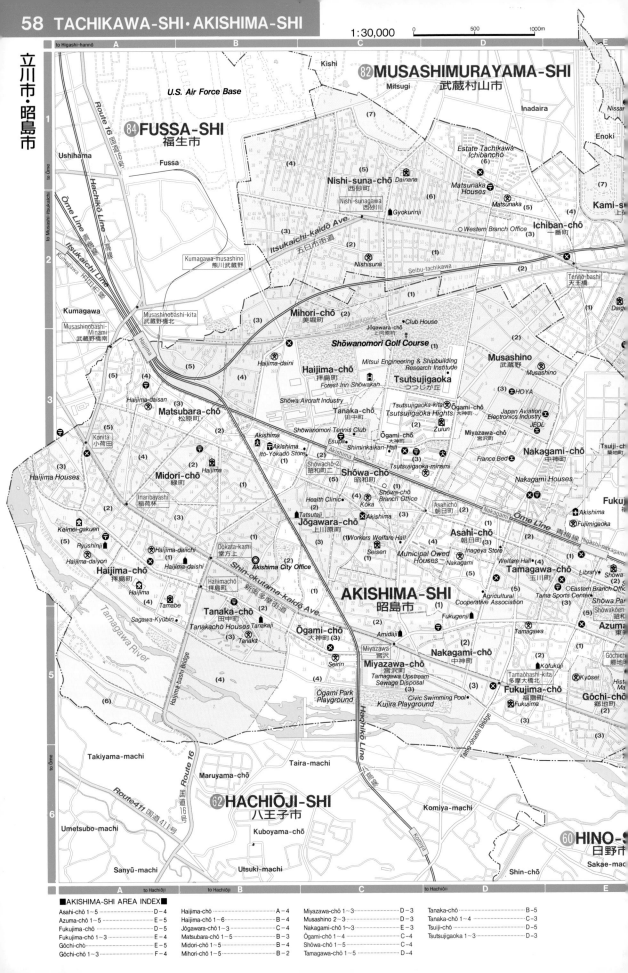

■AKISHIMA-SHI AREA INDEX

Asahi-chō 1～5 ·········· D-4	Haijima-chō ·········· A-4	Miyazawa-chō 1～3 ·········· D-3	Tanaka-chō ·········· B-5
Azuma-chō 1～5 ·········· E-5	Haijima-chō 1～6 ·········· B-4	Mushashino 2～3 ·········· D-3	Tanaka-chō 1～4 ·········· C-3
Fukujima-chō ·········· D-5	Jōgawara-chō 1～3 ·········· C-4	Nakagami-chō 1～3 ·········· C-4	Tsuiji-chō ·········· D-3
Fukujima-chō 1～3 ·········· E-4	Matsubara-chō 1～5 ·········· B-3	Ōgami-chō 1～4 ·········· C-4	Tsutsujigaoka 1～3 ·········· D-3
Gōchi-chō ·········· E-5	Midori-chō 1～5 ·········· B-4	Shōwa-chō 1～5 ·········· C-4	
Gōchi-chō 1～3 ·········· F-4	Mihori-chō 1～5 ·········· B-2	Tamagawa-chō 1～5 ·········· D-4	

立川市・昭島市

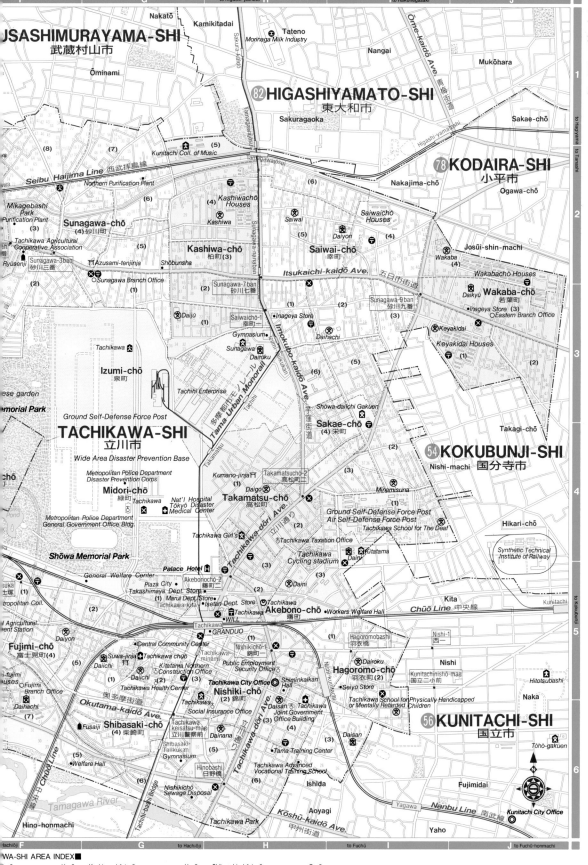

USASHIMURAYAMA-SHI
武蔵村山市

(8)　(7)

Seibu Haijima Line　西武拝島線
Kunitachi Coll. of Music

Northern Purification Plant
(6)
Mikagebashi
Park
Purification Plant
(3)
Tachikawa Agricultural
Cooperative Association
Ryūsenji　Sunagawa-3 ban
砂川三番
(2)

Ōminami

Sunagawa-chō
(4) 砂川町

(5)

Azusami-tenjinja
O Sunagawa Branch Office
Shōbunsha

Kashiwa-chō
柏町(3)

(2)

Daijū

Saiwaichō-1
幸町一

Gymnasium
Sunagawa

Nakatō　Kamikitadai

Tateno
Morinaga Milk Industry
Nangai

Sakuragaoka

Kashiwachō
Houses
(4)
Kashiwa

Sunagawa-nanaban

Sunagawa-7 ban
砂川七番

(1)

Inageya Store

Daiichi

Mukōhara

82 HIGASHIYAMATO-SHI
東大和市

Nakajima-chō

Saiwai

(5)
Saiwai-chō
幸町

Itsukaichi-kaidō Ave.　五日市街道

Daihachi

Dairoku

Sakae-chō

78 KODAIRA-SHI
小平市

Ogawa-chō

Saiwaichō
Houses
(4)

Josūi-shin-machi

Wakaba
(4)

Wakabachō Houses

Daikyū
Inageya Store
Eastern Branch Office

Keyakidai

Keyakidai Houses

Tachikawa

Izumi-chō
泉町

Tachihi Enterprise

TACHIKAWA-SHI
立川市

Wide Area Disaster Prevention Base

Metropolitan Police Department
Disaster Prevention Corps

Midori-chō
緑町

Tachikawa

Metropolitan Police Department
General Government Office Bldg.

Shōwa Memorial Park

ese garden

emorial Park

chō

Pond

tropolitan Coll.

Agricultural
ent Station

Fujimi-chō
富士見町(4)

Fujimi
Branch Office

Daihachi

(7)

Daiyon

Fusaiji
Shibasaki-chō
(4) 柴崎町

Welfare Hall

Hino-honmachi

Kumano-jinja

Daigo
Takamatsuchō-2
高松町

Nat'l Hospital
Tōkyō Disaster
Medical Center

Takamatsu-chō
高松町

Tachikawa Girl's

Palace Hotel
General Welfare Center
Plaza City
Takashimaya Dept. Store

Akebonochō-2
曙町

Marui Dept. Store
Tachikawa-kita
Isetan Dept. Store

Akebono-chō
曙町

Tachikawa

Central Community Center
Suwa-jinja
Tachikawa chūo

Daiichi
Daiichi

Okutama-kaidō Ave.　奥多摩街道

Tachikawa
keisatsu-mae
立川警察前
Shibasaki-
Taiikukan
Gymnasium

Tachikawa-bashi
Bridge

Tamagawa River　多摩川

Tachikawa Park

GRANDUO

Tachikawa
minami

Nishikichō-1
錦町

Public Employment
Security Office

Nishiki-chō
錦町

Tachikawa City Office
Shiminkaikan
Hall

Tachikawa Health Center
Social Insurance Office

Dainana

Hinobashi
日野橋

Nishikichō
Sewage Disposal

Shōwa-daiichi Gakuen

Sakae-chō
栄町

Minamisuna

Ground Self-Defense Force Post
Air Self-Defense Force Post
Tachikawa School for The Deaf

Tachikawa
Cycling stadium

Daini

Tachikawa Taxation Office

Daini

Workers Welfare Hall

Chūō Line　中央線

WILL

Hagoromobashi
羽衣橋

Dairoku

Hagoromo-chō
羽衣町(2)

Seiyu Store

Daisan Tachikawa
Joint Government
Office Building

Daisan

Tama Training Center

Tachikawa Advanced
Vocational Training School

Ishida

Kōshū-kaidō Ave.　甲州街道

54 KOKUBUNJI-SHI
国分寺市

Nishi-machi

Takagi-chō

Hikari-chō

Synthetic Technical
Institute of Railway

Kitatama

Kita

Nishi-1
西一

Nishi

Kunitachinishō-mae
国立二小前

Tachikawa School for
Physically Handicapped
or Mentally Retarded
Children

56 KUNITACHI-SHI
国立市

Daisan

Fujimidai

Nanbu Line　南武線

Yaho

Hitotsubashi

Naka

Tōhō-gakuen

Kunitachi City Office

Aoyagi

Yagawa

■ WA-SHI AREA INDEX ■

ー3	H-5	Kashiwa-chō 1~5 ……… H-2
7	F-5	Midori-chō ……… G-4
1~3	I-5	Nishi-suna-chō 1~7 ……… C-2
1~5	E-2	Nishiki-chō 1~6 ……… H-6
	G-3	Saiwai-chō 1~6 ……… I-2
1~7	F-2	Sakae-chō 1~6 ……… I-3

Shibasaki-chō 1~6 ……… G-6
Sunagawa-chō 1~8 ……… G-2
Takamatsu-chō 1~3 ……… H-4
Wakaba-chō 1~4 ……… J-3

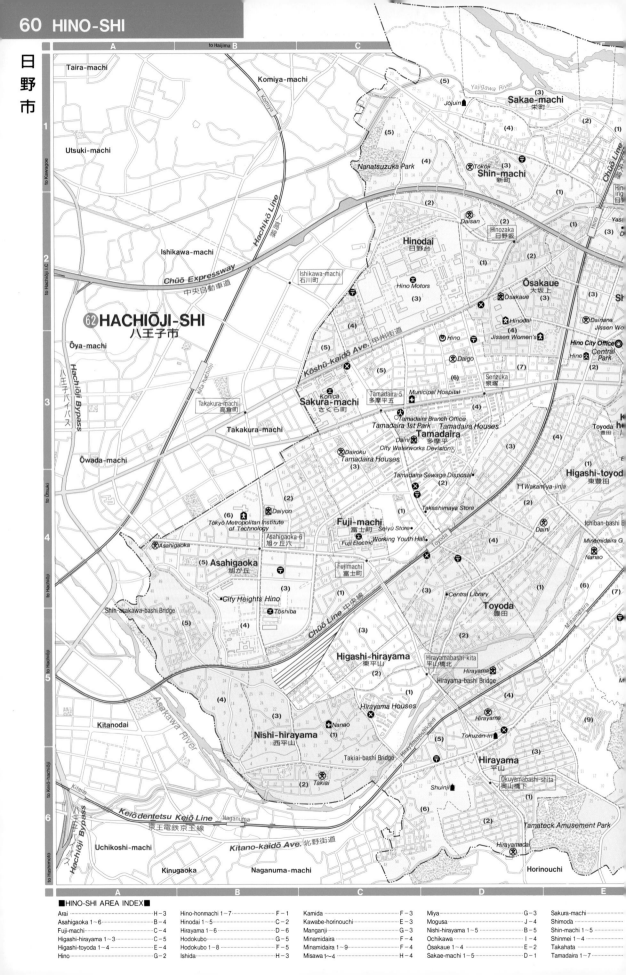

■HINO-SHI AREA INDEX■

Arai	H-3	Hino-honmachi 1~7	F-1	Kamida	F-3
Asahigaoka 1~6	B-4	Hinodai 1~5	C-2	Kawabe-horinouchi	E-3
Fuji-machi	C-4	Hirayama 1~6	D-5	Manganji	G-3
Higashi-hirayama 1~3	C-5	Hodokubo	G-5	Minamidaira	F-4
Higashi-toyoda 1~4	E-4	Hodokubo 1~8	F-5	Minamidaira 1~9	F-4
Hino	G-2	Ishida	H-3	Misawa 1~4	H-4

Miya	G-3	Sakura-machi	
Mogusa	J-4	Shimoda	
Nishi-hirayama 1~5	B-5	Shin-machi 1~5	
Ochikawa	I-4	Shinmei 1~4	
Ōsakaue 1~4	E-2	Takahata	
Sakae-machi 1~5	D-1	Tamadaira	

1 : 25,000

0   250   500   750m

to Fuchū   to Tachikawa

58 TACHIKAWA-SHI
立川市

Ishida

Yagawa

Nishiki-chō

Aoyagi

Fujimidai

Nanbu Line 南武線

Kunitachi City Office

1

Shin-okutama-kaidō Ave. 新奥多摩街道

Shibasaki-chō

Tachikawa Park

Kōshū-kaidō Ave. 甲州街道

Yaho

Nakada (6)
onmachi
野本町

Haneda Flume Pipe

Hinobashi-minami
日野橋南

56 KUNITACHI-SHI
国立市

Playground
(7)

Tama Urban Monorail

Tamagawa River

Ishida
石田

Chūō Expressway
中央自動車道

Izumi

Community Center

Kōshūkaidō

Daiyon

Tamagawa-bashi Bridge

Kunitachi-Fuchū I.C
国立府中IC

2

Hino
日野

Hino
Hino Agricultural Cooperative
ssociation

Snow Brand Milk Products

Manganji
万願寺

Shimoda
下田

Civic Ground

Orient Watch

Manganji
万願寺

Manganji
万願寺

Manganji

Hino

Shimoda

Arai
新井

56 FUCHŪ-SHI
府中市

Nisshin-chō

3

Kamida
上田

Ishida
石田

Ishida
石田

Ishida
石田

Ishida
石田
Ishidaji

Miya
宮

Manganji
万願寺

Hino

Clean Center

Yotsuya

Kamida
上田

Taxation Office

Fureai-bashi Bridge

Arai-bashi Bridge

Asakawa River

Arai
新井

Takahata-bashi Bridge

Juntoku

Mogusaen Houses

Mogusa
百草

Ochikawa
落川

kaidō Ave. 北野街道
(4)

Takahatabashi-minami
高幡橋南

Takahata
高幡

Takahata-fudoson
Keiō Store
Takahatafudō

Misawa
三沢

Hino Health Center

Daihachi

Mogusa
百草

Tama Driving School

4

Minamidaira
南平
(3)

Ōta Store

Misawa

Keiōdentetsu Keiō Line
京王電鉄京王線

Mogusa
三沢

Mogusa
百草

Ochikawa
落川

(1)

Takahata
高幡

Kawasaki-kaidō Ave.
川崎街道

Misawa

Keiō Dobutsuen Line

Nanao Branch Office
(4)

Misawa
三沢
(3)

Misawa
三沢
(3)

Minamidaira
南平

Hodokubo

Mitsui Houses
Hodokubo
程久保

(1)

Misawa
三沢

Seibu Mogusaen Houses(2)

Takahatadai Houses

Mogusadai

Misawa
三沢

Mogusaen Garden

Mogusa-hachimangū

Ichinomiya
一の宮

Ichinomiya
一の宮
Ochikawa
落川

5

Musashidai Houses

Hodokubo
程久保

Takahatadai

Misawadai

Mogusa
百草

Ochikawa
落川

Chōrakuji

Hodokubo
程久保

Mogusa Houses

Nanao School for Physically Handicapped
or Mentally Retarded Children

Mogusa-kannondō

Tōden-gakuen

ogical Park
(2)

Daisan

Nanao Welfare Home

Mogusaen Houses

Higashiteragata

Hodokubo
程久保

2nd Musashidai Houses
(3)

Tama Kōseien

Sugino-gakuen

(4)

Meisei

Ōtsuka

Higashi-nakano

Teikyō

Wada

70 TAMA-SHI
多摩市

6

Chūō
Chūōdaigaku
Meiseidaigaku

Yaen-kaidō Ave. 野猿街道

Ochikawa

F   G   H   I   J

E - 3

D - 4

1:30,000

0   500   1000m

八王子市（Ⅰ）

to Ōme

AKIRUNO-SHI
あきる野市

to Akiruno

Dōwa Mining Central Institute
Central Cemetery
Meiji Mutual Life Insurance Co. Green Land
Kyōrin

Club House
Nishihachiōji
Meidainakano Hachiōji
Kaidō-bashi Bridge
Takiyama-kaidō Ave.

GMG Hachiōji Golf Course

Miyashita-machi
宮下町
Kasumi

Tobuki-machi
戸吹町

Kamikawa-machi
上川町

Musashino Golf Club
Club House
Kasumi Branch C

Kawaguchi-machi
川口町
Club House
Hachiōji Country Club

Kasum
加

Chōrakuji
Kawaguchi Branch Office
Kawaguchi
Takao-kaidō Ave.

Kawaguchi

Takiyama

Kawaguchi River

Inume-machi
犬目町
Tōyō

Akigawa-kaidō Ave.
秋川街道

Hōshōji Houses

Nishiterakata-machi
西寺方町
Hōshōji

Tōkyō Shinsei
Kamiichibunkata
Tōkyō-tenshi
Shimogawa Houses

Hachiōji-kita
Matsue
Gyokuyōkan Asakawaen
Narahara
楢原

Hachiōji-kita Jr.
Toita Women's Jr. C

Miyama-machi
美山町
Ryōhoku-ōhashi Bridge
Matsue Houses
Chūjitsuya Store
Matsue-bashi Bridge

Women's G
Fujiho
婦人補

Motoki
Shimo-ongata-machi
下恩方町

Kami-ichibunkata-machi
上壱分方町

Suwa-machi
諏訪町

Yotsuya-machi
四谷町

Narahara-machi
楢原町

Narahara

Jinba-kaidō Ave.
陣馬街道

Yotsuya

Nibukata-machi
弐分方町

Izumi-chō
泉町

Narahara

Hachiōji Welfare Home
Hachiōji-nishi Health Clinic
Ongata
Ryōhoku
Hachiōji-kōryō

Motohachiōji
Yotsuyamachi
四谷町

Kiyokawa-chō
清川町

Chūjitsuya Store

Kanseiji
Nibukata
Moto-hachiōji Branch Office
Motohachiōji

Motohachiōji-higashi
Sōsokuji
Asakawa-bashi Bridge
Gourmet City

Kanoya-machi
叶谷町

Ongata
Kawa-machi
川町

Green Town Takao

Dairakuji-machi
大楽寺町

Shiroyama
Seirenji

Yokokawa
Yokokawa
Tsurumaki-bashi Bridge
Purification Plant

Hachiōji City Offic
(4)

Matsukomai Houses

Chūō Expressway
中央自動車道
Yokokawabashi Bridge

Moto-hong
元本郷

Municipal Owed Hachiōji Cemetery

Moto-hachiōji-machi
元八王子町
(2)

Motohachinichōme
元八二丁目

Yokokawa-machi
横川町

Midorigaoka Houses
Minase-bashi Bridg

Branch Office of F
Legal Affairs

Tōkyō Cemetery
Management Center
Minamitama Cemetery
Shiroyama

Kyōritsu Women's
Kyōritsu Joshi Daini
Nagafusa
Funada

Nagafusa 1st. Houses
Nagafusa
Fujimori

Hiyoshi-chō
臼井町
Sōkakuin
Daigo
Sennin-chō
千人町
(2)

Hachiōji-kōgyō (3)
Chūjitsuya Store
Central Library

Hachiman-jinja

Nagafusa-machi
長房町

Higashi-yokoyama-bashi Bridge
(4)

Public Er
Minamitama

Goreiya River

Nagafusa-machi
長房町

Keiō Store
Yokoyama-daini

Shiroyamate
城山手
(1)

Namiki-chō
並木町

Sanda-machi
散田町
(3)

Chōsenji
Kōshū-kaidō Ave.
甲州街道

Kasumigaoka Houses

Seiy
(2)

to Sagamiko | to Takao | | to Ōtsuki |

■AREA INDEX■

Akatsuki-chō 1〜3 ·········· 63·G-5	Dairakuji-machi ·········· 62·C-4	Higashi-nakano ·········· 70·D-3	Inume-machi ·········· 62·D-3	Kami-yugi 2·3
Asahi-chō ·········· 63·G-6	Fujimi-chō ·········· 63·H-5	Hiraoka-chō ·········· 63·F-5	Ishikawa-machi ·········· 63·I-4	Kamikawa-machi
Azuma-chō ·········· 63·G-6	Fukiman-chō ·········· 63·F-6	Hiyoshi-chō ·········· 62·E-6	Izumi-chō ·········· 62·D-4	Kanōya-machi
Bessho 1·2 ·········· 70·C-5	Hatsuzawa-machi ·········· 64·B-2	Hon-chō ·········· 63·G-6	Kami-ichibukata-machi ·········· 62·B-3	Kashima
Dai-machi 1〜4 ·········· 65·F-1	Hazama-machi ·········· 64·B-3	Hongō-chō ·········· 63·F-6	Kami-ongata-machi ·········· 94·B-2	Kasumi-machi 1·2
	Higashi-asakawa-machi ·········· 64·C-2	Horinouchi ·········· 70·D-3	Kami-yugi ·········· 65·J-5	Katakura-machi
		Hyōe 1 ·········· 65·G-3		

八王子市（Ⅰ）

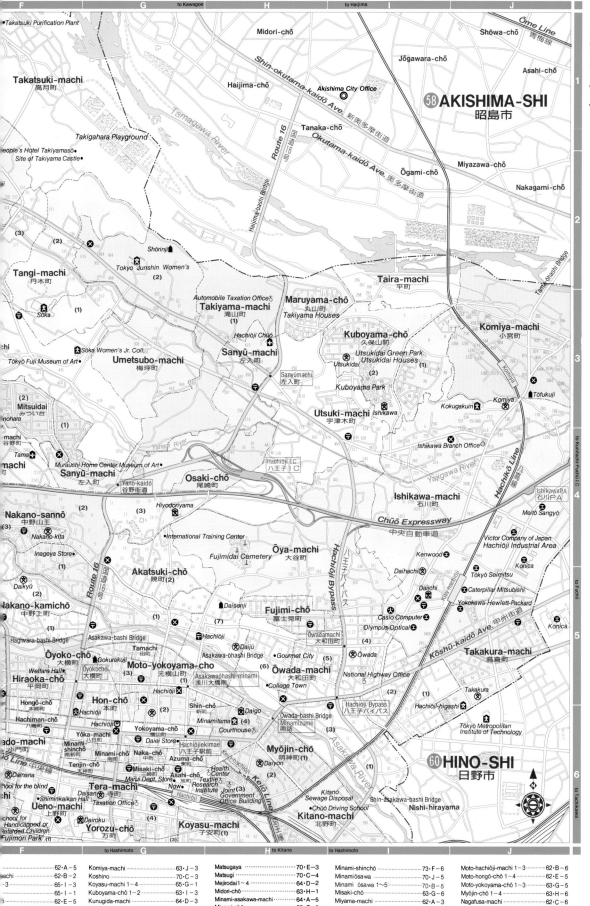

…machi	62・A‑5	Komiya-machi	63・J‑3
…machi	62・B‑2	Koshino	70・C‑3
…3	65・I‑1	Koyasu-machi 1～4	65・G‑1
…machi	62・E‑5	Kuboyama-chō 1～2	63・I‑3
…3	65・F‑3	Kunugida-machi	64・D‑3
		Maruyama-chō	63・H‑3

Matsugaya	70・E‑3	Minami-shinchō	73・F‑6	Moto-hachiōji-machi 1～3	62・B‑6
Matsugi	70・C‑4	Minamiōsawa	70・J‑5	Moto-hongō-chō 1～4	62・E‑5
Mejirodai 1～4	64・D‑2	Minami ōsawa 1～5	70・B‑5	Moto-yokoyama-chō 1～3	63・G‑5
Midori-chō	63・H‑1	Misaki-chō	63・G‑6	Myōjin-chō 1～4	63・H‑6
Minami-asakawa-machi	64・A‑5	Miyama-machi	62・A‑3	Nagafusa-machi	62・C‑6
Minami-chō	63・G‑6	Miyashita-machi	62・E‑1	Naganuma-machi	65・J‑2
Minamino 1・3～6	65・F‑3				

八王子市(II)

1 : 30,000

0 500 1000m

to Hachiōji · to Nishi-akiru | to Fuchū

Chūō Expressway 中央自動車道

Hachiman-jinja
Funada
Nagafusa-daiichi Houses
Fujimori
Higashi-yokoyama-bashi Bridge
Hachiōji-kōgyō
Central Library
Public E Sec
Sennin-chō 千人町
Chūji
Moto-hachiōji-machi 元八王子町
Kasumigaoka Houses
Shiroyamate 城山手
Chōsenji
Nagafusa-machi 長房町
Chūjitsuya Store
Nagafusa-danchi-iriguchi 長房団地入口
Namiki-chō 並木町
Yokoyama-daini
Sanda-machi 散田町
Takaodai Houses
Nagafusa-machi 長房町
Musashiryō Graveyard
Tama-ryō Mausoleum
Musashino-ryō Mausoleum
Tama-higashi-ryō Mausoleum
Fukuju-gakuen
Ryōnan Park
Yokoyama Branch Office
Yokoyama
Shinkakumitsuji
Sanda
Seiy
Forestry and Forest Product Research Institute
Tama Forest Science Garden
Todori-machi 廿里町
Hachiōji-nishi
Keiō-mejirodai Houses
Yamada
Yama
Nishi-asakawa-machi 西浅川町
Machida-kaidō-iriguchi 町田街道入口
Ryōnan
Higashi-asakawa-machi 東浅川町
Keiō Store
Ura-takao-machi 裏高尾町
Asakawa Branch Office
Oki Electric Industry
Mejirodai (2) めじろ台
Chūō Line 中央本線
Takao
Higashiasakawa
Daiei Store
Hazama
Komakino
Asakawa
Tōkyō-kōgyō Junior Coll.
Kunugidamachi 椚田町
Korakuji
Satō Pharmaceutical
Hachiōji-minami Cemetery
Kunugida-machi 椚田町
Asakawa
Hazama-machi 狭間町
Kitano-kaidō Ave. 北野街道
Kunugidai Pla
Takao-machi 高尾町
Hatsuzawa-machi 初沢町
Yokoyama-daiichi
Tate Branch Office
Kunugida
People's hotel Takaosansō
Takao-kōyōdai Houses
Jōsenji
Ryūkenji
Nippon Vehicle Service Coll.
Lift Sanroku Kiyotaki
Cable Railway
Natural Science Museum
Medical Center Attached to Tōkyō Medical Coll.
Kamitate
Tate-machi 館町
Yurinokidai Houses
Asakawa E.S. Annai Annex
Takushoku
Tate
Tatemachi Houses
Haruna-jinja
HACHIŌJI-SHI 八王子市
Tategaoka Houses
Tonoiri
Eimeikan
Green Hill Terada Houses
Terada-machi 寺田町
Ōfuna 大
Minami-asakawa-machi 南浅川町
Tate Incineration Plant
Terada
Inariyama
Hōsei Univ. Ground
Agricultural Cooperative Assn. Chūō Gakuen
Hōsei
Sōbu Country Club
Aihara-machi 相原町
Ōto
Ōyoko-chō
Tōkyō Kasei Gakuin
Motozawa Dam
Shiroyamako Lake
Musashioka
Enrinji
NTT Aihara Relay
SHIROYAMA-MACHI 城山町
Nakazawa
Kawajiri
Wakabadai

■AREA INDEX■

A	B	C	D	E
Naka-chō ·······63·G-6	Nan-yōdai 1~3 ·······65·J-3	Oiwake-chō ·······63·E-6	Ōya-machi ·······63·H-4	Shimo-yugi
Nakano-kamichō 1~5 ·······63·F-5	Narahara-machi ·······62·D-4	Okado-machi ·······63·F-6	Ōyoko-chō ·······63·F-5	Shimo-yugi 2~3
Nakano-machi ·······63·F-4	Nibukata-machi ·······62·B-4	Osaki-chō ·······63·H-4	Sanda-machi 1~5 ·······64·E-1	Shin-chō
Nakano-sannō 1~3 ·······63·F-4	Nishi-Asakawa-machi ·······64·A-2	Otsu-machi ·······64·B-2	Sanyū-machi ·······63·F-3	Shiroyamate 1~2
Nakayama ·······65·I-4	Nishi-Katakura 1~3 ·······65·F-3	Ōtsuka ·······70·E-2	Sennin-chō 1~4 ·······62·E-6	Suwa-machi
Namiki-chō ·······64·D-1	Nishiterakata-machi ·······62·A-3	Ōwada-machi 1~7 ·······63·H-5	Shimo-ongata-machi ·······62·A-1	Taira-machi
Nanakuni 6 ·······65·F-4	Ōfuna-machi ·······64·E-4			

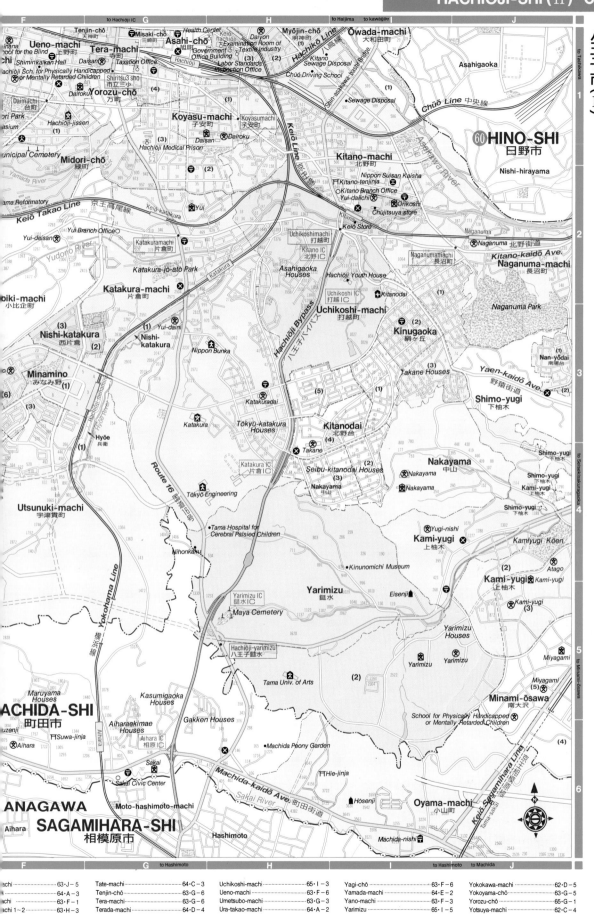

...machi	63·J·5	Tate-machi ·········· 64·C·3	Uchikoshi-machi ········· 65·I·3	Yagi-chō ··············· 63·F·6	Yokokawa-machi ······· 62·D·5
...chi	64·A·3	Tenjin-chō ·········· 63·G·6	Ueno-machi ············· 63·F·6	Yamada-machi ·········· 64·E·2	Yokoyama-chō ········· 63·G·5
...chi	63·F·1	Tera-machi ·········· 63·G·6	Umetsubo-machi ······· 63·G·3	Yano-machi ············· 63·F·3	Yorozu-chō ············· 65·G·1
...chi 1~2	63·H·3	Terada-machi ······· 64·D·4	Ura-takao-machi ······· 64·A·2	Yarimizu ··············· 65·I·5	Yotsuya-machi ········· 62·C·4
...chi	63·G·5	Tobuki-machi ······· 62·C·1	Utsuki-machi ··········· 63·I·1	Yarimizu 2 ············· 65·I·5	Mitsuidai 1~2 ·········· 63·F·3
...1~3	63·F·2	Todori-machi ········ 64·B·2	Utsunuki-machi ········ 65·F·4	Yōka-machi ············· 63·G·6	

調布市・狛江市

1:27,000

0   400   800m

54 **KOGANEI-SHI**
小金井市
Higashi-chō

Jindaiji

Luther Gakuin
Tōkyō Union Theological Seminary

International Christian

Fuji Heavy Industries

Nozaki

Nozaki-nishi
野崎西

Mitaka City Office

Kōkūken-mae
航空研究所

Nozakihachiman-mae
野崎八幡前

(8)

Aerospace Research Institute

52 **MITAKA-SHI**
三鷹市

Tōhachi-dōro Ave. 東八道路

Ōsawa

Chōfu-kita
(5)

Kichijōji
(4)

(7)

Jindaiji-higashi-machi
深大寺東町

Fire Defence C
Fire Research Ins

Nogawa Park
Nomizu
野水

American School

Tama-machi

Hitomi-kaidō Ave. 人見街道

National Astronomical Observatory

Nogawa River

Jindaiji-kita-machi
深大寺北町
(3)

Sengen-jinja
(1)

(7)

Kitanodai

Shokubutsukōen-mae
植物公園前

Jindai Botanical Garden
(5)

Jindaiji
深大寺

Synthetic Gymnasium

(6)

Purification Plant No.3

Aoi-jinja
Jindaiji Jindaiji

(1)

Jindaiji-minami-machi
深大寺南町

Nomizu
野水
(1)

Chōfu Airfield

Chōfu Airfield Office

Asahi-chō

Nishi-machi
西町

Chōfu

(4)

(8)

Jindaiji-moto-machi
深大寺元町
(1)

(2)

Jindaiji Natu

Kashiwano
(2)

Kohaku-jinja
(2) Gionji

56 **FUCHŪ-SHI**
府中市

Tokyo Stadium

Kōshū-kaidō Ave. 甲州街道

Purification Plant No.1

Ishiwara

Fujimi-chō
富士見町
(1)

Hashutsusho-mae
派出所前

Chōfugaoka
調布ヶ丘

Kita-tama
The Univ. of
Electro Communications

Kōrakuen Shopping Center

(3)

Shiraitodai

Kami-ishiwara
上石原
(1)

Yakushidō

Kami-ishiwara-1
上石原一

Chōfu I.C
調布

Chōfu

Kojimachō
小島町

Chōfu
Daiichi

Fuda-jinja
Fuda-chō

Chōfu School for Physically
Handicapped or Mentally Retarded Children

Shimo-

Yagum

Musashinodai

Seichōnoie Exercise Hall

Tobitakyū

Keiōdentetsu Keiō Line 京王電鉄京王線

Nishi-chofu

Seiyū Store

(2)

Kurumagaeshi Houses

Tobitakyū
飛田給

Daisan

Tobitakyū

Shimo-ishiwara
下石原

Tsurukawa-kaidō
鶴川街道

Store
Parco

Chōfu
Cooperative Association
Culture Hall

Civic Welfare Hall
Civic Center

Fuda
布田

(3)

Chōfu City Hall

Tōkyū Shopping Center

Oshitate-chō

Chūō Expressway 中央自動車道

Kami-ishiwara
上石原

Wakamiyahachiman-jinja

Daigo

Aoki

Chōfu

Kojima-chō
小島町

Chōfueki-minamiguchi
調布駅南口

**CHŌFU-
調布**

(6)

Koyanagi-chō

Inagi-bashi Bridge

Fujimidai

Local Museum

Komae-chōfu Health Center

Tōhō Chōfu
Golf Course
(2)

Tamagawa

Tamagawa
多摩川

Daiei Studio

Chōfu-minami

Fuda

Inageya Fu

Shimo-ishihara
下石原

Oshitate

Keiōkaku
Cycling Stadium

Keiō Tennis Club
Keiō Swimming Pool

(7)

Tamagawa

Tamagawa Amusement Park

Civic Ground

Kamifuda-chō
上布田町

Kojima-chō
小島町

68 **INAGI-SHI**
稲城市

Yanokuchi

Nanbu Line 南武線

Suge-notoro

Tamagawa River

Suge-inadazutsumi

Higashinaganuma

Kawasaki-kaidō Ave. 川崎街道

Yanokuchi

Suge

Inadazutsumi

KANAGAW

Inagi-naganuma

■**CHŌFU-SHI AREA INDEX**■

Chōfugaoka 1~4 ··············· D-4
Fuda 1~6 ······················· E-4
Fujimi-chō 1~4 ················ C-4
Higashi-tsutsujigaoka 1~3 ··· G-3
Irima 1~3 ······················· C-4
Jindaiji-higashi-machi 1~8 ··· E-1

Jindaiji-kita-machi 1~7 ······· D-1
Jindaiji-minami-machi 1~5 ··· D-2
Jindaiji-moto-machi 1~5 ····· D-3
Kami-ishiwara 1~3 ············ C-4
Kikunodai 1~3 ················· F-3
Kojima-chō 1~3 ··············· D-4

Kokuryō-chō 1~8 ·············· F-4
Midorigaoka 1~2 ·············· G-1
Nishi-machi ···················· B-3
Nishi-tsutsujigaoka 1~4 ····· G-3
Nomizu 1~2 ···················· A-2
Sazu-machi 1~5 ··············· E-3

Sengawa-chō 1~3 ············· G-2
Shibasaki 1~2 ················· F-3
Shimo-ishiwara 1~3 ·········· C-4
Somechi 1~3 ··················· F-5
Tamagawa 1~7 ················ D-5
Tobitakyū 1~3 ················· B-4

Wakaba-chō 1~3 ··············
Yagumodai 1~2 ···············

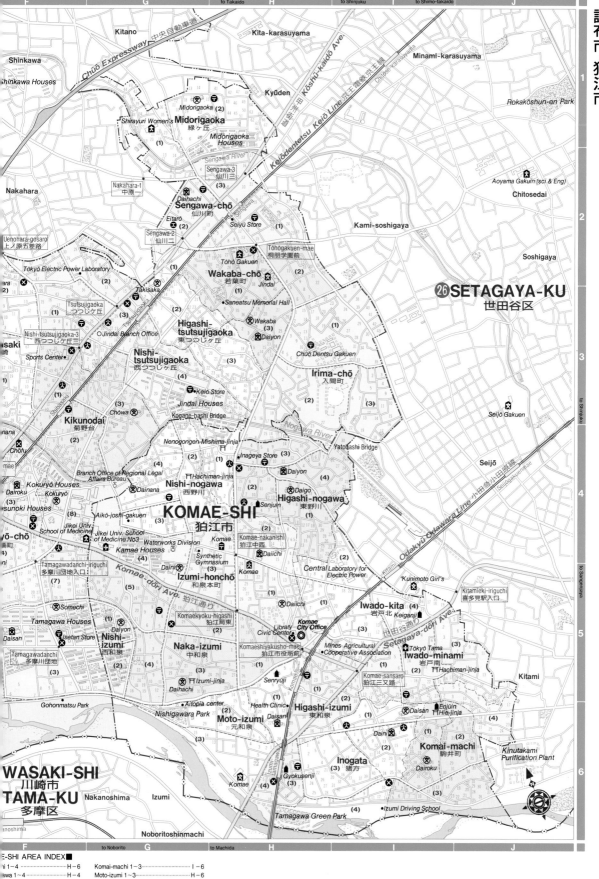

調布市・狛江市

to Takaido
to Shinjuku
to Shimo-takaido

Kitano
中央自動車道
Kita-karasuyama
Minami-karasuyama

Shinkawa
Chūō Expressway
京王電鉄京王線
Rokakōshun-en Park

Shinkawa Houses
Keiōdentetsu Keiō Line
Chitose-karasuyama
1

Kyūden

Midorigaoka (2)
Shirayuri Women's
Midorigaoka
緑ヶ丘
Midorigaoka Houses
(1)
Aoyama Gakuin (sci & Eng)

Sengawa River
Chitosedai

Nakahara
Sengawa-3
仙川三 (3)
Kami-soshigaya

Nakahara-1
中原一
Daihachi
Sengawa-chō
仙川町
Kami-soshigaya

Uenohara-gosaro
上ノ原五差路
Eitarō
Seiyu Store
Sengawa-2
仙川二

Tōhōgakuen-mae
桐朋学園前

Tōkyō Electric Power Laboratory
(1)
Tōhō Gakuen
Wakaba-chō
若葉町
Jindai

Takisaka
Saneatsu Memorial Hall

Tsutsujigaoka
つつじヶ丘 (3)
Wakaba
Daiyon
26 SETAGAYA-KU
世田谷区

Nishi-tsutsujigaoka-3
西つつじヶ丘三
(1)
Jindai Branch Office
Higashi-tsutsujigaoka
東つつじヶ丘
(3)

Sports Center
Nishi-tsutsujigaoka
西つつじヶ丘 (4)
Chūō Dentsu Gakuen
Irima-chō
入間町
(3)

Keiō Store
Jindai Houses
(2)
Seijō Gakuen

Kikunodai
菊野台
Chōwa
Kogane-bashi Bridge

Nogawa River

Nenogongen-Mishima-jinja
Inageya Store
Yatobashi Bridge
Seijō

Chōfu
Hachiman-jinja
Nishi-nogawa
西野川
Daiyon

Branch Office of Regional Legal Affairs Bureau
Dainana
Daigo
Higashi-nogawa
東野川

Kokuryō Houses
Kokuryō
Dairoku
KOMAE-SHI
狛江市
Senjuin

Kusunoki Houses
(8)
Aikō-joshi-gakuen
Komae
Komae-nakanishi
狛江中西

Jikei Univ. School of Medicine
Jikei Univ. School of Medicine No3
Waterworks Division
Daiichi

ryō-chō
Kamae Houses
Synthetic Gymnasium
Komae
Central Laboratory for Electric Power

Dairoku
Dalni
Izumi-honchō
和泉本町
Kunimoto Girl's
Kitamieki-iriguchi
喜多見駅入口

Tamagawadanchi-iriguchi
多摩川団地入口 (7)
Daiichi
Iwado-kita
岩戸北
Keiganji

Somechi
Komaekyoku-higashi
狛江局東
Komae City Office
Tōkyō Tama

Tamagawa Houses
Daiyon
Library
Komae Civic Center
Mines Agricultural Cooperative Association
Iwado-minami
岩戸南

Daisan
Isetan Store
Nishi-izumi
西和泉
Naka-izumi
中和泉
Komaeshiyakusho-mae
狛江市役所前
Komae-sansaro
狛江三叉路
Hachiman-jinja
Kitami

Tamagawadanchi
多摩川団地
Izumi-jinja
Daihachi
Senryūji
Health Clinic
Higashi-izumi
東和泉
Daisan
Eqiuin
Hie-jinja

Gohonmatsu Park
Aifopia center
Nishigawara Park
Moto-izumi
元和泉
Daisan
Daini
Komai-machi
駒井町
Kinutakami Purification Plant

WASAKI-SHI
川崎市
TAMA-KU
多摩区
Nakanoshima
Izumi
Gyokusenji
Inogata
猪方 (3)
Dairoku

Komae
Tamagawa Green Park
Izumi Driving School

Noboritoshinmachi
to Noborito
to Machida

E-SHI AREA INDEX
Komai-machi 1~3 .... I-6
awa 1~4 .... H-6
Moto-izumi 1~3 .... H-6
4 .... I-6
Naka-izumi 1~5 .... G-5
i 1~4 .... I-5
Nishi-izumi 1~2 .... G-5
i 1~4 .... I-5
Nishi-nogawa 1~4 .... G-4
ō 1~5 .... H-5

1:25,000

稲城市

Keiō Line

Seiseki Sakuragaoka

Sekido

Tamagawa River

Suntory

Fujitsu

Iōji

Minam

Clean Center Tamagawa
Minamitama Sewage Disposal

Municipal Hospita

Sakuragaoka

Kawasaki-kaidō Ave.

川崎街道

Renkōji

Sakuragaoka Country Club

Ōmaru
大丸

U.S Army Tama Service

2nd Inagi Tunnel

Tama New Town-dōri Ave.

多摩ニュータウン通り

to Takahatafudō

Kaidori

⑦**TAMA-SHI**
多摩市

Ichinomiya

Higashinaganuma
東長沼

(4)

(5)

Kōyōdai
向陽台

Ribere Kōyōdai

(3)

Da

Tama City Office

Kōyōdai

Kata-jinja

U.S Army Tama
Golf Course

Tama Country Club

Inagi Central Park

to Tama Center

Hijirigaoka

Club House

Nagamine
長峰
Nagamine

(1)

(3)

to Tama Center

Keiō-nagayama

Ōdakyū-nagayama

(2)

Hōzòin

Kōshōji

(4)

Suwa

Tama-higashi Park

Inagidai

Wakabadai
若葉台

(1)

(3)

Daini

Keiō Sagamihara Line

富士相模原線

Nagayama

(3)

(2)

Tenman-jinja

Wakabadai
BranchOffice

Sakahama
坂浜

Clu

Inagi

Wakabadai

Daini

Purification Plant No.2

Ōdakyū Tama Line

小田急多摩線

Kurokawa

Minami-kurokawa

Nihon Univ. Ground

Hirao
平尾

Sugiyama-jinja

Tsurukawa-kaidō Ave.

鶴川街道

Kurikidai

Daigo

Hirao Branch Office

(3)

Hira

Onoji-machi

Kuriki

Kurihira

Kurihira

Shiratori

Gorikida

⑦**MACHIDA-SHI**
町田市

Shinkōji-machi

■AREA INDEX

Higashinaganuma	D – 2	Oshitate	H – 1	
Hirao	E – 6	Sakahama	E – 4	
Kōyōdai 1~6	E – 2	Yanokuchi	H – 3	
Momura	F – 2	Wakabadai	C – 4	
Nagamine 1~3	D – 1			
Ōmaru	D – 1			

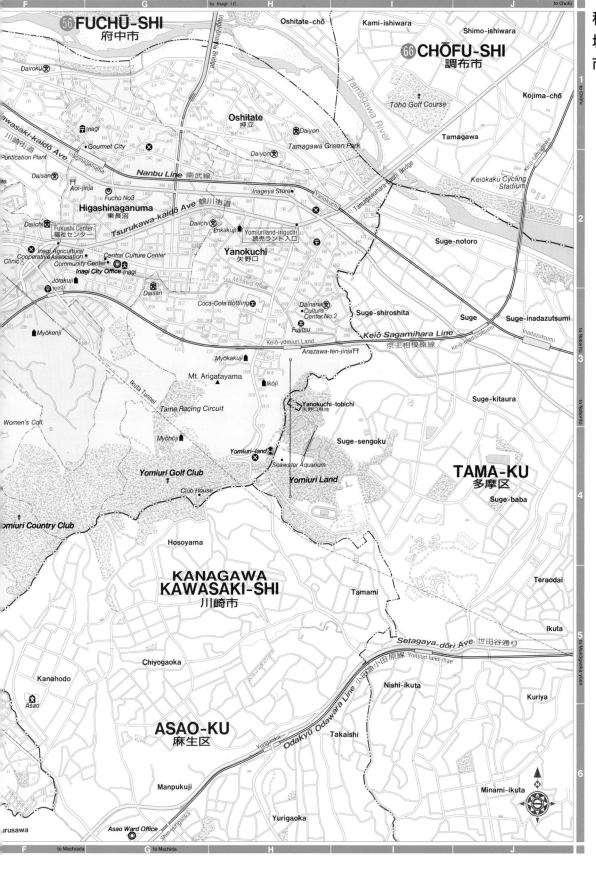

F　to Inagi I.C.　G　to Chofu J

56 FUCHŪ-SHI
府中市

Oshitate-chō

Kami-ishiwara

Shimo-ishiwara

66 CHŌFU-SHI
調布市

Kojima-chō

Dairoku

Oshitate
押立

Daiyon

Toho Golf Course

Tamagawa River

Tamagawa

Inagi

Gourmet City

597

Daiyon

Tamagawa Green Park

Purification Plant

川崎街道

Kawasaki-kaidō Ave.

Inaginaganuma

Nanbu Line 南武線

1440

Keiōkaku Cycling Stadium

Daisan

Aoi-jinja

Fuchū No3

1130

Inageya Store

Yanokuchi

Tamagawahara-ōhashi Bridge

Suge-notoro

Higashinaganuma
東長沼

Tsurukawa-kaidō Ave. 鶴川街道

Daiichi

Enkakuji

Yomiuriland-iriguchi
読売ランド入口

213

740

Daiichi

Fukushi Center
福祉センター

Yanokuchi
矢野口

Suge-shiroshita

Inagi Agricultural Cooperative Association

Central Culture Center

Misawa River

Suge

Suge-inadazutsumi

Clinic

Community Center

Inagi City Office Inagi

Daisan

Inadazutsumi

Jōrakuji

Inagi

Coca-Cola Bottling

Dainana Culture Center No.2

Keiō Sagamihara Line

Fujitsu

京王相模原線

Myōkenji

Anazawa-ten-jinja

Keiō-yomiuri Land

Myōkakuji

Suge-kitaura

Mt. Arigatayama

Ikoji

Ikuta Tunnel

Tama Racing Circuit

Yanokuchi-tobichi
矢野口飛地

Women's Coll.

Myōhōji

Suge-sengoku

Yomiuri-land

TAMA-KU
多摩区

Yomiuri Golf Club

Seawater Aquarium

Yomiuri Land

Suge-baba

Club House

Yomiuri Country Club

Hosoyama

Teraodai

**KANAGAWA
KAWASAKI-SHI**
川崎市

Tamami

Ikuta

Chiyogaoka

Setagaya-dōri Ave. 世田谷通り

Kanahodo

Odakyū Odawara Line 小田急小田原線

Yomiuri land-mae

Nishi-ikuta

Kuriya

Asao

ASAO-KU
麻生区

Takaishi

Yurigaoka

Manpukuji

Shin-yurigaoka

Minami-ikuta

urusawa

Asao Ward Office

Yurigaoka

F　to Machiada　G　to Machida　H　I　J

多摩市

1:30,000

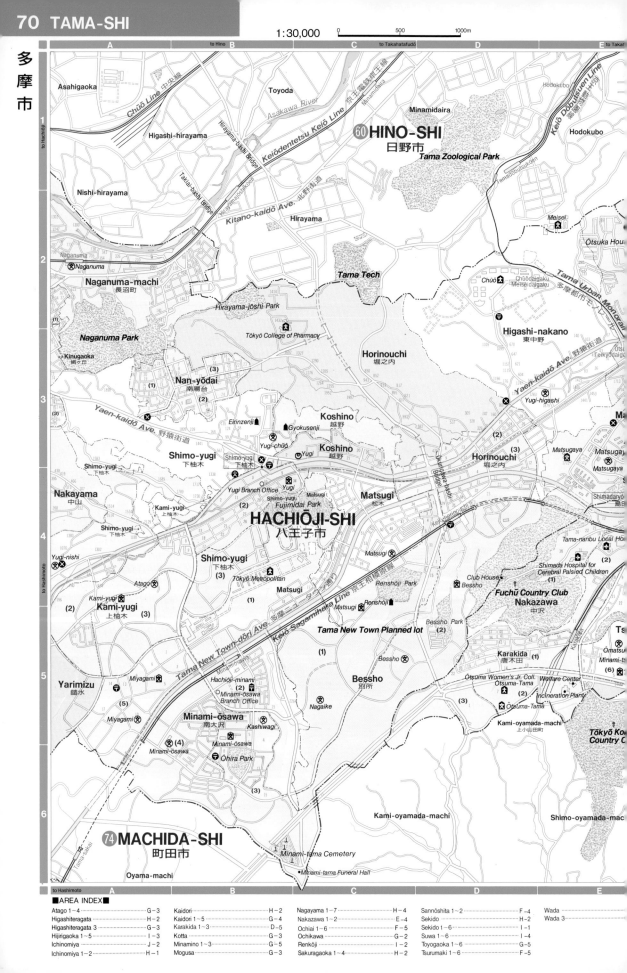

Asahigaoka

Chūō Line 中央線

Toyoda

Minamidaira

Keiōdentetsu Keiō Line 京王電鉄京王線

Minamidaira

⑥HINO-SHI
日野市

Hodokubo

Keiō Dobutsuen Line 京王動物園線

Hodokubo

Higashi-hirayama

Tama Zoological Park

Hirayama-bashi Bridge

Asakawa River

Nishi-hirayama

Takiai-bashi Bridge

Meisei

Ōtsuka Hou

Kitano-kaidō Ave. 北野街道

Hirayama

Tama Urban Monorail 多摩都市モノレール

Naganuma

Naganuma

Naganuma-machi
長沼町

Tama Tech

Chūō

Chūōdaigaku
Meiseidaigaku

Hirayama-jōshi Park

Naganuma Park

Kinugaoka
絹ヶ丘

Tōkyō College of Pharmacy

Horinouchi
堀之内

Higashi-nakano
東中野

Teikyōdaigaku

Nan-yōdai
南陽台

Yaen-kaidō Ave. 野猿街道

Yaen-kaidō Ave. 野猿街道

Eirinzenji

Koshino
越野

Gyokusenji

Yugi-higashi

Yugi-chūō

Koshino
越野

Yugi

Matsugaya

Matsugaya

Shimo-yugi
下柚木

Shimo-yugi
下柚木

Horinouchi
堀之内

Matsugaya

Shimo-yugi
下柚木

Yugi Branch Office

Shimo-yugi

Yugi
Fujimidai Park

Matsugi
松木

Nakayama
中山

Kami-yugi
上柚木

Shimadaryō

Shimo-yugi
下柚木

HACHIŌJI-SHI
八王子市

Matsugi

Tama-nanbu Local Ho

Yugi-nishi

Shimo-yugi
下柚木

Matsugi

Club House

Shimada Hospital for
Cerebral Palsied Children

Atago

Tōkyō Metropolitan

Club House
Bessho

Kami-yugi
上柚木

Matsugi

Renshōji Park

Fuchū Country Club
Nakazawa
中沢

Kami-yugi
上柚木

Renshōji

Matsugi

Bessho

Karakida
唐木田

Ōmatsu

Minami-ts

Keiō Sagamihara Line 京王相模原線

Tama New Town Planned lot

Bessho Park

Tama New Town-dōri Ave. 多摩ニュータウン通り

Bessho

Ōtsuma Women's Jr. Coll.
Ōtsuma-Tama

Welfare Center

Yarimizu
鑓水

Miyagami

Hachiōji-minami

Bessho
別所

Otsuma-Tama

Incineration Plant

Nagaike

Kami-oyamada-machi
上小山田町

Minami-ōsawa
Branch Office

Ōtsuma-Tama

Tōkyō Ko
Country C

Miyagami

Minami-ōsawa
南大沢

Kashiwagi

Minami-ōsawa

Minami-ōsawa

Ohira Park

Shimo-oyamada-mac

Kami-oyamada-machi

⑦MACHIDA-SHI
町田市

Minami-tama Cemetery

Tama-sakai

Oyama-machi

Minami-tama Funeral Hall

■AREA INDEX■

Atago 1~4	G-3	Kaidori	H-2	Nagayama 1~7	H-4	Sannōshita 1~2	F-4	Wada
Higashiteragata	H-2	Kaidori 1~5	G-4	Nakazawa 1~2	E-4	Sekido	H-2	Wada 3
Higashiteragata 3	G-3	Karakida 1~3	D-5	Ochiai 1~6	F-5	Sekido 1~6	I-1	
Hijirigaoka 1~5	I-3	Kotta	G-3	Ochikawa	G-2	Suwa 1~6	I-4	
Ichinomiya	J-2	Minamino 1~3	G-5	Renkōji	I-2	Toyogaoka 1~6	G-5	
Ichinomiya 1~2	H-1	Mogusa	G-3	Sakuragaoka 1~4	H-2	Tsurumaki 1~6	F-5	

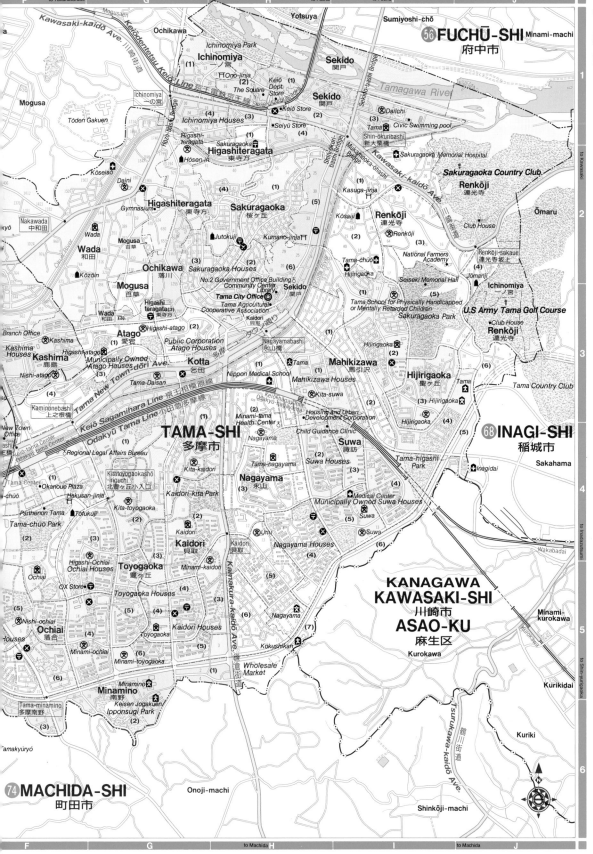

to Takahatafudō   to Fuchū   to Fuchū

Kawasaki-kaidō Ave.

Mogusaen

Keiōdentetsu Keiō Line 京王電鉄京王線

Hozu-bashi Bridge

Ichinomiya
一ノ宮
(1)

Ichinomiya Park

Yotsuya

Sumiyoshi-chō

56 FUCHŪ-SHI
府中市 Minami-machi

Ochikawa

Ono-jinja
(2)

Keiō Store

Sekido
関戸
(1)

The Square

Keiō
Dept.
Store

Keiō Store

Sekido
関戸

Sekido-bashi Bridge

Tamagawa River

to Kawasaki

Mogusa

Tōden Gakuen

Ichinomiya Houses
(4)

(3)

Seiyū Store

(4)

Daiichi

Tama

Civic Swimming pool

Shin-ōkuribashi
新大栗橋

Sakuragaoka Memorial Hospital

Sakuragaoka Country Club

Kōseiso

Daini

Higashi-
teragata

Sakuragaoka

Higashiteragata
東寺方

Hōsen-in

Mukōhooka-ōhashi
bridge

Kawasaki-kaidō Ave. 三鷹街道

Renkōji
連光寺

Ōmaru

Nakawada
中和田

Gymnasium

Higashiteragata
東寺方

(4)

Sakuragaoka
桜ヶ丘

(1)

Kumano-jinja

(5)

Kasuga-jinja

Kōsaiji

Renkōji
連光寺

Renkōji

Club House

Wada
和田

Wada

Mogusa
百草

Jutokuji

Kumano-jinja

(2)

Tama-chūo

(3)

National Farmers
Academy

Renkōji-sakaue
連光寺坂上

Renkōji
連光寺

Ichinomiya
一ノ宮

Jōmanji

Ochikawa
落川

Sakuragaoka Houses
(4)

(5)

(6)

Hijirigaoka

Seiseki Memorial Hall

(5)

U.S. Army Tama Golf Course

Mogusa
百草

No.2 Government Office Building
Community Center
Library

Tama City Office

Sekido
関戸

Tama School for Physically Handicapped
or Mentally Retarded Children

Sakuragaoka Park

Club House

Renkōji
連光寺

Higashi
teragata
(3) 東寺方

Tama Agricultural
Cooperative Association

Kaidori
貝取

(1)

Tama

Tama Country Club

Atago
愛宕

Higashi-atago

Public Corporation
Atago Houses

Nagayamabashi
永山橋

(1)

Hijirigaoka

Hijirigaoka
聖ヶ丘

Branch Office

Kashima

Higashi-atago

Municipally Owned
Atago Houses

Tama New Town-dōri Ave.

(3)

Tama

Tama

Mahikizawa
馬引沢

(3) Hijirigaoka

(6)

Kashima
鹿島

Nishi-atago

Kotta
乞田

Tama-Daisan

Nippon Medical School

Mahikizawa Houses

Kita-suwa

(2)

Hijirigaoka

Kashima
Houses

(4)

Keiō Sagamihara Line 京王相模原線

Odakyū-Nagayama

Housing and Urban
Development Corporation

INAGI-SHI
稲城市

68

Kaminonebashi
上之根橋

Odakyū Tama Line 小田急多摩線

(1)

Minami-tama
Health Center

(2)

(3)

Tama-higashi
Park

New Town
Office

Odakyū Tama Center

(1)

TAMA-SHI
多摩市

Child Guidance Clinic

Nagayama

Suwa
諏訪

Sakahama

(1)

Regional Legal Affairs Bureau

(1)

Tama-nagayama

Suwa Houses

(3)

Inagidai

(5)

to Inadazutsumi

Tama Center

Kita-kaidori

Nagayama
永山

(4)

to Shin-yurigaoka

Okanoue Plaza

Hakusan-jinja

Kitatoyogaokashō
-iriguchi
北豊ヶ丘小入口

Kaidori-kita Park

Medical Center

Municipally Owned Suwa Houses

Minami-
kurokawa

chū

Pārthenon Tama

Tōfukuji

Kita-toyogaoka

Kaidori

Uriu

Suwa

(5)

Suwa

(6)

Wakabadai

Tama-chūo Park

(2)

(3)

(2)

Kaidori
貝取

Kaidori
貝取

Nagayama Houses

(2)

Higashi-Ochiai
Ochiai Houses

Toyogaoka
豊ヶ丘

Minami-kaidori

(4)

**KANAGAWA
KAWASAKI-SHI**
川崎市
ASAO-KU
麻生区

OX Store

Toyogaoka Houses

(3)

(5)

Nishi-ochiai

Ochiai
落合

(4)

Kaidori Houses

(6)

Nagayama

Kokushikan

Kurokawa

(5)

Minami-ochiai

(7)

Kurikidai

Houses

Toyogaoka

Minami-toyogaoka

(6)

Wholesale
Market

Kuriki

(1)

Minamino
南野

Kankamura-kaidō Ave. 鎌倉街道

Tama-minamino
多摩南野

Minamino

Keisen Jogakuen
Ipponsugi Park

(3)

(2)

Tsurukawa-kaidō Ave. 鶴川街道

Tamakyūryō

74 MACHIDA-SHI
町田市

Onoji-machi

Shinkōji-machi

to Machida   to Machida

町田市（Ⅰ）

1:30,000

0   500   1000m

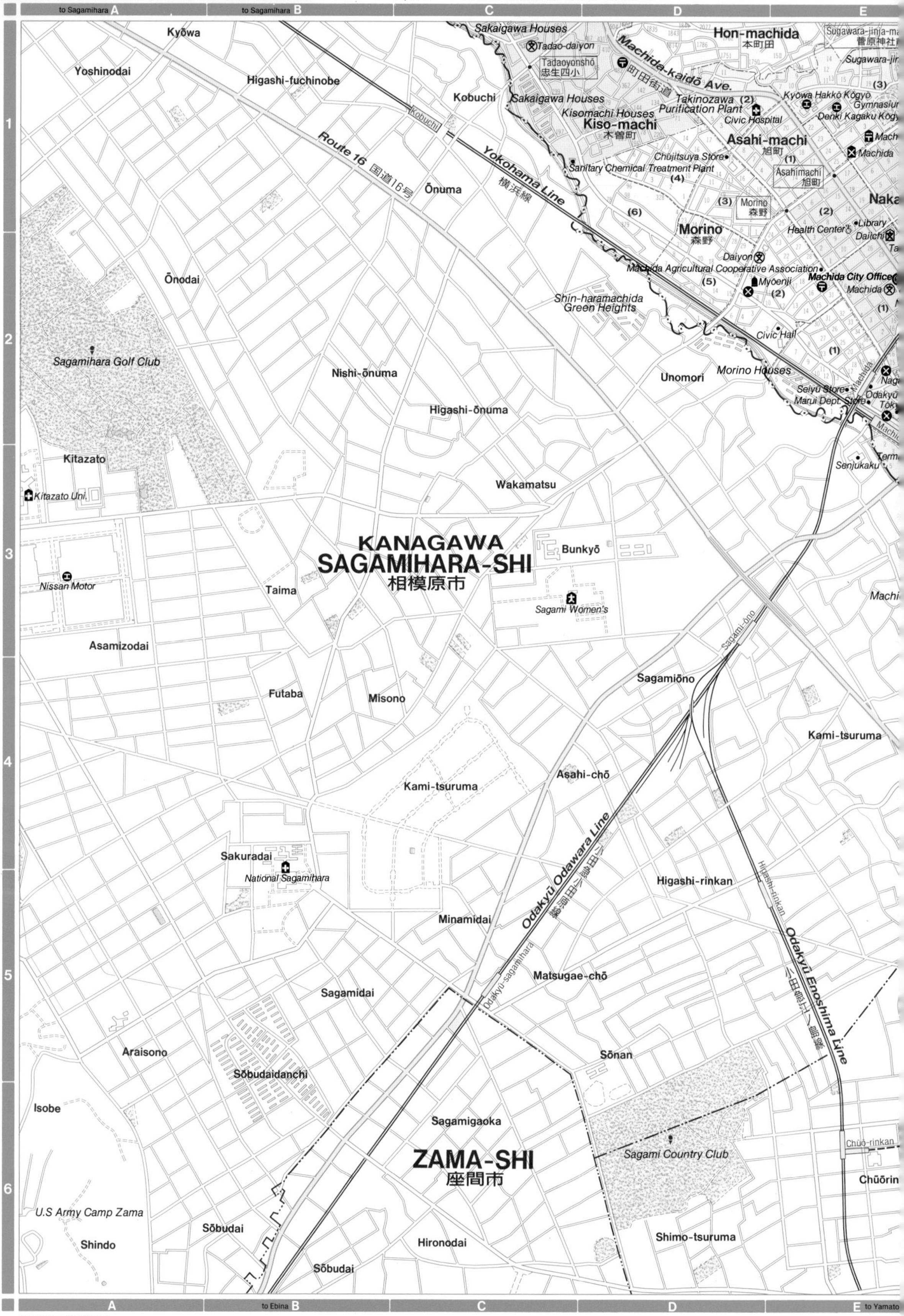

Map labels (reading across the map):

to Sagamihara — A — to Sagamihara — B — C — D — E

Kyōwa
Yoshinodai
Higashi-fuchinobe
Kobuchi
Sakaigawa Houses
Tadao-daiyon
忠生四小
Sakaigawa Houses
Kisomachi Houses
Kiso-machi
木曽町
Machida-kaidō Ave.
Hon-machida
本町田
Sugawara-jinja-m
菅原神社
Sugawara-jir
Kyōwa Hakkō Kōgyō
Takinozawa (2)
Purification Plant
Civic Hospital
Gymnasiur
Denki Kagaku Kōg
Asahi-machi
旭町
(1)
Mach
Machida
Route 16 国道16号
Ōnuma
Yokohama Line
横浜線
Sanitary Chemical Treatment Plant
Chūjitsuya Store
(4)
Asahimachi
旭町
(3)
Morino
森野
(6)
Morino
森野
Health Center
Library
Daiichi
Ta
Naka
Ōnodai
Shin-haramachida
Green Heights
Machida Agricultural Cooperative Association
(5)
Daiyon
Myōenji
(2)
Machida City Office
Machida
(1)
Nishi-ōnuma
Sagamihara Golf Club
Higashi-ōnuma
Unomori
Morino Houses
Civic Hall
(1)
Seiyu Store
Marui Dept. Store
Odakyū
Tok
Nag
Kitazato
Wakamatsu
Kitazato Uni.
Senjukaku
Term
Nissan Motor
Taima
**KANAGAWA
SAGAMIHARA-SHI
相模原市**
Bunkyō
Machi
Sagami Women's
Asamizodai
Futaba
Misono
Sagamiōno
Kami-tsuruma
Kami-tsuruma
Asahi-chō
Sakuradai
National Sagamihara
Higashi-rinkan
Minamidai
Odakyū Odawara Line
小田急小田原線
Odakyū Enoshima Line
小田急江ノ島線
Sagamidai
Matsugae-chō
Araisono
Sōnan
Chūō-rinkan
Isobe
Sōbudaidanchi
Sagamigaoka
**ZAMA-SHI
座間市**
Sagami Country Club
Chūōrin
U.S Army Camp Zama
Sōbudai
Hironodai
Shimo-tsuruma
Shindo
Sōbudai

to Ebina — B — C — D — E — to Yamato

■AREA INDEX■

Aihara-machi	64·D-5	Kami-oyamada-machi	74·A-2
Asahi-machi 1~3	72·E-1	Kanai1~8	75·F-4
Haramachida 1~6	73·F-4	Kanai-machi	75·G-4
Higashi-tamagawagakuen 1~4	73·G-1	Kanamori	73·F-3
Hirohakama-machi	75·H-2	Kanamori 1	73·G-4
Hon-machida	74·E-5	Kiso-machi	74·C-5

Kōgasaka	73·F-2	Morino 1~6	72·D-2
Minami-Naruse 1~7	73·H-3	Naka-machi 1~4	72·E-1
Minami-tsukushino 1~4	73·H-5	Naruse	73·H-2
Minamiōya	73·F-1	Naruse 1~3	73·H-2
Miwa-machi	75·J-4	Narusedai 1~4	73·H-1
Miwa-midoriyama 1~4	75·J-4	Narusegaoka 1~3	73·G-3

Negishi-machi	
Nōgaya-machi	
Nozuta-machi	
Ogawa	
Ogawa 1~4	
Ōkura-machi	

町田市(Ⅰ)

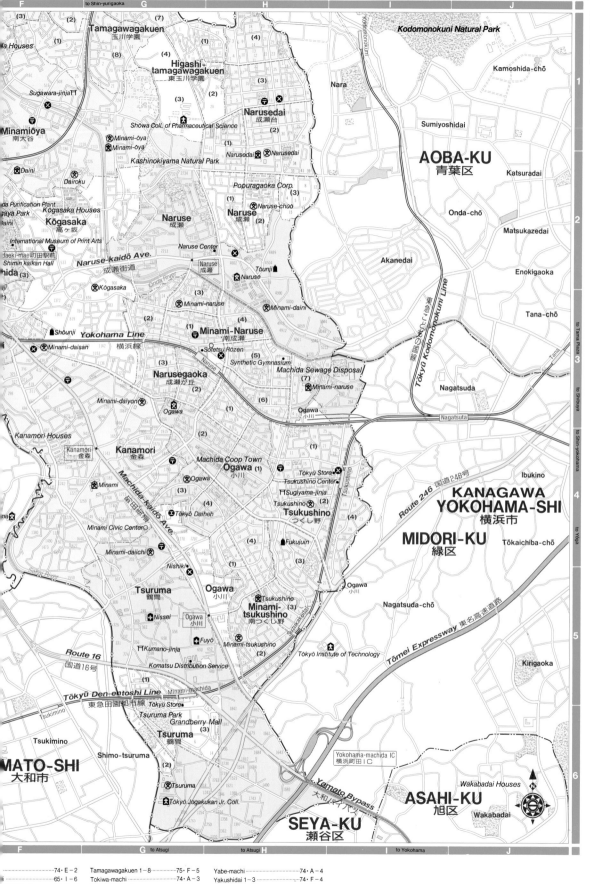

Kodomonokuni Natural Park

Kamoshida-chō

Sumiyoshidai

AOBA-KU
青葉区

Katsuradai

Nara

Onda-chō

Matsukazedai

Akanedai

Tana-chō

Enokigaoka

Nagatsuda

Nagatsuta

Ibukino

KANAGAWA
YOKOHAMA-SHI
横浜市

MIDORI-KU
緑区

Tōkaichiba-chō

Tamagawagakuen
玉川学園

Higashi-
tamagawagakuen
東玉川学園

Sugawara-jinja

Minami-ōya

Minamiōya
南大谷

Showa Coll. of Pharmaceutical Science

Narusedai
成瀬台

Daini

Dairoku

Kashinokiyama Natural Park

Narusedai

Narusedai

da Purification Plant

gaya Park

Kōgasaka Houses

Kōgasaka
高ヶ坂

Naruse
成瀬

Naruse-chūo

Popuragaoka Corp.

Naruse
成瀬

International Museum of Print Arts

Naruse Center

Naruse-kaidō Ave.
成瀬街道

Onda River

Tōunji

daeki-mae 町田駅前

Shimin kaikan Hall

Naruse

Kōgasaka

Minami-naruse

Minami-daini

Shounji

Yokohama Line
横浜線

Minami-Naruse
南成瀬

Minami-daisan

Narusegaoka
成瀬が丘

Sōtetsu Rōzen

Synthetic Gymnasium

Machida Sewage Disposal

Minami-daiyon

Ogawa

Minami-naruse

Ogawa
小川

Kanamori Houses

Kanamori
金森

Kanamori
金森

Machida Coop Town

Ogawa
小川

Tōkyū Store

Tsukushino Center

Ogawa

Sugiyama-jinja

Minami

Ogawa

Tsukushino
つくし野

Tōkyō Daiheh

Tsukushino

Minami Civic Center

Tsukushino

Fukujuin

Minami-daiichi

Nishiki

Ogawa

Tsuruma
鶴間

Ogawa
小川

Tsukushino

Minami-
tsukushino
南つくし野

Nissei

Ogawa
小川

Fuyō

Nagatsuda-chō

Tōkaichiba-chō

Tōkyō Institute of Technology

Kirigaoka

Kumano-jinja

Minami-tsukushino

Komatsu Distribution Service

Route 16
国道16号

Minami-machida

Tōmei Expressway 東名高速道路

Tōkyū Den-entoshi Line
東急田園都市線

Tōkyū Store

Tsukimino

Tsuruma Park
Grandberry Mall

Tsuruma
鶴間

Shimo-tsuruma

MATO-SHI
大和市

Yamato Bypass
大和バイパス

Yokohama-machida IC
横浜町田IC

Wakabadai Houses

Tsuruma

Tokyo Jogakukan Jr. Coll.

ASAHI-KU
旭区

Wakabadai

SEYA-KU
瀬谷区

to Shin-yurigaoka

to Atsugi

to Atsugi

to Yokohama

...............................74・E-2
Tamagawagakuen 1〜8........75・F-5
Yabe-machi................74・A-4
i...............65・I-6
Tokiwa-machi...............74・A-3
Yakushidai 1〜3............74・F-4
uradai 1〜2.................74・A-3
Tsukushino 1〜4...........73・H-4
Yamasaki-machi...........74・D-4
da-machi..................74・B-2
Tsurukawa 1〜6...........75・G-3
Zushi-machi..............74・C-3
ji...........75・G-1
Tsuruma..................73・H-5
74・C-4
Tsuruma 1〜3..............73・G-6

町田市（II）

1:30,000

0 500 1000m

to Seisekisakuragaoka

A B C D E

1

Ōtsuma Women's Jr. Coll.
Ōtsuma-Tama
Karakida

Club House

Tsurumaki

Ochiai

Toyogaoka

Kaidori

Nagayam

⑦ **TAMA-SHI**
多摩市

Tōkōji
On

Tokyo Kokusai Country Golf Course

Keisen Jogakuen
Minamino

Kamakura-kaidō Ave.

2

Kami-Oyamada-machi
上小山田町

Shōzanji

Tamakyūryō

Machida Cemetery

Onoji-machi
小野路町

Daisenji

Shimo-Oyamada-machi
下小山田町

Shimizu Construction Grou
Seikō Grou

Yōjuin

Oyamada

Ono-jinja

Oyamada Green Park

Manshōji

Health Facilities for Ag
Machida Sakuran

Shinmei-jinja

Nozuta Playground

Nozuta Park

Nichidai-daisan

Nippon School for The Deaf and Dumb

Nozuta

Oyamada-sakuradai
小山田桜台
Oyamada-minami

Archaeological Museum

Machida School for Physically Handicapped
or Mentally Retarded Children

Kegon

3

Oyamada

Recycle Culture Center

Zushi-machi
図師町

Nozuta
野津田

Indoor Pool

Tokiwa-machi
常盤町

Tokiwa

Kumano-jinja

Tsurumi River

Minken-no

Kami-yabe

Enpukuji

Municipally owned Yamasakimachi
Apartment

Yakushigaoka

Negishi-machi

Shibamizo-kaidō Ave. 芝溝街道

Zushiohashi
図師大橋

Yakushida
Yakus

Ōbirin

(4)

Tadao-Daiichi

4

Yabe-machi
矢部町

Negishi-nishi
根岸西

Tadao Civic Center

Machida Agricultural
Cooperative Association

(2)

Yamasaki

Kiso-machi
木曽町

Negishi
根岸

Tadao (3)

Yamazaki

Yamasaki

Tadao-Dainana

Negishi-machi
根岸町

Tadao
忠生

Machida Kōgyō

Kōyōji

Yamasaki-machi
山崎町

Tadao-Dairoku

(1)

Tadao Park

Yamasaki Houses

Imaiyato
今井谷戸

Fuchinobe

Fuchinobe-hon-chō

Tadao

Hon-machida

Hon-ma

5

**KANAGAWA
SAGAMIHARA-SHI**
相模原市

Negishi-machi
根岸町

Tadao-Daigo

Kiso-yamasaki Center

Hon-machida-nishi

Hinata

Kiso

Christian Hospital
Daimaru Peacock

Machi

Kiso-machi
木曽町

Kiso
木曽

Public Corporation Kiso Houses

Kiso

Midorigaoka

Kyōwa

Sakaigawadanchi-iriguchi
境川団地入口

Odakyū OX

Hara

Hon-machida
本町田

Tadao-Daisan

Midorigaoka Houses

Sugawarajinja
菅原神

Sakaigawa Houses

Machida-Daisan

Sugawara-

(3)

6

Yoshinodai

Higashi-fuchinobe

Tadao-Daiyon

Takizawa
滝沢

Kyōwa Hakkō Kōgyō

Machida Ce
Gymnas

Route 16 国道16号

Yokohama Line 横浜線

Takinosawa Purification Plant

Civic Hospital

(1)

Denki Kagaku Kōgy

Ōnodai

Kiso-Morino Houses

(3)

Asahi-machi
旭町

Machida

Kobuchi

Sanitary Chemical Treatment Plant

Chūjitsuya

Asahimachi
旭町

Naka-n
中

Ōnuma

Ōnuma

Kobuchi

Morino
森野

(4)

(2)

(6)

(3)

to Aihara
to Sagamihara
to Hashimoto

A B C D E
to Yokohama I.C
to Machida

町田市(II)

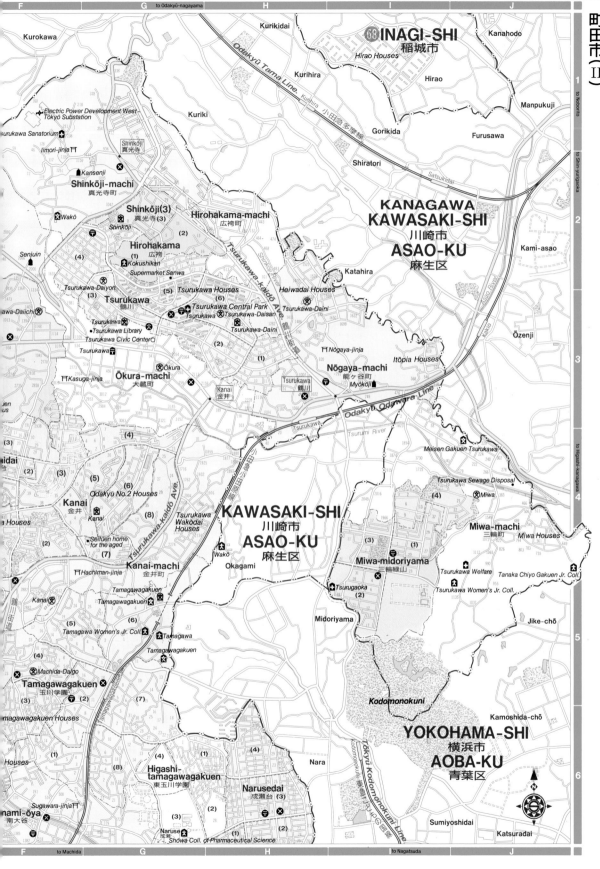

西東京市

1:30,000

0 500 1000m

80 HIGASHIKURUME-SHI
東久留米市

80 NERIMA 練馬

SAITAMA NIIZA-SHI 新座市

Koyama
Hikawadai
Kanayama-chō
Shinhō-chō
Higashi-honchō
Daimon-chō
Kurihara
Nodera
Katay

Saiwai-chō
Hon-chō
Shinkawa-chō
Musashino Substation
Nishi-

Higashikurume City Office
Sengen-chō
Seiran
Kita-machi 北町
Tenjinji
Fukusenji

Chūō-chō
Gaguen-chō
Jiyū-gakuen
Hibarigaoka-kita ひばりが丘北
Sakae
Sakae-chō 栄町
Shimo-hōya 下保谷
Library Shimo-hōya Welfa

Minami-sawa
Hibarigaoka Plaza Seiyū Store
Inari-jinja
Hōya-daiichi
Hōya Kōsei
Hōya

Maesawa
Hibarigaoka ひばりが丘
Nakahara
Matarokujizō 又六地蔵
Hōya
Sumiyoshi-chō 住吉町
Hōya-nakamachi 保谷町中丁
Seiyū

Hibarigaoka-danchi
Hibarigaoka Houses
Seiyū Store
Yato-chō 谷戸町
Sumiyoshi
Welfare Hall
Jōdono-jinja
Hōya-chūō
Bunridai Park
Higashi-chō 東町
Meiho

Minami-chō
Higashihonganji
Sumitomo Heavy Industries
Hibarigaoka
Tōzenji
Izumi-chō 泉町
Hōya Government Office Bldg.
Higashi

Higashihonganji Cemetery
Tanashi
Yato-daini
Yato Branch Office
Hōshōin
Nyoirinji
Hōjuin
Naka-machi 中町

Univ. of Tōkyō Institute for Nuclear Study
Yato
Midori-chō 緑町
Tanashi-daini
Hōya
Hōya Health Clinic
Midoriyama

Minami-chō
Bunka Girl's
Nishihara Green Heights
Nishihara Houses
Nishihara-chō 西原町
Univ. of Tōkyō Farm
Kitahara-chō 北原町
Hōya-chō 保谷町
Higashifushimi Houses

Hanakoganei
West Tōkyō Sky Tower
Tama Rokuto Science Center
Nishihara
Nishihara-Daini
Tanashi-Daisan
Nishihara-chō 西原町
Kitahara 北原
Henryūji
Inageya Store
Hōya-honchō 保谷本町
Hōya Honchō
Fuji-kaidō Ave. 富士街道
Fujimachi-4 富士町四
Tai 高

Waterworks Division
Tanashi Agricultural Cooperative Association
Yato-shindō 谷戸新道
Hōya-shindō 保谷新道
Fuji-machi 富士町
Higashi-fushimi

Kita-shibakubo 北芝久保
Municipal Owed Apartment
Hashiba 橋場
Tanashi
Tanashi
St. Joseph Home

Shibakubo
Ōme-kaidō Ave. 青梅街道
Tanashi-chō 田無町
Sasa
Sōjiji
Tanashi-jinja

Shibakubo-chō 芝久保町
Citizen Watch
Health Center
Shiminkaikan Hall
Tanashi
Itō-Yōkadō Store
Seibu Dept. Store
Seibu-yagisawa
Hikawa-jinja
Waseda Univ. Ground
Ice Arena
Musashi Park

Daiichi
Branch Office of Regional Legal Affairs Bureau
Tanashi
Yamada
Higashifushimiinari-jinja
Higashifushimi

Kodaira
Seibu Shinjuku Line 西武新宿線
Central Community Center
Nishitōkyō City Office
Tōkyō Gas
Higashi-fushimi 東伏見
Sekimac

Sankyō
Tanashi-daiichi
Gymnasium
Minami-chō 南町
Hōya-higashifushimi 保谷東伏見
Ōme-kaid

78 KODAIRA-SHI 小平市
Kamimukōdai
Tanashi sch. for Physically Handicapped or Mentally Retarded Children
Civic Park
Mukōdai
Yagisawa
New Yagisawa Houses
Hōya-daini
Yagisawa
Sekir mina

Hanakoganei-minami-chō
Gymnasium
Mukōdai-chō 向台町
Tanashi
Sports Center
Tanashi-daiyon
Yagisawa
Yagisawa
Musashino Joshi Gakuin
NTT Research and Development Center
Sekir

Koganei Park
Tanashi
Ishikawajima-Harima Heavy Industries
Joshigakuin-mae 女子学院前
Musashino Central Park
Musashino City Office
Midori-chō

Tamako Cycling Path 多摩湖自転車道
Awasu-jinja
Yanagibashi Branch Office
Yahata-chō

Sekino-chō
Shin-machi 新町
Yanagibashi 柳橋
Itsukaichi-kaidō Ave. 五日市街道
Kichijōji-kita

54 KOGANEI-SHI 小金井市
Sakurazutsumi
Sekimae
52 MUSASHINO-SHI 武蔵野市
Nishikubo-chō

Itsukaichi-kaidō Ave. 五日市街道
Midori-chō
Hōsei (Eng.)
Sakaibashi 境橋
Imokashira-dōri Ave. 井ノ頭通り
Sakai Purification Plant
Naka-chō

Kajino-chō
Tamagawajōsui Irrigation Canal

■NISHITŌKYŌ-SHI AREA INDEX■

Fuji-machi 1~6 ········· E-4	Hōya-chō 1~6 ········· D-4	Mukōdai-chō 1~6 ········· B-5	Shin-machi 1~6 ········· B-6
Hibarigaoka 1~4 ········· B-3	Izumi-chō 1~6 ········· D-3	Naka-machi 1~6 ········· E-3	Sumiyoshi-chō 1~6 ········· D-3
Hibarigaoka-kita 1~4 ········· C-2	Kitahara-chō 1~3 ········· C-4	Nishihara-chō 1~5 ········· B-4	Tanashi-chō 1~7 ········· B-4
Higashi-chō 1~6 ········· E-3	Kita-machi 1~6 ········· E-2	Sakae-chō 1~3 ········· D-2	Yagisawa 1~6 ········· D-5
Higashi-fushimi 1~6 ········· E-5	Midori-chō 1~3 ········· C-3	Shibakubo-chō 1~5 ········· A-4	Yato-chō 1~3 ········· C-3
	Minami-chō 1~6 ········· C-5	Shimo-hōya 1~5 ········· E-2	

to Tokorozawa, to Ōme, to Kodaira, to Hajima, to Kichijōji

1:30,000

0　500　1000m

A　B　to Kawagoe　C　D　to Urawa　E

Minami-nagai

Kamegaya

o-arai

Hibita

Urawa Tokorozawa Bypass 浦和所沢バイパス

Tokorozawa IC
所沢IC

Sakanoshita

Owada

Shimo-yasumatsu

1

Kiyose
Purification Plant

(3)

No.3 Playground

Matsugō

Higashi-tokorozawa

SAITAMA
TOKOROZAWA-SHI
所沢市

Shiro
Takinojoshi Park

No.2 Playground

Shitajuku-3
下宿三

(6)

(4)

Higashi-tokorozawa

Musashino Line 武蔵野線

Hachiman-jinja

Matsumiyainari-jinja

Hongō

Higashi-tokorozawa

Shitajuku
Playground

Entsūji

Daikyū

(2)

(5)

Gymnasium

Shitajuku
下宿

(3)

Daigo

Uemiyainari-jima

Asahigaoka
旭が丘

Daigo

2

Shizuokaya Store

(1)

Asahigaoka
Houses

(2)

Sugasawa

Kiyosedai Houses

(1)

Daisan

(6)

Orimoto

Shimo-yasumatsu

Kanayama Green Park

Ōbayashi Institute

Atago

Kiyose Houses

Nakazato Houses

(4)

Kiyose

Nakazato
中里

(5)

Daihachi

(4)

Yakumo-jinja

(5)

3

Kiyose

Kiyose City Office
Naka-kiyoto Houses

(2)

Chōgenji

Shimo-kiyoto
下清戸

Kiyose-noshio
Houses

Tōkōin

Daiyon

Hikawa-jinja

Fujisan-jinja

(3)

Kiyose

Chōmeiji

(4)

Shima-kiyoto

(3)

Meiji College of Pharmacy

(2)

Kiyoseyakushi

(2)

Local Museum

Mitake-jinja

Hie-jinja

(2)

Green Town Kiyoto Houses

Noshio Area Civic Center

Daiyon

Kiyose Health Clinic

Zenryūji

Naka-kiyoto
中清戸

(1)

Inageya Store

Noshio
野塩

Yakushidō

Meteorological Satellite Center

(5)

Kiyose higashi

4

Enpukuji

Yūbinkyoku-mae
郵便局前

Kiyose

(3)

Fujimi

(1)

Hachiman-jinja

Kami-kiyoto
上清戸

Daiju

NIIZA-SHI
新座市

Nishibori

Takeya

Daigo

Shibayama

(2)

Central Park

Moto-machi
元町

Civic Center

Uenohara

Shin-ai

Seiyū Store

Ishigami

Tōsei-gakuen

Nurses' School Attached to
Tokyō Hospital

Central Library

Dairoku

Shibayama
芝山

(3)

Daini

Umezono
梅園

Institute of Tuberculosis
Matsuyama Area Civic Institute

Fukūjūji

Kanayama-chō

Bethlehem-no-sono

Kiyose Children's
Hosp.

Industrial Safety Institute

Saty Store

Shinbori

Shinhō-chō

Seikōkai

Kunpūen

Salvation Army

Kiyose

5

GASHI-
URAYAMA-SHI
村山市

Yamazaki

Kiyose School for Physically Handicapped
or Mentally Retarded Children

Daisan

Dainana

Kiyoseuemiya

(3)

National Sanatoria
Tokyō

Matsuyama
松山

Higashi-honchō

Daimon-chō

Zenseien

Takeoka
竹丘

Japan Coll. of Social Work

Kurumegaoka

Hikawadai

Kiboen Nursing
Home

Takeoka
Area
Civic Center

Koyama

Takeoka
Houses

Tokyō Office
Workers' Hospital

(2)

Saiwai-chō

Nobidome

Kurume River

Shinkawa-chō

Zenseien-higashi
全生園東

Nobidome Irrigation Canal

-chō

Aobachō.1
青葉町一

Shimosato

Tokorozawa-kaidō Ave.

Hachiman-chō

80 HIGASHIKURUME-SHI
東久留米市

Chūō-chō

Hon-chō

Higashikurume City Office

Sengen-chō

Kurihara

6

Saibu Ikebukuro Line 西武池袋線

Koganei-kaidō Ave. 小金井街道

Minamisawa

Gakuen-chō

A　to Tanashi　B　to Fuchū　C　D　E to Ikebukuro

-SHI AREA INDEX■

~6 ····· E-2
~2 ····· C-4
~3 ····· B-5
~2 ····· B-4
~5 ····· D-4
~6 ····· C-3

Noshio 1~5 ····· A-4
Shimo-kiyoto 1~5 ····· E-3
Shitajuku 1~3 ····· D-2
Takeoka 1~3 ····· A-5
Umezono 1~3 ····· A-4

小平市

1:27,000

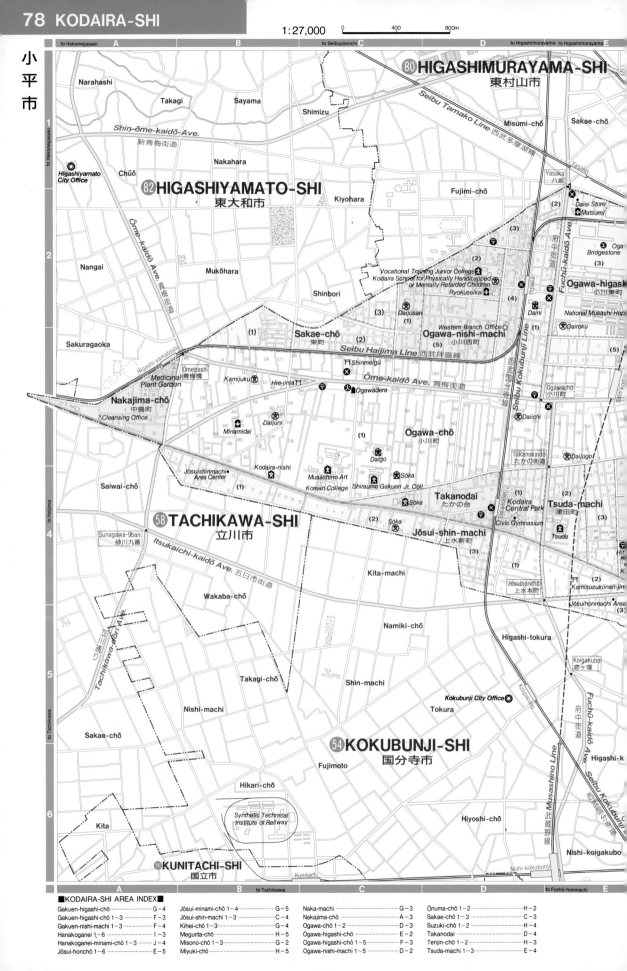

■KODAIRA-SHI AREA INDEX■

Gakuen-higashi-chō	G-4	Jōsui-minami-chō 1～4	G-5	Naka-machi	G-3	Ōnuma-chō 1～2	H-2
Gakuen-higashi-chō 1～3	F-3	Jōsui-shin-machi 1～3	C-4	Nakajima-chō	A-3	Sakae-chō 1～3	C-3
Gakuen-nishi-machi 1～3	F-4	Kihei-chō 1～3	G-4	Ogawa-chō 1～2	D-3	Suzuki-chō 1～2	H-4
Hanakoganei 1～6	I-3	Megurita-chō	H-5	Ogawa-higashi-chō	E-2	Takanodai	D-4
Hanakoganei-minami-chō 1～3	J-4	Misono-chō 1～3	G-2	Ogawa-higashi-machi 1～5	F-3	Tenjin-chō 1～3	E-4
Jōsui-honchō 1～6	E-5	Miyuki-chō	H-5	Ogawa-nishi-machi 1～5	D-2	Tsuda-machi 1～3	E-4

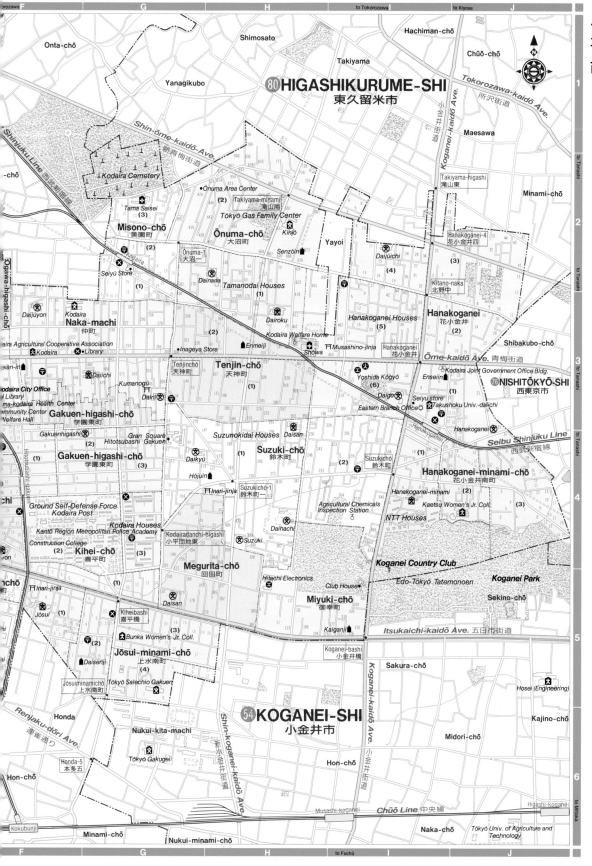

Onta-chō

Shimosato

Hachiman-chō

Takiyama

Chūō-chō

Yanagikubo

80 **HIGASHIKURUME-SHI**
東久留米市

Tokorozawa-kaidō Ave.

Koganei-kaidō Ave.

Maesawa

Shin-ōme-kaidō Ave.
新青梅街道

Shinjuku Line 西武新宿線

Kodaira Cemetery

Takiyama-higashi
滝山東

Minami-chō

Ōnuma Area Center

(2) Takiyama-minami
滝山南

Hanakoganei-4
花小金井四

Tama Saisei
(3)

Tōkyō Gas Family Center

Misono-chō
美園町

Ōnuma-chō
大沼町

Kinjō

Yayoi

Daijūichi

(2)

Ōnuma-1
大沼一

Senzōin

(3)

Seiyū Store

Dainana

Tamanodai Houses

(4)

Kitano-naka
北野中

(1)

Daijūyon

Kodaira
Naka-machi
仲町

Dairoku

Hanakoganei Houses
(5)

Hanakoganei
花小金井

(2)

Shibakubo-chō

ira Agricultural Cooperative Association

Kodaira
Library

Inageya Store

Enmeiji

Musashino-jinja

Showa

Hanakoganei
花小金井

Ōme-kaidō Ave. 青梅街道

Kodaira Joint Government Office Bldg.

Tenjinchō
天神町

Tenjin-chō
天神町

Yoshida Kōgyō

Enseiin

NISHITŌKYŌ-SHI
西東京市

Kodaira City Office

Daiichi

Kumanogū

Dairi

(1)

(6)

Daigo

Seiyū store

Takushoku Univ.-daiichi

(1)

Gakuen-higashi-chō
学園東町

Suzunokidai Houses

Daisan

Eastern Branch Office

Hanakoganei

Gakuenhigashi
(2)

Gran Square
Hitotsubashi Gakuen

(1)

Suzuki-chō
鈴木町

Seibu Shinjuku Line
西武新宿線

(1)

Gakuen-higashi-chō
学園東町

Daikyū

(3)

Hōjuin

Suzukichō
鈴木町

(2)

Suzukichō
鈴木町

(1)

Hanakoganei-minami-chō
花小金井南町

Inari-jinja

Suzukichō-1
鈴木町一

Hanakoganei-minami

(2)

Ground Self-Defense Force
Kodaira Post

Agricultural Chemicals
Inspection Station

Kaetsu Women's Jr. Coll.

(3)

Kanto Region Metropolitan Police Academy

NTT Houses

Construction College

Kodaira Houses

Daihachi

Kihei-chō
喜平町

Kodairadanchi-higashi
小平団地東

Suzuki

Megurita-chō
回田町

Koganei Country Club

Koganei Park

(1)

Daisan

Hitachi Electronics

Miyuki-chō
御幸町

Edo-Tōkyō Tatemonoen

Sekino-chō

Inari-jinja

Club House

Jōsui

(1)

Kiheibashi
喜平橋

Kaiganji

Itsukaichi-kaidō Ave. 五日市街道

(2)

Bunka Women's Jr. Coll.

(3)

Koganei-bashi
小金井橋

Sakura-chō

Jōsui-minami-chō
上水南町

Daisenji

(4)

Hosei (Engineering)

Jōsuiminamichō
上水南町

Tōkyō Salechio Gakuen

Renjaku-dōri Ave.
連雀通り

Honda

54 **KOGANEI-SHI**
小金井市

Kajino-chō

Nukui-kita-machi

Midori-chō

Honda-5
本多五

Tōkyō Gakugei

Hon-chō

Hon-chō

Kokubunji

Minami-chō

Nukui-minami-chō

Musashi-koganei

Chūō Line 中央線

Higashi-koganei

Naka-chō

Tōkyō Univ. of Agriculture and Technology

to Tokorozawa

to Kiyose

to Fuchū

東久留米市・東村山市

to Nishitokorozawa   to Hannō   to Iruma   to Honkawagoe

Kotobuki-chō
Moto-machi
Hoshinomiya
Nishi-sumiyoshi
Hiyoshi-chō
Kusunokidai
Minami-sumiyoshi
Higashi-sumiyoshi

Kami-

Kita-akitsu

西武狭山線
Seibu Sayama Line
西武池袋線
Seibu Ikebukuro Line
Seibu Shinjuku Line
所沢街道
Tokorozawa-kaidō Ave.

Seibu Railway Ground

Yamaguchi

Shimo-yamaguchi

**SAITAMA
TOKOROZAWA-SHI
所沢市**

Matsugaoka

Jimyōin

Akitsu-chō
秋津町

(4)

Akitsu-higas

Arahata

Seibuen Golf Course

Akitsuchō-3
秋津町三
(5)

Kumegawachō
久米川町

(4)
Akitsu

Seibuen Park

Seibuen Cycling Studium

Shin-yamate

Hakujūji

Suwa-chō
諏訪町

Tokuzōji

Baiganji

Daini

Yamazaki Baking

Culture Center

Dairoku

Seibuen Park

Yuenchi-mae

Seibuen
(4)

Seibu Seibuen Line 西武西武園線

Kitayama Park

Kitayama

(1)

Kumegawatsuji
久米川辻

Kumegawa-chō
久米川町

Renown Look

Tamako Lake

Social Welfare Center

Shōfukuji

Kasei

Kumegawa-higashi

Aobachō Houses

(2)

Tamako-chō
多摩湖町

Daiyon

(3)

Noguchi-chō
野口町

Kita-kumega

(4)

Honchō-2
本町二

Kumegawa

**HIGASHIMURAYAMA-SHI
東村山市**

Aobachō-2
青葉町二

Higash
Home

Sayama Park

Megurita

(2)

Central Community Center

Civic Sports Center

Higashimurayama

Daigo

(5)

Kanayamajinja-mae
金山神社前

Nikkisō

Higashimurayama
Health Center

Itōyōkadō Store
Higashimurayama

Higashimurayama Taxation Office

Onta

Nobidome

Tamako

**Megurita-chō
廻田町**

(1)

Dainana

Civic Center

Central Library

Hon-chō
本町

Ontachō
恩多町

**Onta-chō
恩多町**

Higashi

(3)

Sayama

Shimizu

Higashimurayama
Purification Plant

Misumi-chō
美住町

Higashimurayama City Office

Higashimurayama
Municipal Owed Kumegawa Houses

(4)

Musashiyamatoeki-mae
武蔵大和駅前

Higashimurayama

(2)

Noguchibashi
野口橋

Yasaka-jinja

(4)

Public Corporation
Kumegawa Houses

Yasaka

Sakaechō-1
栄町一

(2)

新青梅街道
Shin-ōme-kaidō Ave.

Higashimurayama-
nishi

Training Institute of International
Trade and Industry

Higashimurayama

**Sakae-chō
栄町**

Daisan

Kumegawaeki-higashi Houses
Higashi-hagiyama

Seibu Tamako Line 西武多摩湖線

Nakahara

(3)

Fujimi

Higashimurayama
Central Park

**Fujimi-chō
富士見町**

(5)

Yasakaeki-kita
八坂駅北

Kumegawa

**Hagiyama-chō
萩山町**

Kodaira Cemetery

(3)

**82 HIGASHI
YAMATO-SHI
東大和市**

Meihō

Minamidai

Seibu Chūō

(1)

Yasaka
八坂

Ryokufūsō

Itsumi

Hagiyama

Kiyohara

Daiichi

Oka Girl's
Meiji Gakuin Higashimurayama

Daiei Store

Culture Center

Mukōhara

Bridgestone

Hagiyama Business School

Kodaira

Shinbori

Higashimurayama Welfare Home

Misono

Tamako Cycling
Kodaira

Sakae-cho

Seibu Haijima Line 西武拝島線

Ogawa-nishi-machi

Ogawa-higashi-chō

**78 KODAIRA
小平市**

to Hajima

Tachikawa-dōri Ave.
立川通り

Ōme-kaidō Ave. 青梅街道

Ogawa-chō

Naka-machi

Shin-kodaira

Ōme-kaidō

to Kokubunji   to Nishi-kokubunji   to Kokubunji

■HIGASHIMURAYAMA-SHI AREA INDEX■

Akitsu-chō 1~5 ···················· E-2
Aoba-chō 1~4 ···················· E-3
Fujimi-chō 1~5 ···················· B-5
Hagiyama-chō 1~5 ············ D-5
Hon-chō 1~4 ···················· C-4
Kumegawa-chō 1~5 ············ D-3

Megurita-chō 1~4 ·············· B-4
Misumi-chō 1~2 ················ B-4
Noguchi-chō 1~4 ················ B-3
Onta-chō 1~5 ···················· E-4
Sakae-chō 1~3 ·················· C-4
Suwa-chō 1~3 ·················· C-2

Tamako-chō 1~4 ················ A-3

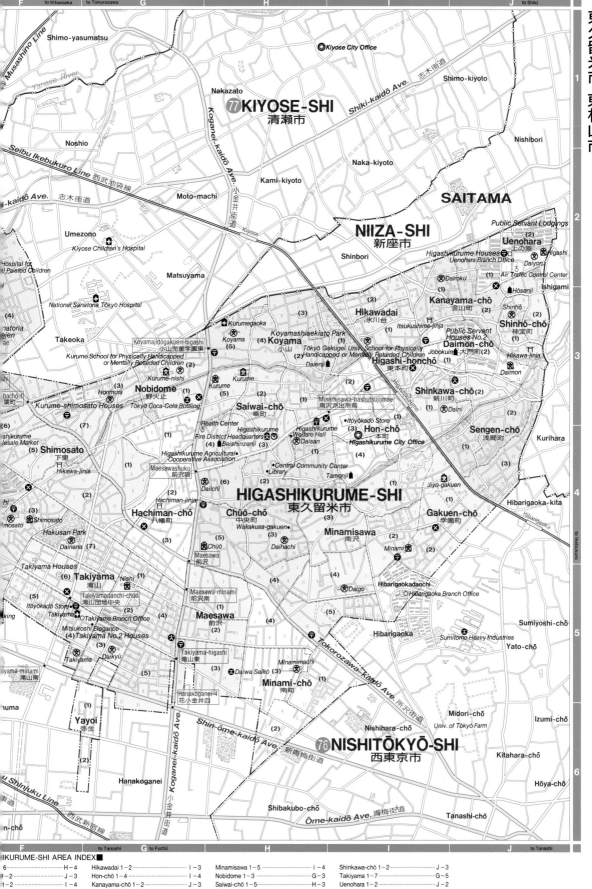

F to Kitaasaka   to Tokorozawa G   H   I   J to Shiki

Shimo-yasumatsu

Kiyose City Office

Nakazato
KIYOSE-SHI
77 清瀬市

Noshio

Shimo-kiyoto

Naka-kiyoto

Shiki-kaidō Ave. 志木街道

Nishibori

Seibu Ikebukuro Line 西武池袋線

Kami-kiyoto

Moto-machi

SAITAMA

志木街道 -kaidō Ave.

Umezono

Kiyose Children's Hospital

Hospital for Palsied Children

Matsuyama

NIIZA-SHI
新座市

Shinbori

Public Servant Lodgings

Uenohara
上の原
(2)

Higashikurume Houses
Uenohara Branch Office

Higashi
Daiyon

Dairoku

Air Traffic Control Center

Ishigami

National Sanatoria Tōkyō Hospital

Hōsenji

Kanayama-chō
金山町
(1)

Shinhō
神宝町

Shinhō-chō

Takeoka

Sanatoria
eien

(4)

Hikawadai
氷川台

Kurumegaoka
Koyama
(5)

Koyamashisekiato Park

Koyama
(4) 小山

Itsukushima-jinja

Tōkyō Gakugei Univ. School for Physically
Handicapped or Mentally Retarded Children

Daimon-chō
大門町

Hikawa-jinja
Daimon

Kurume School for Physically Handicapped
or Mentally Retarded Children

Koyamajidōgakuen-higashi
小山児童学園東

Higashi-honchō
東本町

Kurume-nishi

Daienji

Kurume

(5)

Minamimisawa-hashutsujomae
南沢出所前

Shinkawa-chō
新川町

Nobidome
野火止

Honmura
Tōkyō Coca-Cola Bottling

Daini

Kurume-shimosato Houses

Saiwai-chō
幸町

Health Center

Higashikurume
Fire District Headquarters

Itōyōkadō Store

Hon-chō
本町

Higashikurume City Office

Sengen-chō
浅間町

Kurihara

bachō-
葉町

Beishinzenji

Daisan

Daini

Higashikurume Agricultural
Cooperative Association

Maesawashuku
前沢宿

Central Community Center
Library

Daisan

Tamonji

Jiyū-gakuen

Shimosato
下里

Daiichi

Hachiman-jinja

HIGASHIKURUME-SHI
東久留米市

Gakuen-chō
学園町

Hibarigaoka-kita

Shimosato

Hachiman-chō
八幡町

Chūō-chō
中央町

(3)

Minamisawa
南沢

Hakusan Park

Dainana

Wakakusa-gakuen

Hibarigaoka

Dainichi

Chūō

Daihachi

Minami

Takiyama Houses

Maesawa
前沢

Daigo

Hibarigaokadanchi

Sumiyoshi-chō

Takiyama
滝山

Nishi

Takiyamadanchi-chūō
滝山団地中央

Hibarigaoka Branch Office

Sumitomo Heavy Industries

Yato-chō

Itōyōkadō Store
Takiyama

Maesawa
前沢

Mitsukoshi Elegance
Takiyama No.2 Houses

Takiyama Branch Office

king

Maesawa-minami
前沢南

Takiyama

Daikyū

Takiyama-higashi
滝山東

Daiwa Seikō

Minamimachi
南町

iyama-minami
滝山南

Hanakoganei-4
花小金井四

Minami-chō
南町

Midori-chō

Univ. of Tōkyō Farm

Yayoi
弥生

Nishihara-chō

Izumi-chō

Kitahara-chō

Hanakoganei

Shin-ōme-kaidō Ave. 新青梅街道

76 **NISHITŌKYŌ-SHI**
西東京市

Hōya-chō

u Shinjuku Line 西武新宿線

Shibakubo-chō

Ōme-kaidō Ave. 青梅街道

Tanashi-chō

n-chō

F   to Tanashi   G to Fuchū   H   I   to Tanashi   J

IKURUME-SHI AREA INDEX■

6 ··· H-4	Hikawadai 1~2 ··· I-3	Minamisawa 1~5 ··· I-4	Shinkawa-chō 1~2 ··· J-3
-2 ··· J-3	Hon-chō 1~4 ··· I-4	Nobidome 1~3 ··· G-3	Takiyama 1~7 ··· G-5
-2 ··· J-3	Kanayama-chō 1~2 ··· J-3	Saiwai-chō 1~5 ··· H-3	Uenohara 1~2 ··· J-2
3 ··· G-4	Koyama 1~5 ··· H-3	Sengen-chō 1~3 ··· J-4	Yanagikubo 1~5 ··· E-5
danchi ··· I-5	Maesawa 1~5 ··· H-5	Shimosato 1~7 ··· F-4	Yayoi 1~2 ··· G-6
hō ··· I-3	Minami-chō 1~4 ··· H-5	Shinhō-chō 1~2 ··· J-3	

東大和市・武蔵村山市

IRUMA-SHI
入間市

Ishihata

to Hakonegasaki

◎ Mizuho Town Office

86 **MIZUHO-MACHI**
瑞穂町

to Hakonegasaki

(4)

(4)

(5)

Kishi
岸
(3)

Playground

Murayama-toride

(4)

(2)

● Zenshōji

Noyama-Kita Park

(6)

Tonogaya

Ōme-kaidō Ave.

(3)

(5)

Musashi

(3)

(5)

Historical Folk Material Hall ●

● Inageya Store

Mizuho-tonogaya
瑞穂殿ヶ谷

(5)

▲ Yakushido

Mitsugi
三ツ木

Junisho-jinja ⛩

Hon-machi
本町

(3)

● Chōenzenji

(4)

Naka
中原
(3)

Shin-ōme-kaidō Ave.

(1)

ⓧ

(2)

ⓧ Daini

(1)

Hall of Commerce and Industry

● Kisshōin

⛩ Hiyoshi-jinja

Shinpukuji
ⓧ Daisan

Chūō
中央 (3)

(3)

Green Town Musashimurayama

(3)

Ⓣ

ⓧ Musashimurayama

Musashimurayama Agricultural Cooperative
Association Daiichi

Ⓣ ⓧ Yakushido

Nakahara
中原

(1)

ⓧ

Musashimurayama City Office Daiichi

MUSASHIMURAYAMA-SH

(3)

(2)

Shimin-kaikan Hall ●

(1) 武蔵村山市

ⓧ Daijū

ⓧ Daigo

Mitsugi
三ツ木

(3)

(2)

Murayamaitchū-nishi
村山一中西

Murayama Health Clinic
● Welfare Hall

(4)

Shin-zanboribashi
新残堀橋

● Daihachi

Mitsufuji
三ツ藤

Mitsugienoki
三ツ樫

Murayamaryō
村山療養所

(5)

(2)

(1)

(3)

ⓧ Daikyū

National
Muraya

Zanbori
残堀

Zanbori
残堀

Gakuen
学園

(5)

(2)

(1)

(5)

National Institute of N

Mizuho-machi-
tobichi

(4)

● Inageya Store

Enoki
榎

Murayama School for Physically Handicapped
or Mentally Retarded Children

Tōkyō Keizai

Kishi
岸

(6)

ⓧ

(1)

Children's H
the Severel

**U.S. Air Force
Yokota Base**

(1)

Enoki
榎

Edo-kaidō Ave.
江戸街道

Daiyon

84 **FUSSA-SHI**
福生市

Mitsugi
三ツ木

Inadaira
伊奈平

(1)

(1)

Fussa

(2)

Nissan Motor Test Course

(4)

(3)

(1)

(1)

Enoki
榎

ⓧ Nissan Motor

Nishi-suna-chō

Itsukaichi-kaidō Ave.
五日市街道

Ichiban-chō

Musashi-sunagawa

58 **TACHIKAWA-SHI**
立川市

Sunag

Kami-suna-chō

Seibu-tachikawa

Tamagawa-jōsui

Mihori-chō

58 **AKISHIMA-SHI**
昭島市

to Haijima

■ MUSASHIMURAYAMA-SHI AREA INDEX ■

Chūō 1~5 ············· D−3	Kishi 1~5 ················· B−2	Ōminami 1~5 ············· E−5
Enoki 1~3 ············· D−4	Midorigaoka ············· F−4	Shinmei 1~4 ············· E−3
Gakuen 1~5 ············· E−4	Mitsufuji 1~3 ············· C−3	Zanbori 1~5 ············· B−4
Hon-machi 1~6 ············· D−2	Mitsugi 1~5 ············· C−2	
Inadaira 1~6 ············· C−4	Nakahara 1~5 ············· A−3	
Kishi ············· A−4	Nakatō 1~5 ············· E−2	

to Haijima

東大和市・武蔵村山市

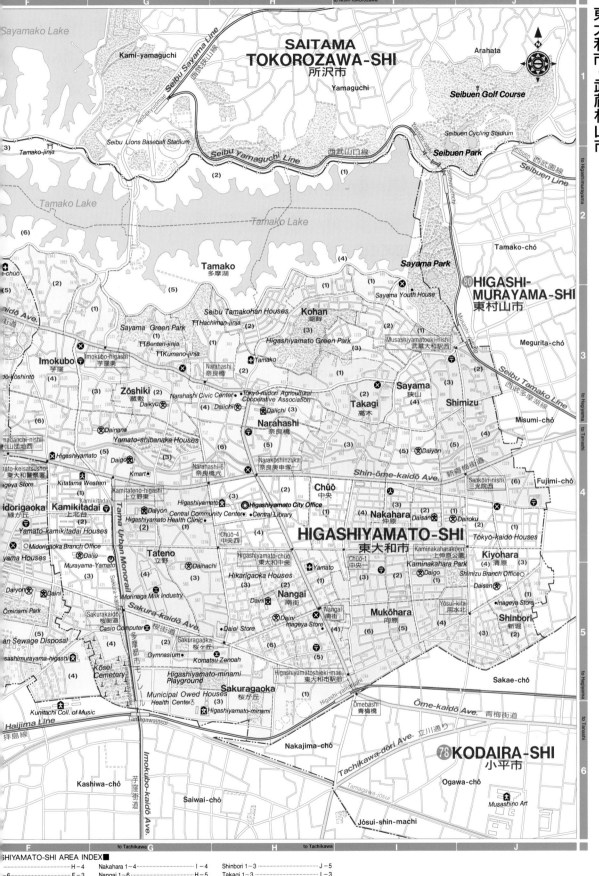

SAITAMA
TOKOROZAWA-SHI
所沢市

Kami-yamaguchi

Yamaguchi

Arahata

Seibuen Golf Course

Sayamako Lake

Seibu Lions Baseball Stadium

Seibuen Cycling Stadium

Tamako-jinja

Seibu Yamaguchi Line 西武山口線

Seibuen Park

Seibuen Line

Tamako Lake

Tamako Lake

Tamako-chō

Tamako
多摩湖

Sayama Park

HIGASHI-MURAYAMA-SHI
東村山市

Sayama Youth House

Megurita-chō

Kohan
湖畔

Seibu Tamakohan Houses
Hachiman-jinja

Higashiyamato Green Park

Musashiyamatoeki-nishi
武蔵大和駅西

Sayama Green Park
Benten-jinja
Kumano-jinja

Imokubo
芋窪
Imokubo-higashi
芋窪東

Tamako

Sayama
狭山

Shimizu
清水

Misumi-chō

Zōshiki
蔵敷
Daikyu

Narahashi Civic Center
Tōkyō-midori Agricultural
Cooperative Association
Daiichi

Takagi
高木

Narahashi
奈良橋

Yamato-shibanaka Houses

Daigo

Narakoshinzuka
奈良庚申塚

Daiyon

Higashiyamato
Kitatama Western

Narahashi-6
奈良橋六

Shin-ōme-kaidō Ave.
新青梅街道

Sankōin-nishi
三光院西

Fujimi-chō

Kamitateno-higashi
上立野東

Higashiyamato

Chūō
中央

Kamikitadai
上北台

Daiyon

Central Community Center
Higashiyamato Health Clinic

Higashiyamato City Office
Central Library

Nakahara
仲原

Daisan

Dairoku

Tōkyō-kaidō Houses

Yamato-kamikitadai Houses

Chūō-4
中央西

HIGASHIYAMATO-SHI
東大和市

Kaminakaharakōen
上仲原公園

Kiyohara
清原

Midorigaoka Branch Office
Daiju

Tateno
立野

Daihachi

Higashiyamato-chūō
東大和中央

Chūō-1
中央

Kaminakahara Park

Daigo

Shimizu Branch Office

Murayama-Yamato

Hikarigaoka Houses

Yamato

Daisan

Daiyon
Daini

Morinaga Milk Industry

Daini

Nangai
南街

Mukōhara
向原

Shinbori
新堀

Sakurakaidō
桜街道

Casio Computer

Daini
Inageya Store

Inageya Store

Sakuragaoka
桜ヶ丘

Daiei Store

Yōsui-kita
用水北

Sewage Disposal
sashimurayama-higashi

Gymnasium

Komatsu Zenoah

Higashiyamatoshieki-mae
東大和市駅前

Sakae-chō

Kōsei Cemetery

Higashiyamato-minami
Playground

Municipal Owed Houses
Health Center

Sakuragaoka
桜ヶ丘

Higashiyamato-minami

Kunitachi Coll. of Music

Ōmebashi
青梅橋

Ōme-kaidō Ave. 青梅街道

Haijima Line
拝島線

Nakajima-chō

Tachikawa-dōri Ave. 立川通り

KODAIRA-SHI
小平市

Kashiwa-chō

Saiwai-chō

Ogawa-chō

Musashino Art

Jōsui-shin-machi
Tamagawa-jōsui

■HIGASHIYAMATO-SHI AREA INDEX

SHIYAMATO-SHI	H-4	Nakahara 1~4	I-4	Shinbori 1~3	J-5
~6	F-3	Nangai 1~6	H-5	Takagi 1~3	I-3
ai 1~6	F-4	Narahashi 1~6	H-3	Tamako 1~6	G-2
~4	J-3	Sakuragaoka 1~4	H-5	Tateno 1~4	G-4
	H-3	Sayama 1~5	I-3	Zōshiki 1~3	G-3
1~6	I-5	Shimizu 1~6	J-3		

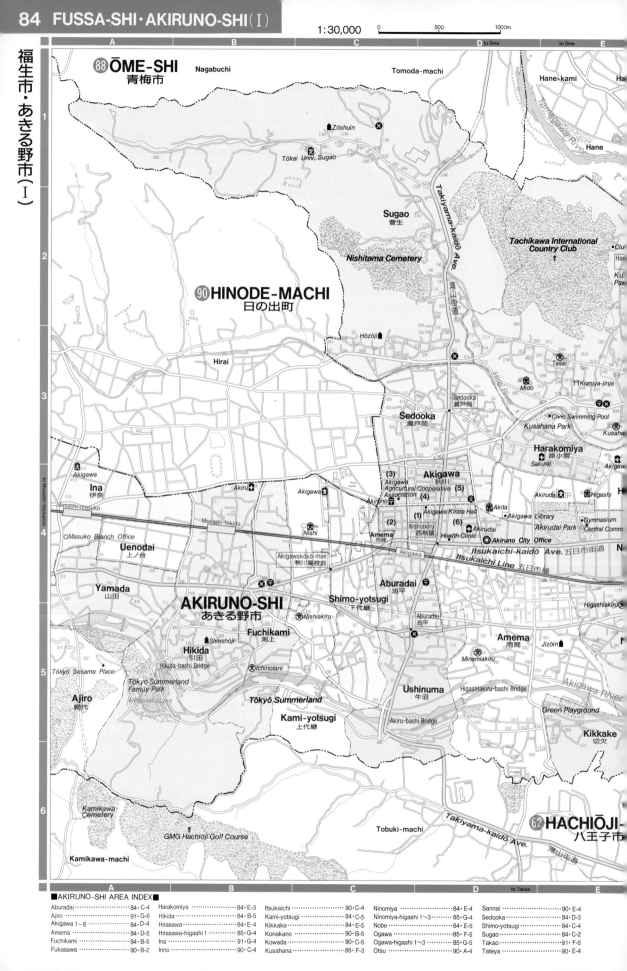

福生市・あきる野市（Ⅰ）

■AKIRUNO-SHI AREA INDEX■

Aburadai ·············· 84·C-4	Harakomiya ·············· 84·E-3	Itsukaichi ·············· 90·C-4
Ajiro ·············· 91·G-6	Hikida ·············· 84·B-5	Kami-yotsugi ·············· 84·C-5
Akigawa 1~6 ·············· 84·D-4	Hirasawa ·············· 84·E-4	Kikkake ·············· 84·E-5
Amema ·············· 84·D-5	Hirasawa-higashi 1 ·············· 85·G-4	Konakano ·············· 90·B-5
Fuchikami ·············· 84·B-5	Ina ·············· 91·G-4	Kowada ·············· 90·C-5
Fukasawa ·············· 90·B-2	Irino ·············· 90·C-4	Kusahana ·············· 85·F-3

Ninomiya ·············· 84·E-4	Sannai ·············· 90·E-4
Ninomiya-higashi 1~3 ·············· 85·G-4	Sedooka ·············· 84·D-3
Nobe ·············· 84·E-5	Shimo-yotsugi ·············· 84·C-5
Ogawa ·············· 85·F-5	Sugao ·············· 84·C-2
Ogawa-higashi 1~3 ·············· 85·G-5	Takao ·············· 91·F-5
Otsu ·············· 90·A-4	Tateya ·············· 90·E-4

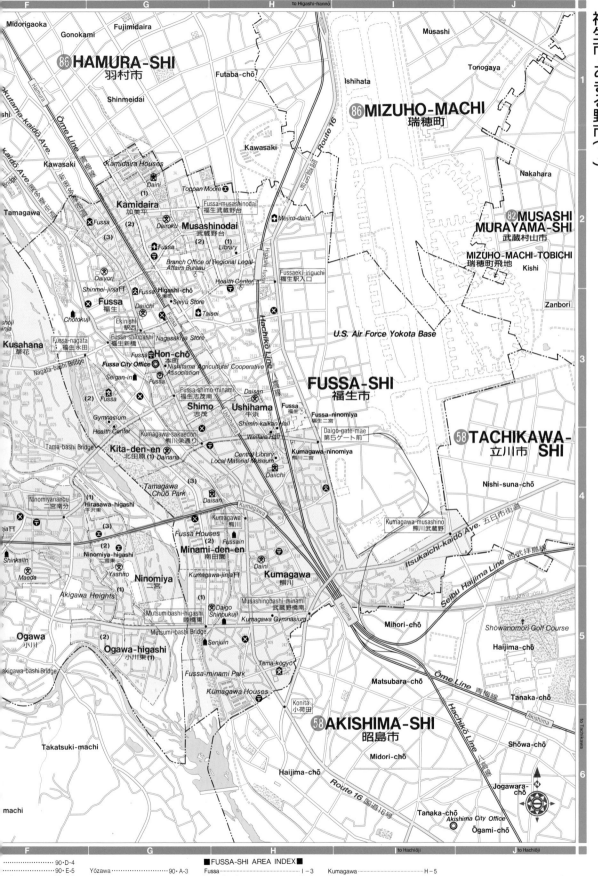

Midorigaoka
Gonokami
Fujimidaira

㊌HAMURA-SHI
羽村市

Shinmeidai

Ōme Line

Kawasaki

Kamidaira Houses

Daini
(1)

Toppan Moore

Fussa-musashinodai
福生武蔵野台

Kamidaira
加美平
(2)

Dairoku

Musashinodai
武蔵野台
(2)

Library

Mejiro-daini

Branch Office of Regional Legal-
Affairs Bureau

Fussaeki-iriguchi
福生駅入口

Health Center

Daiyori

Shinmei-jinja

Higashi-chō
東町

Seiyu Store

Fussa
福生

Daichi

Taisei

Chōtokuji

Ekinishi
駅西

Nagasakiya Store

Fussa-shinbashi
福生新橋

Hon-chō
本町

Nishitama Agricultural Cooperative
Association

Fussa City Office

Seigan-in

Fussa

Fussa-shimo-minami
福生志茂南

Daisan

Shimo
志茂

Ushihama
牛浜

Gymnasium

Health Center

Kumagawa-sakaedōri
熊川栄通り

Shimin-kaikan Hall

Welfare Hall

Kita-den-en
北田原
(1)

Dainana

Central Library
Local Material Museum

Daiichi

Tamagawa
Chūō Park

Daisan

Kumagawa

Hirasawa-higashi
平沢東

Kumagawa
熊川

Ninomiyananbu
二宮南分

Fussa Houses

Fussain

Shinkairin

Ninomiya-higashi
二宮東

Maeda

Yashiro

Minami-den-en
南田園

Kumagawa-jinja

Kumagawa
熊川

Ninomiya
二宮

Daigo
Shinpukuji

Mutsumibashi-higashi
睦橋東

Musashinobashi-minami
武蔵野橋南

Ogawa
小川

Mutsumi-bashi Bridge

Kumagawa Gymnasium

Ogawa-higashi
小川東 (1)

Senjuin

Fussa-minami Park

Tama-kogyō

Kumagawa Houses

Konita
小荷田

㊄AKISHIMA-SHI
昭島市

Midorigaoka

Kawasaki

to Higashi-hannō

Ishihata

Route 16

Musashi

Tonogaya

Nakahara

㊏MIZUHO-MACHI
瑞穂町

㊓MUSASHI
MURAYAMA-SHI
武蔵村山市

MIZUHO-MACHI-TOBICHI
瑞穂町飛地
Kishi

Zanbori

Higashi-fussa

Hachikō Line

U.S. Air Force Yokota Base

FUSSA-SHI
福生市

Fussa
福生

Fussa-ninomiya
福生二宮

Daigo-gate-mae
第5ゲート前

Kumagawa-ninomiya
熊川二宮

㊅TACHIKAWA-
立川市 SHI

Nishi-suna-chō

Kumagawa-musashino
熊川武蔵野

Itsukaichi-kaidō Ave. 五日市街道

Seibu Haijima Line 西武拝島線

Tamagawa-jōsui

Haijima

Mihori-chō

Shōwanomori Golf Course

Haijima-chō

Ōme Line 青梅線

Hachikō Line 八高線

Akishima

Matsubara-chō

Tanaka-chō

Shōwa-chō

to Tachikawa

Jogawara-
chō

Route 16 国道16号

Tanaka-chō
Akishima City Office

Haijima-chō

Midori-chō

Ōgami-chō

to Hachiōji

machi

F ....90・D-4
......................90・E-5
......................90・A-5
......................91・H-4
......................84・D-5
......................91・H-5
......................91・F-4

G Yōzawa ....90・A-3

H ■FUSSA-SHI AREA INDEX■
Fussa ....I－3
Fussa-ninomiya ....H－3
Higashi-chō ....G－3
Hon-chō ....G－3
Kamidaira 1-4 ....G－2
Kita-den-en 1-2 ....G－3

Kumagawa ....H－5
Kumagawa-ninomiya ....H－4
Minami-den-en 1-3 ....G－4
Musashinodai 1-2 ....G－2
Shimo ....G－3
Ushihama ....H－3

羽村市・瑞穂町

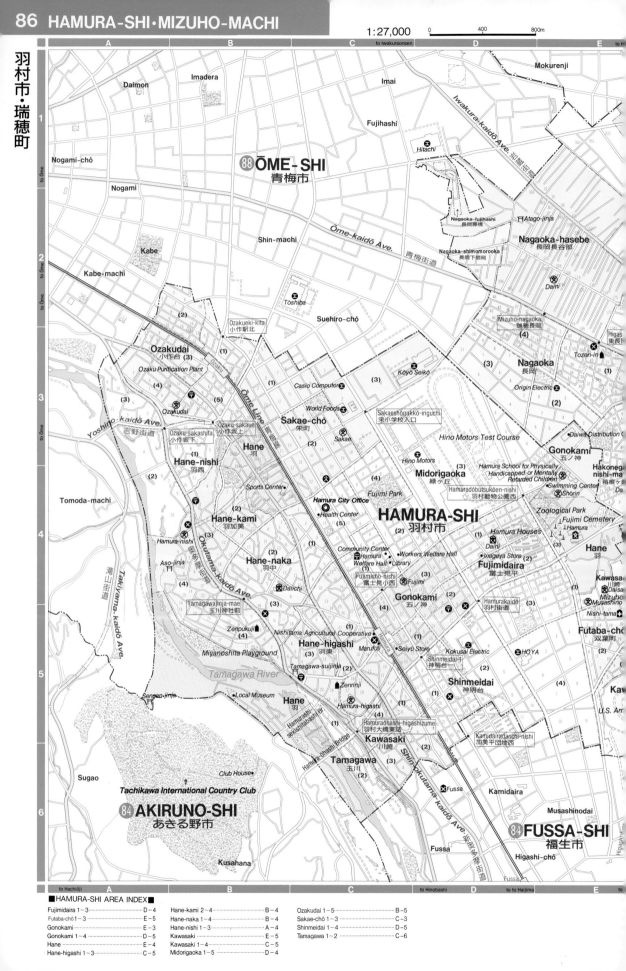

■HAMURA-SHI AREA INDEX■

Fujimidaira 1~3	D-4	Hane-kami 2~4	B-4	Ozakudai 1~5	B-5
Futaba-chō 1~3	E-5	Hane-naka 1~4	B-4	Sakae-chō 1~3	C-3
Gonokami	E-3	Hane-nishi 1~3	A-4	Shinmeidai 1~4	D-5
Gonokami 1~4	D-5	Kawasaki	E-5	Tamagawa 1~2	C-6
Hane	E-4	Kawasaki 1~4	C-5		
Hane-higashi 1~3	C-5	Midorigaoka 1~5	D-4		

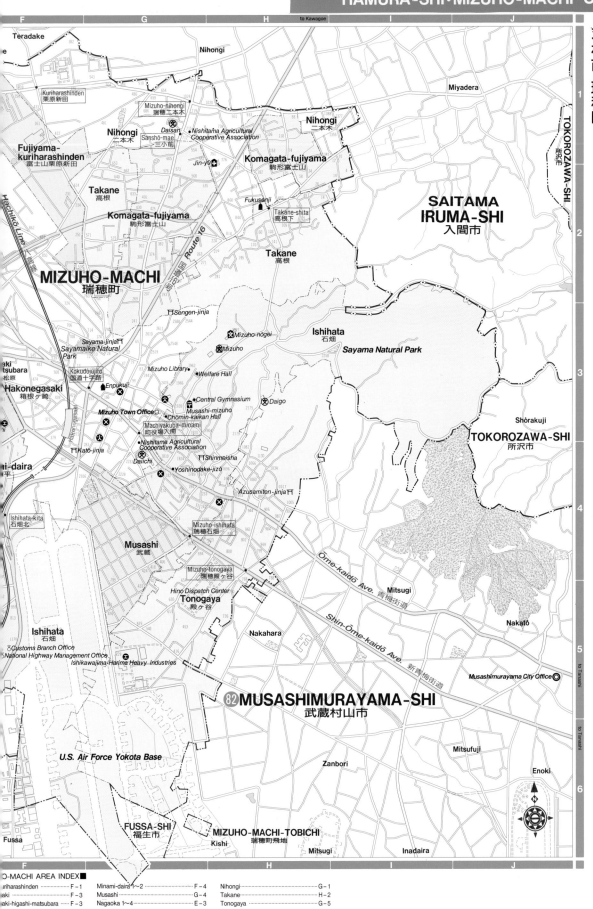

Teradake

Nihongi

Kuriharashinden
栗原新田

Mizuho-nihongi
瑞穂二本木

Nihongi
二本木

Daisan
三小前

Sanshō-mae
三小前

Nishitama Agricultural
Cooperative Association

Miyadera

Nihongi
二本木

Jin-yū

Komagata-fujiyama
駒形富士山

Fujiyama-
kuriharashinden
富士山栗原新田

Takane
高根

Fukusenji

Takane-shita
高根下

**SAITAMA
IRUMA-SHI
入間市**

Komagata-fujiyama
駒形富士山

Takane
高根

Route 16

Sengen-jinja

**MIZUHO-MACHI
瑞穂町**

Mizuho-nōgei

Ishihata
石畑

Sayama Natural Park

Sayama-jinja
Sayamaike Natural
Park

Mizuho

Hakonegasaki
箱根ヶ崎

Kokudōjūjiro
国道十字路

Mizuho Library

Welfare Hall

Enpukuji

Central Gymnasium

Daigo

Shōrakuji

**TOKOROZAWA-SHI
所沢市**

Mizuho Town Office

Musashi-mizuho

Chōmin-kaikan Hall

Machiyakuba-minami
町役場入南

Katō-jinja

Nishitama Agricultural
Cooperative Association

Shinmeisha

Daichi

Yoshinodake-jizō

Azusamiten-jinja

Ishihata-kita
石畑北

Mizuho-ishihata
瑞穂石畑

**Musashi
武蔵**

Ōme-kaidō Ave. 青梅街道

Mitsugi

Mizuho-tonogaya
瑞穂殿ヶ谷

Hino Dispatch Center

**Tonogaya
殿ヶ谷**

Shin-Ōme-kaidō Ave. 新青梅街道

Nakatō

**Ishihata
石畑**

Customs Branch Office
National Highway Management Office
Ishikawajima-Harima Heavy Industries

Nakahara

Musashimurayama City Office

82 **MUSASHIMURAYAMA-SHI
武蔵村山市**

U.S. Air Force Yokota Base

Zanbori

Mitsufuji

Enoki

**FUSSA-SHI
福生市**

Fussa

Kishi

**MIZUHO-MACHI-TOBICHI
瑞穂町飛地**

Mitsugi

Inadaira

■O-MACHI AREA INDEX■

riharashinden	F-1	Minami-daira 1〜2	F-4	Nihongi	G-1
aki	F-3	Musashi	G-4	Takane	H-2
aki-higashi-matsubara	F-3	Nagaoka 1〜4	E-3	Tonogaya	G-5
aki-nishi-matsubara	E-4	Nagaoka-fujihahashi	D-2		
	H-3	Nagaoka-hasebe	E-2		
ujiyama	H-1	Nagaoka-shimomorooka	D-2		

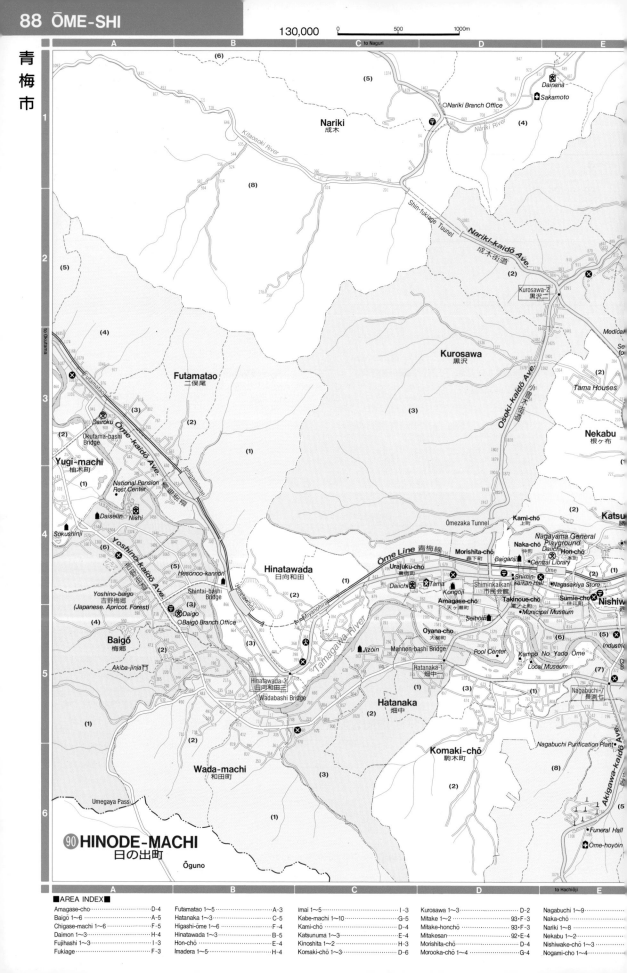

青梅市

130,000

Nariki 成木
Kurosawa 黒沢
Nekabu 根ヶ布
Futamatao 二俣尾
Yugi-machi 柚木町
Hinatawada 日向和田
Baigō 梅郷
Hatanaka 畑中
Komaki-chō 駒木町
Wada-machi 和田町

⑨⓪ **HINODE-MACHI** 日の出町

■AREA INDEX■

Amagase-chō	D-4
Baigō 1~6	A-5
Chigase-machi 1~6	F-5
Daimon 1~3	H-4
Fujihashi 1~3	I-3
Fukiage	F-3
Futamatao 1~5	A-3
Hatanaka 1~3	C-5
Higashi-ōme 1~6	F-4
Hinatawada 1~3	B-5
Hon-chō	E-4
Imadera 1~5	H-4
Imai 1~5	I-3
Kabe-machi 1~10	G-5
Kami-chō	D-4
Katsunuma 1~3	E-4
Kinoshita 1~2	H-3
Komaki-chō 1~3	D-6
Kurosawa 1~3	D-2
Mitake 1~2	93·F-3
Mitake-honchō	93·F-3
Mitakesan	92·E-4
Morishita-chō	D-4
Morooka-chō 1~4	G-4
Nagabuchi 1~9	
Naka-chō	
Nariki 1~8	
Nekabu 1~2	
Nishiwake-chō 1~	
Nogami-chō 1~4	

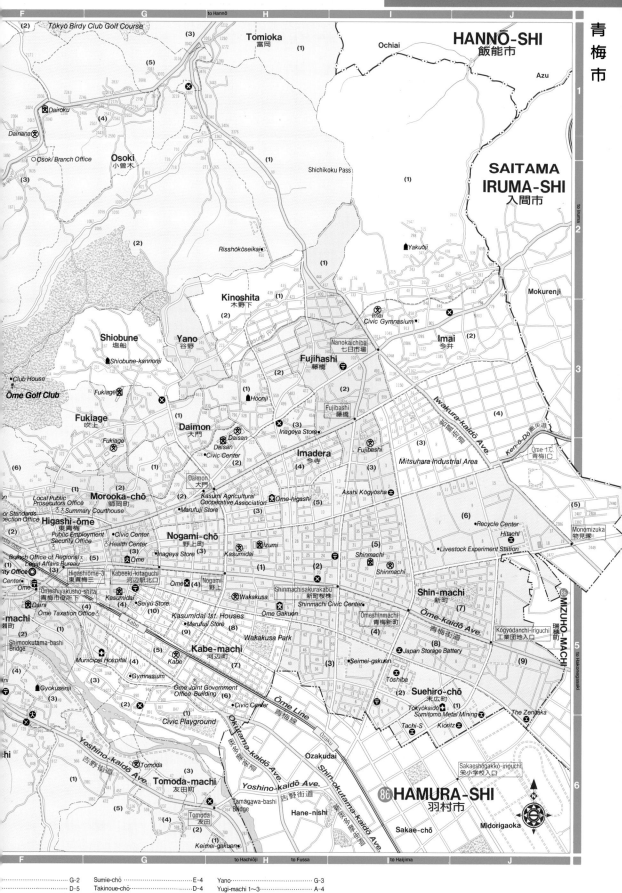

青梅市

·········G-2	Sumie-chō ·········E-4	Yano ·········G-3		
·········D-5	Takinoue-chō ·········D-4	Yugi-machi 1~3 ·········A-4		
93·F-3	Tomioka 1~3 ·········H-1			
~9 ·········I-5	Tomoda-machi 1~5 ·········G-6			
·········G-3	Urajuku-chō ·········C-4			
~2 ·········I-5	Wada-machi 1~2 ·········B-6			

あきる野市（Ⅱ）・日の出町

Ōguno ☖

Ōguno
大久野

Taiheiyō Cement 井

Ⓣ Hakusan-ji

Asano PC Concrete 井

Kōshin
幸神

⊗ Ōguno
Ⓣ

Ⓣ Kōshin-jinja

Taiheiyō Cement Clinic 井

Yōzawa
養沢

⊕ Ōguno

井 Shinkōji

Fukasawa
深沢

Nanseien Home for the Aged ●

Taiheiyō Cement

Irino
入野

Sannai
三内

Konpira Park

Tateyadai
舘谷台

● Hoshitake Campsite

Itsukaichi Home for the Aged ●

Otsu
乙津

AKIRUNO-SHI
あきる野市

Itsukaichi
五日市

⊗ Itsukaichi ●

● Tokura Campsite

⊗ Itsukaichi

Itsukaichi ☖

Hinohara-Kaidō Ave.
檜原街道

Kaikōin ☖

Itsukaichi
Government Office Bldg.

Workers Welfare Hall

Itsukaichi Ⓣ

Konakano
小中野

Itsukaichi ●
Local Museum

Branch Office of Regional Legal
Affairs Bureau

Akigawabashi
Riverbed Park

Tateya
舘谷

☖ Sh

⊗ Gyokurinji

Ⓣ

Akigawa Health Center

⊗ Tokura

Kōgenji ☖

Akigawa River

Todohara
留原

秋
川
街
道

● Youth House

Tokura
戸倉

Bonbori River

Public Ground

HOYA ☖

Kōtokuji ☖

Kowada
小和田

Kominedai
小峰台

Komine Industri

Shisuien Home for the Aged ●

⑥② HACHIŌJI-SHI
八王子市

Kamikawa-machi

E to Hachi

■AKIRUNO-SHI AREA INDEX■

Aburadai	84・C－4	Harakomiya	84・E－3	Itsukaichi	90・C－4
Ajiro	91・G－6	Hikida	84・B－5	Kami-yotsugi	84・C－5
Akigawa 1~6	84・D－4	Hirasawa	84・E－4	Kikkake	84・E－5
Amema	84・D－5	Hirasawa-higashi 1	85・G－4	Konakano	90・B－5
Fuchikami	84・B－5	Ina	91・G－4	Kowada	90・C－5
Fukasawa	90・B－2	Irino	90・C－4	Kusahana	85・F－3

Ninomiya	84・E－4	Sannai	
Ninomiya-higashi 1~3	85・G－4	Sedooka	
Nobe	84・E－5	Shimo-yotsugi	
Ogawa	85・F－5	Sugao	
Ogawa-higashi 1~3	85・G－5	Takao	
Otsu	90・A－4	Tateya	

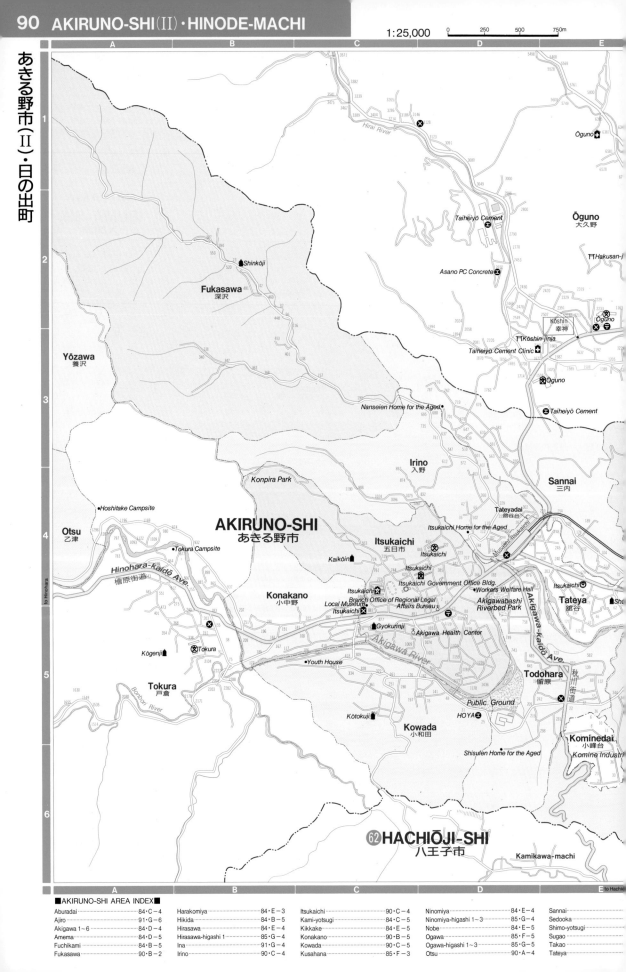

あきる野市（II）・日の出町

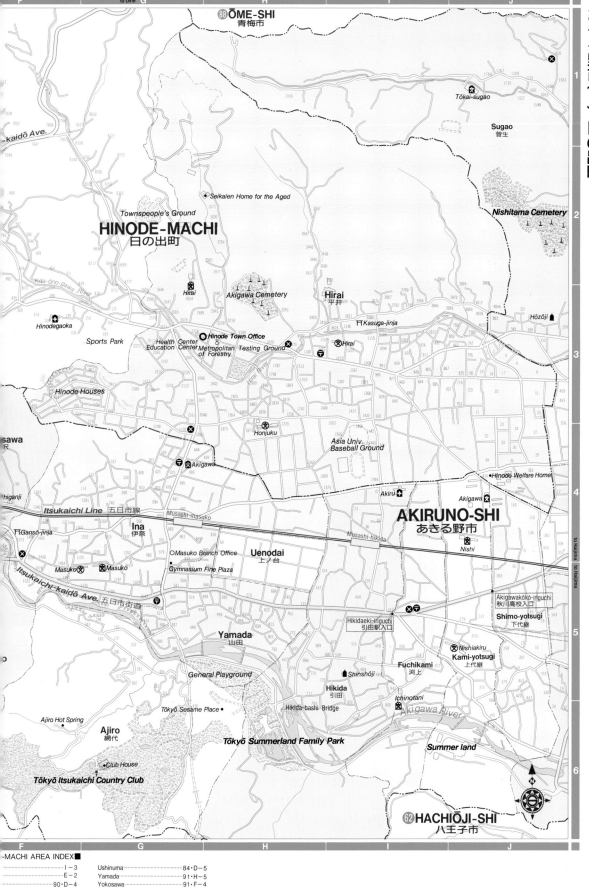

F to Ōme G H I J

89 **ŌME-SHI**
青梅市

Tōkai-sugao

Sugao
菅生

• Seikaien Home for the Aged

Nishitama Cemetery

Townspeople's Ground

HINODE-MACHI
日の出町

Hirai

Akigawa Cemetery

Hirai
平井

Kita-ōno-gawa River

Hirai

Kasuga-jinja

Hōzōji

Hinodegaoka

Sports Park

Health Center
Education Center

Hinode Town Office

Metropolitan Testing Ground
of Forestry

Hirai

Hinode Houses

Honjuku

Asia Univ.
Baseball Ground

Hinode Welfare Home

Akigawa

Akiru

Akigawa

Itsukaichi Line 五日市線

Musashi-masuko

Musashi-hikida

AKIRUNO-SHI
あきる野市

Ina
伊奈

Gansō-jinja

Masuko

○Masuko Branch Office

○Gymnasium Fine Plaza

Uenodai
上ノ台

Nishi

Akigawakōkō-inguchi
秋川高校入口

Shimo-yotsugi
下代継

Itsukaichi-kaidō Ave. 五日市街道

Hikidaeki-iriguchi
引田駅入口

Nishiakiru

Kami-yotsugi
上代継

Yamada
山田

General Playground

Shinshōji

Hikida
引田

Fuchikami
渕上

Ichinotani

Akigawa River

Tōkyō Sesame Place •

Ajiro Hot Spring

Hikida-bashi Bridge

Ajiro
網代

Tōkyō Summerland Family Park

Summer land

• Club House

Tōkyō Itsukaichi Country Club

62 **HACHIŌJI-SHI**
八王子市

to Hajima

-MACHI AREA INDEX■

	I－3	Ushinuma	84・D－5
	E－2	Yamada	91・H－5
	90・D－4	Yokosawa	91・F－4
	90・E－5	Yōzawa	90・A－3
	90・A－5		
	91・H－4		

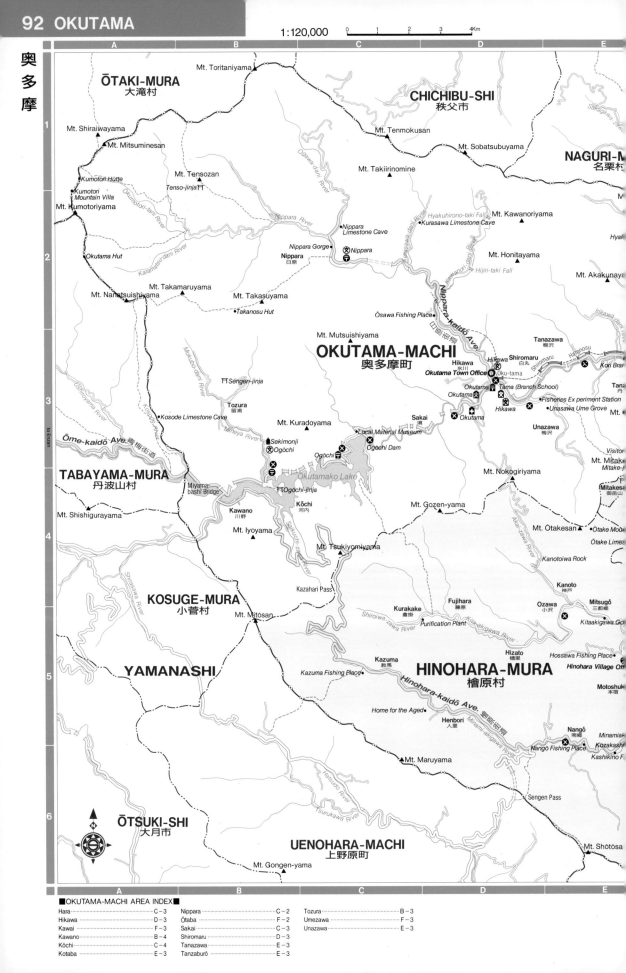

奥多摩

1:120,000

0 1 2 3 4Km

■OKUTAMA-MACHI AREA INDEX■

Hara	C – 3	Nippara	C – 2	Tozura	B – 3
Hikawa	D – 3	Ōtaba	F – 2	Umezawa	F – 3
Kawai	F – 3	Sakai	C – 3	Unazawa	E – 3
Kawano	B – 4	Shiromaru	D – 3		
Kōchi	C – 4	Tanazawa	E – 3		
Kotaba	E – 3	Tanzaburō	E – 3		

奥多摩

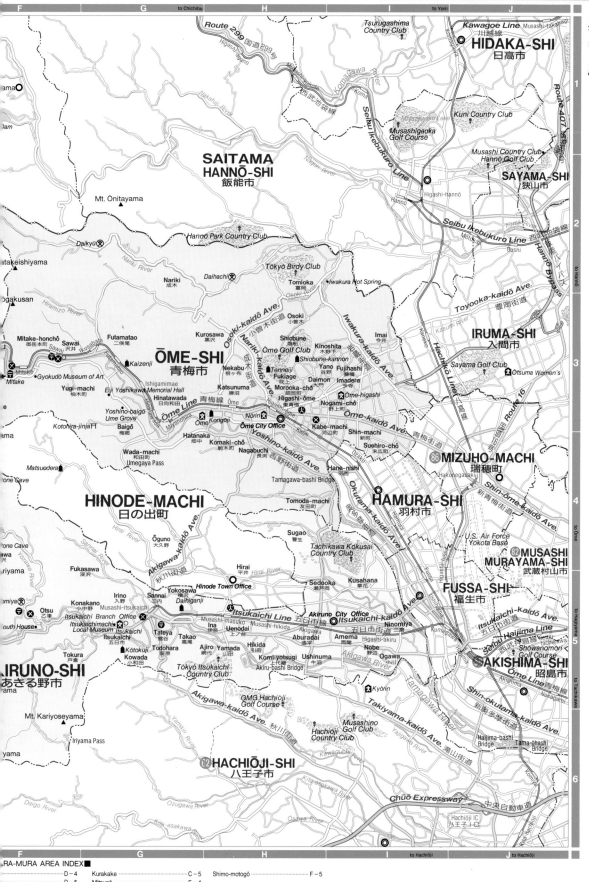

to Chichibu · to Yorii

Tsurugashima Country Club

Kawagoe Line Musashi-takahama

◉ **HIDAKA-SHI** 日高市

Route 299 国道299号 Higashi-Agano Seibu Ikebukuro Line 西武池袋線 Koma River Komagawa

Nakatsuji River Koma Koma River

Miyazawako Lake

Kuni Country Club

Musashigaoka Golf Course

SAITAMA HANNŌ-SHI 飯能市

Nagura River

Musashi Country Club Hanno Golf Club

◉ **SAYAMA-SHI** 狭山市

Mt. Onitayama ▲

Higashi-hanno

Hanno

Seibu Ikebukuro Line 西武池袋線 Irum... Moto...

Bushi

to Hannō

Hannō Bypass 飯能バイパス

Daikyū ⊗

Hanno Park Country Club

Osoki-kaidō Ave.

Toyooka-kaidō Ave. 豊岡街道

Nariki River Nariki 成木 Daihachi

Tokyo Birdy Club

Tomioka 富岡

Iwakura Hot Spring

Osoki River

Kasumi River

IRUMA-SHI 入間市

ⓧ Hiramizo River

Osoki-kaidō Ave.

Iwakura-kaidō Ave. 飯山街道

Imai 今井

Kurosawa 黒沢 Osoki 小曽木 Shiobune Kinoshita 木野入

Sayama Golf Club

Futamatao 二俣尾

ŌME-SHI 青梅市

Ōme Golf Club

Shiobune-kannon Yano Fujihashi 藤橋

⊗ Ōtsuma Women's

Mitake-honchō 御岳本町 Sawai 沢井 Kaizenji

Nekabu 根ヶ布 Shiobune 塩船 Tenneiji Fukiage 吹上

Daimon Imadera 今寺

Hachikō Line 八高線 Route 16

⊗ Mitake 御岳 ⓧ

Gyokudō Museum of Art Yugi-machi 柚木町

Eiji Yoshikawa Memorial Hall Hinatawada 日向和田

Katsunuma 勝沼 Moroka-chō 師岡町

Higashi-ōme 東青梅 Nogami-chō 野上町 Ōme-higashi 青梅東

Ōme Line 青梅線 Ōme 青梅 Miyanoira

Kongoji Ōme City Office Kabe-machi 河辺町 Shin-machi 新町

86 **MIZUHO-MACHI** 瑞穂町

Yoshino-baigō Ume Grove Baigō 梅郷

Norin Kabe Suehiro-chō 末広町

Ōme-kaidō Ave. 青梅街道

Kotohira-jinja 琴平神社

Hatanaka 畑中 Komaki-chō 駒木町 Nagabuchi 長渕

Hane-nishi 羽西

Hakonegasaki Shin-ōme-kaidō Ave. 新青梅街道

Matsuodera ▲

Wada-machi 和田町 Umegaya Pass

Tamagawa-bashi Bridge

Tomoda-machi 友田町

HAMURA-SHI 羽村市

U.S. Air Force Yokota Base

...one Cave

HINODE-MACHI 日の出町

Sugao 菅生

Okutama-kaidō Ave.

Hamura

82 **MUSASHI MURAYAMA-SHI** 武蔵村山市

Akigawa-kaidō Ave. 秋川街道

Ōguno 大久野

Tachikawa Kokusai Country Club

...one Cave

Hirai River Sannai River

Hirai 平井 Hirai River

Sedooka 瀬戸岡

Kusahana 草花

FUSSA-SHI 福生市

Fukasawa 深沢

Yokosawa Hinode Town Office

Itsukaichi-kaidō Ave.

...riyama ⓧ

Konakano 小中野 Irino 入野 Musashi-itsukaichi

Sannai 三内 Daihiganji

Itsukaichi Line 五日市線 Akiruno City Office Itsukaichi-kaidō Ave. Ninomiya 二宮

to Haijima

Itsukaichi Branch Office Itsukaichimachi Local Museum

Tateya Takao 高尾 Ina 伊奈 Uenodai 上ノ台 Musashi-masuko Musashi-hikida Higashi-akiru 東秋留

Haijima Line

Shōwanomori Golf Course

Otsu 乙津 ⓧ

Itsukaichi 五日市 Kōtokuji

Todohara 留原 Ajiro 網代 Yamada 山田 Hikida 引田 Amema 雨間 Nobe 野辺 Ogawa 小川

Ōme Line 青梅線

◉ **AKISHIMA-SHI** 昭島市

South House ⊗

Tokura 戸倉 Kowada 小和田

Komi-yotsugi 小美四 Ushinuma 牛沼 Aburadai 油平

Kyōrin

Akigawa River

Akishima Nakagami

to Tachikawa

IRUNO-SHI あきる野市

Mt. Kariyoseyama ▲

Tōkyō Itsukaichi Country Club

Akiru-bashi Bridge

Tamagawa River

Shin-okutama-kaidō Ave. 新奥多摩街道

Iriyama Pass

Akigawa-kaidō Ave. 秋川街道

GMG Hachiōji Golf Course

Takiyama-kaidō Ave. 滝山街道

Yaigawa River

Takiyama-kaidō Ave. 滝山街道

Daigo River

Musashino Golf Club

Hachiōji Country Club

Yamen River

Haijima-bashi Bridge

Tama-ōhashi Bridge

72 **HACHIŌJI-SHI** 八王子市

Kita-asakawa River

Ozugawa River

Osawa River

Kita-asakawa River

Chūō Expressway 中央自動車道

Hachiōji IC 八王子IC

to Hachiōji · to Hachiōji

...RA-MURA AREA INDEX ■

...	D – 4	Kurakake	C – 5	Shimo-motogō	F – 5
...	D – 5	Mitsugō	E – 4		
...	D – 5	Motoshuku	E – 5		
...	E – 5	Nangō	E – 5		
...	E – 4	Ōdake	E – 4		
C – 5		Ozawa	E – 5		

八王子市・町田市

1:120,000

0　1　2　3　4km

to Ōme

A

HINOHARA-MURA
檜原村

Mt. Kariyoseyama

Iriyama Pass

Mt. Ichimichiyama

Kozakashi River

Daigo River

Jinba-kaidō Ave.

Wada Pass

Mt. Jinbasan

Mt. Jinbasan
陣馬山

Mt. Kagenobuyama

Tochiya River

Kobotoke Pass

Sagamiko IC
相模湖IC

Sagamiko East Exit Ramp
相模湖東出口

to Ōtsuki

Fujino

Sagamiko Lake
相模湖

FUJINO-MACHI
藤野町

Sagamiko Lake
相模湖

to Dōshi

Mt. Yakeyama

Sagamiko Country Club

Doshi River

Route 413 国道413号

B

Itsukaichi Line 五日市線

Musashi-masuko
Musashi-hikida

Itsukaichi-kaidō Ave.

Tōkyō Itsukaichi Country Club

Itsukaichi Youth House
Imakuma-jinja
Kamikawa-machi
上川町
Teikyō Hachiōji

Kamikawa

Kamikawaguchi

Miyama-machi
美山町

Daikōji

Miyama

Hirakawa

Hōshōji
Hōshinji

Otsu-machi
小津町

Motoki

Yuyakekoyake-no-hi Monument

Ongata-daini

Ongata

Ongata-daiichi

Kami-ongata-machi
上恩方町

Ongata Branch Office

Shimo-ongata-machi

St. Paul Gakuen

Takizawa River

Hachiōjijō Remains

Ura-takao-machi
裏高尾町

Chūō Expressway
中央自動車道

Hōshūji

Asakawa Kaminagafusa Branch School

Meijinomori Takao Semi-national Park
明治の森高尾国定公園

Busshariō Pagoda
Mt. Takaosan

Takao-machi
高尾町
Takaosan

Takosan

Ōdarumi Pass

Mt. Takaosan
高尾山

Yakuōin

Shunsenji

Takao Kōsei

Minami-asakawa-machi
南浅川町

Sagamiko-ohashi Br.

Mt. Arashiyama

Sagamiko Picnic Land
相模湖ピクニックランド

Shindōshi-bashi Br.

Kōshū-kaidō Ave.

SAGAMIKO-MACHI
相模湖町

Tsukuiko Country Club

Nakatsu Gorge
中津渓谷

Mt. Takahatayama

C

五日市
Akigawa

Akasuka

Akigawa River

AKIRUNO-SHI
あきる野市
Summerland

Tobuki-machi
戸吹町

GMG Hachiōji
Golf Course

Miyashita-machi

Musashino Golf Club

Hachiōji Country Club

Kawaguchi-machi
川口町

Takiyama-kaidō Ave.

Yakugawa River

Nishiterakata-machi
西寺方町

Kami-ichibukata-machi
上壱分方町

Narahara-machi
楢原町

Nibukata-machi
犬分方町

HACHIŌJI-SHI
八王子市

Akigawa-kaidō Ave.

Hachiōji Cemetery

Tōkyō Univ. of Art and Design

Kyōritsu Women's

Nagafusa-machi
長房町

Musashino-ryō Mound

Tama-ryō Mound

Todori-machi
廿里町

Chūō Line 中央本線

Takaosanguchi

Kiyotaki

Takushoku

Animal and Plant Park

Aihara-machi
相原町

Hōsei

Sōbu Country Club

Tōkyō Kasei Gakuin

Tsukuiko Lake

Shiroyamako Lake

SHIROYAMA-MACHI
城山町

Shiroyama Dam

KANAGAWA

Tsukuiko Country Club

Nagatake Country Club

TSUKUI-MACHI
津久井町

Shiokawa-taki Fall

Mt. Kyōgatake

KIYOKAWA-MURA
清川村

Mt. Kegon-yama

Insawa River

Nakagawa River

D

to Ōme

Ushihama

Tamabashi

Tama River

Higashi-akiru

84 90

Takatsuki-machi
高月町

Kasumi-machi
加住町

Tangi-machi
丹木町

Inume-machi
犬目町

Sōka

Yano-machi
谷野町

Kogakuin

Toita Women's Jr. Coll.

Nakano-machi
中野町

Nakano-sannō
中野山王

Hachiōji IC
八王子IC

Yokokawa-machi
横川町

Hachiōji City Office
八王子市役所

Dai-machi
台町

Midori-chō
緑町

Sanda-machi
散田町

Keiō Takao Line 京王高尾線

Hazama

Mejirodai

Yamada

Tōkyō Technical Jr. Coll.

Kobiki-machi
小比企町

Tate-machi
館町

Ōfuna-machi
大船町

Terada-machi
寺田町

Utsunuki-machi
宇津貫町

Machida-kaidō Ave.

Tōkyō Engineering

Yokohama Line

SAGAMIHARA-SHI
相模原市

Route 129 国道129号

Sagamino Country Club

Osagami Country Club

Tōmei-atsugi Country Club

Route 412

Sagami River

AIKAWA-MACHI
愛川町

Nakatsugawa Country Club

Nakatsu Industrial Area

Ōatsugi Country Club

ATSUGI-SHI
厚木市

Takada-bashi Br.

to Atsugi

E

FUSSA
福生

AKISHIMA
昭島市

Takiyama-kaidō Ave.

Tōkyō Junshin Women's

Takiyama-machi

Kita- takakura

Ōya

Ōwada-machi
大和田町

Ōwada-bashi Br.

Dai-machi

Koyasu-machi
子安町

Nippon Bunka

Katakura-machi
片倉町

Hachiōji Bypass

Yarimizu

Tama

Kashimofuji

Route 129

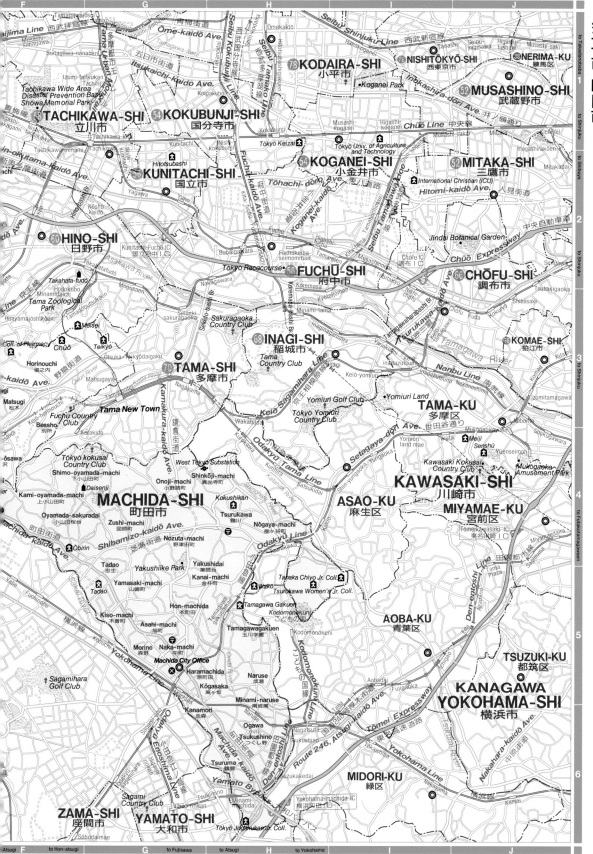

1:12,000

西区（横浜市）

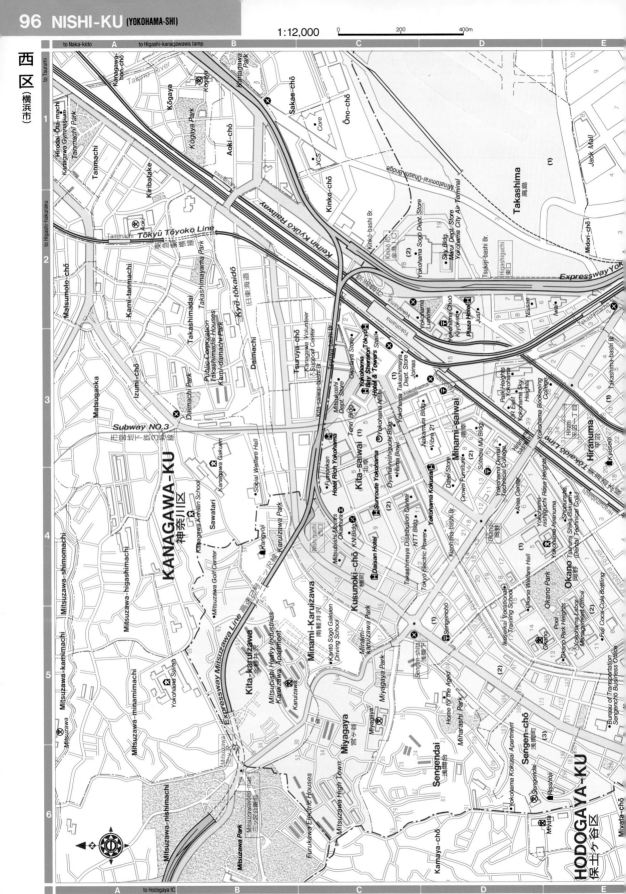

■AREA INDEX■

AKamon-chō 2	J–8	Hanasaki-chō 4～7 ············ G–2
Azumagaoka ············ I–2	Higashi-kubo-chō ············ H–6
Chūō 1～2 ············ F–4	Hiranuma 1～2 ············ E–3
Fujidana-chō 1～2 ············ H–5	Ise-chō 1～3 ············ G–3
Goshoyama-chō ············ F–3	Kasumigaoka ············ I–3
Hamamatsu-chō ············ G–5	Kita-karuizawa ············ B–5

Kita-saiwai 1～2 ············ C–3	Minami-sengen-chō ············ F–6	Nishi-hiranuma-chō ············
Kubo-chō ············ H–5	Minatomirai 1～5 ············ F–1	Nishi-tobe-chō 1～3 ············
Kusunoki-chō ············ C–4	Miyagaya ············ C–5	Nishimae-chō 2～3 ············
Midori-chō ············ E–2	Miyazaki-chō ············ H–2	Oimatsu-chō ············
Minami-karuizawa ············ C–5	Momijigaoka ············ I–5	Okano 1～2 ············
Minami-saiwai 1～2 ············ D–3	Moto-kubo-chō ············	Sakainotani ············

西区（横浜市）

F — to Yokōhamakōen — G — to Kannai — H — I — to Isezaki-chōjachō — J

to Bandobashi
to Yokosuka
to Koganechō

NAKA-KU 中区

NISHI-KU 西区

MINAMI-KU 南区

Minatomirai
みなとみらい

Landmark Tower
Royal Park Hotel Nikko
Mitsubishi Heavy Industries Bldg (2)

Negishi Line 根岸線
Keikyū Line
Seaside Railway

Uchida-chō 内田町
Sakuragi-chō 桜木町
Noge-chō 野毛町
Miyagawa-chō
Hanazaki-chō
Miyazaki-chō 宮崎町
Oimatsu-chō 老松町
Tobe-chō 戸部町
Goshoyama-chō 御所山町
Ise-chō 伊勢町
Chūō 中央
Nishimae-chō 西前町
Nishi-tobe-chō 西戸部町
Fujidana-chō 藤棚町
Kubo-chō 久保町
Hamamatsu-chō 浜松町
Higashi-kubo-chō 東久保町
Moto-kubo-chō 元久保町
Nishikubo-chō 西久保町
Minami-sengen-chō 南浅間町
Nishi-niranuma-chō 西平沼町
Tennō-chō 天王町
Iwama-chō 岩間町

Kasumigaoka 霞ヶ丘
Azumagaoka 東ヶ丘
Azuma 東町
Akamon-chō 赤門町
Tofukuji
Miharudai
Nishinaka-chō 西中町
Hirode-chō 緋代町
Hanabusa-chō
Hatsune-chō 初音町
Kogane-chō 黄金町
Wakabe-chō
Sakaōdō
Sakainotani 境之谷
Fushimi-chō 伏見町
Enjōji
Kanoedai
Shimizugaoka
Iwai-chō 岩井町

Nogeyama Park
Nogeyama Zoo
Kamon-yama Park
Momijigaoka
City Library
Nogeyama-Kōdai-Jinpū
Young Workers Center
New Nogeyama Apartment
Nogeyama Guest House
Nogeyama Swimming Pool

Nishi-ku Medical Center
Nishi Ward Office
Yokohama Uehara Church
Customs House
Nishi-tobe Public Servant House
Prefectural Fujidana Apts
Education Hall
Kuboyama Cemetery
Public Corporation Shimizugaoka Houses

Route 16
Route X

5 4~7 .... G–1
1~5 .... D–6
~2 .... D–6
~2 .... D–2
~7 .... G–2
ō F–3

中区（横浜市）

1:20,000

0　200　400　600m

■AREA INDEX■

Aioi-chō 1~6 .... C-2	Chōja-machi 1~9 .... B-3	Hatsune-chō 1~3 .... A-4	Honmoku-makado G-5	Ikebukuro F-5	Kominato-chō 1~3 .... E-5
Akamon-chō 1 .... A-4	Fujimi-chō B-3	Hinode-chō 1~2 .... A-3	Honmoku-manzaka F-4	Isezaki-chō 1~7 .... B-3	Kotobuki-chō 1~4 .... C-3
Akebono-chō 1~5 .... B-4	Fukutomichō-higashi-dōri B-3	Hinodaigaoka H-3	Honmoku-midorigaoka G-4	Ishikawa-chō 1~5 .... D-3	Mameguchidai ....
Bandai-chō 1~5 .... B-3	Fukutomichō-naka-dōri B-3	Hongō-chō 1~3 .... F-4	Honmoku-miyabara G-3	Kaigan-dōri 1~5 .... C-2	Masago-chō 1~4 ....
Benten-dōri 1~6 .... C-2	Fukutomichō-nishi-dōri B-3	Honmoku-arai H-3	Honmoku-motomachi H-4	Kamome-chō D-4	Matsukage-chō 1~4 ....
Chidori-chō G-2	Furō-chō 1~3 .... D-3	Honmoku-futō H-2	Honmoku-sannotani H-3	Kashiwaba D-4	Minami-nakadōri 1~5 ....
Chitose-chō 1~3 .... C-3	Hagoromo-chō 1~4 .... B-3	Honmoku-hara H-4	Honmoku-wada G-4	Kitagata-chō 1~2 .... F-3	Minosawa ....
Chiyozaki-chō 1~4 .... F-3	Hanabusa-chō A-4	Honmoku-jūniten G-3	Hōrai-chō 1~3 .... B-3	Kogane-chō 1~2 .... A-3	Miyagawa-chō 1~3 ....

to Yokosuka

to Ōfuna

to Yokohama to Higashiguchi Ramp

中区（横浜市）

1

Symbol Tower

Branch Office of Customhouse

Shin-yamashita
新山下

...ashita
...下

Minami-bashi Br.

Kamome-bashi Br.

(3)

Honmoku-bashi Br.

Keihin Port Construction Office

Branch Office of Customhouse

Honmoku-futō
本牧ふ頭

Honmoku-futō
本牧ふ頭

2

Sea-fishing Pier

Harbors Vocational Traning
Jr. Coll.

-chō

...pon-suijō-gakuen

Public Corporation
Kominato Houses

Central Sewage Disposal

Honmoku-jūniten
本牧十二天

Nishikichō
錦町

Honmoku Harbors Houses

Expressway Bayshore Line

Nissan Motor Wharf

3

...ijirizaka Sch. for Physically
...andicapped or Mentally Retarded Children

(1)

Washinzaka

(4)

Kitagata-chō
北方町

Kawahira

(3) 小港町 (2)

Kominato-chō

Kominato
小港

Yamate

Honmoku

...i-chō

(2)

Honmoku-chō
本牧町

Medical Center

Library

Honmoku-
miyahara
本牧宮原

Honmoku-hara
本牧原

Le Phare Honmoku

Mycal Honmoku

Nishiki-chō
錦町

...church

...ongō-chō
本郷町

(1)

(2)

Honmoku Church

Tentokuji

Ōtori

(3)

Otori

Honmoku

Naka Library
District Center

Wadayama
和田山

Honmoku-jinja

Azuma-jinja

Honmoku-motomachi

Tamon-in

Honmoku-
manzaka
本牧満坂

Honmoku-wada
本牧和田

本牧通り

Welfare Culture Center

Honmoku-
motomachi
本牧元町

Environmental Cleaning Projects
Bureau Naka Office

4

Mitsubishi Heavy Industries
Yokohama Dockyard

...al Yokohama-midorigaoka

...nmoku-
...origaoka
...牧緑ヶ丘

Honmoku-arai
本牧荒井

Honmoku

Honmoku-dōri Ave.

(1)

Honmoku-
sannotani
本牧三之谷

Honmoku Megumi Church

Honmoku-minami

Kamome-chō
かもめ町

...ai

...untry Club

Tōfukuin

Makado

Honmoku-Makado
本牧間門

Honmoku-
ōsato-chō
本牧大里町

Bureau of Transportation
Honmoku Office

Hasseiden

5

...kebukuro
池袋

...c Servant's Houses

Kōnan

(2)

Makado

Prefectural Yokohama-tateno

Sankeien Garden

Honmoku Seaside Park

Civic Swimming Pool

Yokohama Immigrants' Asylum

Toyoura-chō
豊浦町

Makado
間門

Route 357 国道357号

Tōkeiji

Honmoku Civic Park

Sumitomo Metal Industries

Chidori-chō
千鳥町

Nippon Petroleum Refining, Negishi Oil Factory

6

Negishi Bay

		Negishidai	D-6	Onoe-chō 1-6	C-3	Sumiyoshi-chō 1-6	C-2	Uchida-chō	A-2	Yamashita-chō	D-2
...5	E-2	Nihon-ōdōri	D-2	Ōshibadai	C-5	Suwa-chō	E-3	Uchikoshi	C-4	Yamate-chō	F-3
...1-4	E-2	Nishi-takenomaru	D-2	Ōta-chō 1-6	C-2	Takenomaru	D-2	Ueno-chō 1-4	A-2	Yamato-chō 1-4	E-4
...4	E-4	Nishiki-chō	I-4	Sagiyama	E-4	Takinoue	E-6	Wadayama	G-4	Yayoi-chō 1-5	B-4
...3	E-6	Nishinoya-chō	E-4	Sakuragi-chō 1-3	A-2	Tateno	D-5	Wakaba-chō 1-3	B-3	Yokohama-kōen	C-2
...3	E-2	Noge-machi 1-4	A-3	Shin-yamashita 1-3	F-2	Terakubo	D-5	Yaguchidai	F-5	Yokohama-machi	B-3
...5	E-6	Ōgi-chō 1-4	C-3	Shinkō 1-2	B-1	Tokiwa-chō 1-5	B-3	Yamabuki-chō	B-3	Yoshida-machi	B-3
...3	E-6	Ōhira-chō	D-5	Suehiro-chō 1-3	B-3	Toyoura-chō	I-5	Yamada-chō	C-4	Yoshihama-chō	D-3
...1-2	C-3	Okina-chō 1-2	C-3	Sueyoshi-chō 1-4	B-3	Tsukagoshi	C-5	Yamamoto-chō 1-5	D-3		

F G H I J

つくば市

1:45,000

Kawasaki-machi
Takarada 高良田
Hachiman-jinja Kashima-jinja
Eikōji
Azuma-chō
MITSUKAIDŌ-SHI 水海道市
Ōsaki-machi
Katori-jinja
Fukuoka-ozeki Sluice
Takasuka 高須賀
Nabenuma Community Center
Nabenuma-shinden 鍋沼新田
Nabenuma-shinden 鍋沼新田
Mase
Mase 真瀬
Fujimi Houses
Mase-iriguchi 真瀬入口
Tōkōji
National House Industrial
Kamakura Community Center Mase
Dai
Fukuoka
Fukuoka
YAWARA-MURA 谷和原村
Sakano-shinden
Minami
Kubota
Hanashima-shinden 花島新田
Kami-kayamaru 上萱丸
Shimo-kayamaru
Kashima-jinja
Shimo-kayamaru 下萱丸
Itoh Iron and Steel works
Nishi-kuriyama 西栗山
Katada 片田
Hachiman-jinja
Tōkin
Nakano 中野
Atago-jinja
Jōban Expressway 常磐自動車道
Jōyō Country Club
Club House
Tsukuba-kōka
Iida 飯田
Club House
Ibaraki Golf Club (East)
INA-MACHI 伊奈町
Tsukuba Country Club (East)
Kasuga-jinja
Takaoka 高岡
Furudate 古館
Nesaki 根崎
Hachiman-jinja
Yatobe-minami
Sakaida 境田
Sakaimatsu 境松
Midorigaoka 緑ヶ丘
Nekōji

Kamigō 上郷
Naka-beppu 中別府
Shimo-beppu 下別府
Shimo-kawarazaki 下河原崎
Kami-kawarazaki 上河原崎
Saifukuji
Shimo-kawarazaki Community Center
Takayama
Shimana
Zentokuji
Shimo-kawarazaki 下河原崎
Takayama
Nakanishi Community Center
Jingūji
Myōtokuji
Kitahara-jinja
Hachiman-jinja
Shimana 島名
Taira Community Center
Taira 平
Ōjirahazama 大白硴
Kojirahazama 小白硴
Hachimandai 八幡台
Yanagihashi 柳橋
Kashima-jinja
Yagihashi
Yōgai Houses
Kasuga-jinja
Kami-kayamaru
Yatabe 谷田部
Yatabe
Regional Legal Affairs Bureau
Health & Education Center
Yatabe Branch Office
Tsukuba City Office
Yatabe Clinic
City Agricultural Cooperative
Dōrinji
Yatabe
Gokakudō
Yatabe
Welfare Center
Hall of Commerce & Industry
Honshūji
Ichijōin
Chōtokuji
Hachimangū
Local Food Agency Office
Komagata Houses
Yatabe I.C. 谷田部IC
Imaizumi 今泉
Imaizumi Community Center
Tsukuba-gakuen Hosp.
Hanare-Kannondō
Royal Tennis Club
Hanare 羽成
Hanare Park
Kannondai 観音台
Nat'l Institute of Animal Health
Nat'l Agriculture Research Center
Higashi-maruyama 東丸山
Kukizaki-machi 茎崎町
Wakaguri
Kōyadai 高野台
Shimo-yo 下

Hakke 百家
Atago-jinja
Kannonji
Saken 酒
Onigakubo Community Center
Tsuchida 土田
Onigakubo 鬼ヶ窪
Tokodai Playing
Tenjingu
Hachinosu Park
Intel Japan
Tōkōc 東光
Takata 高田
Nippon Sheet Glass
Fujisawa Pharmaceutical
Tōkyō Timber Mutural Market
Minami-tsukuba Golf Club
Club House
Tsukuba Shūei
Atago-jinja
Kitahara Community Center
Sekinodai Community Center
Hachiman-jinja
Omonoi 面野井
Japan Automobile Institute Inc.
Shimana
Ōjirahazama 大白硴
Nishioka 西岡
Miyukigaoka 御幸ヶ丘
NEC
West Tsukuba Industria
Mizubori 水堀
Kyowa Hakkō Kōgyō
Yamanouchi Pharmaceutical
Daikin Industries
Tsukuba EXPO Mem. Park
Tōyō Soda Manufactu
Texas Instruments Japan
Nat'l Institute of Health
Nat'l Institute of Hygienic Science
Hachimandai 八幡台
Yagihashi Golf Practice Range
Ōwashi
Arai 新井
Yamanaka 山中
Nat'l Institute of Sericult
Entomological Science
Japan International Research Center for Agricultural Science
Nat'l Center for Seeds and Seedlings
Kami-yokoba 上横場
Fujimoto 藤本
Imamiya-jinja
Hachiman-jinja
Enokido 榎戸
Onogawa Substation
Kongō
Nat'l Research Institute of Agricultural Engineering
Nat'l Food Research Institute
Agriculture, Forestry & Fisheries Research Council
Kita-nakazuma 北中妻
Minami-nakazuma 南中妻
National Institute of Agro-Environment Science
Central Town

■AREA INDEX■

Akatsuka	F-6	Furuku	I-4	Higashi-maruyama	C-6	Kami-kawarazaki	C-1	Kise	I-5	Matsunoki
Amakubo 1~4	G-2	Hachimandai	I-4	Higashioka	H-3	Kami-kayamaru	B-4	Kita-nakazuma	E-6	Matsushiro 1~5
Arai	E-4	Hanamuro	H-3	Iida	B-5	Kami-yokoba	D-5	Kitasato	G-1	Matsuzuka
Aranakida	F-3	Hanare	C-6	Imaizumi	D-5	Kamizakai	I-2	Kojirahazama	D-4	Midorigaoka
Azuma 1~4	G-3	Hanashima-shinden	B-4	Inaoka	F-6	Kannondai 1~3	D-6	Konda	D-5	Minami-nakazuma
Enokido	E-5	Hara	F-3	Inarimae	F-5	Karima	F-3	Kōyadai 1~3	D-6	Miyukigaoka
Fujimoto	E-5	Higashi 1~2	G-5	Kajiuchi	E-6	Kasuga 1~4	G-2	Kurakake	I-1	Mizubori
Furudate	B-6	Higashi-arai	G-4	Kamihara	F-5	Katada	A-5	Kurihara	H-1	Nabenuma-shinden
		Higashi-hiratsuka	G-2	Kami-hirooka	I-5	Katsuragi-nesaki	F-3	Mase	B-3	Nagamine

to Mitsukaido

to Yawara

to Ushiku

to Ushiku

つくば市

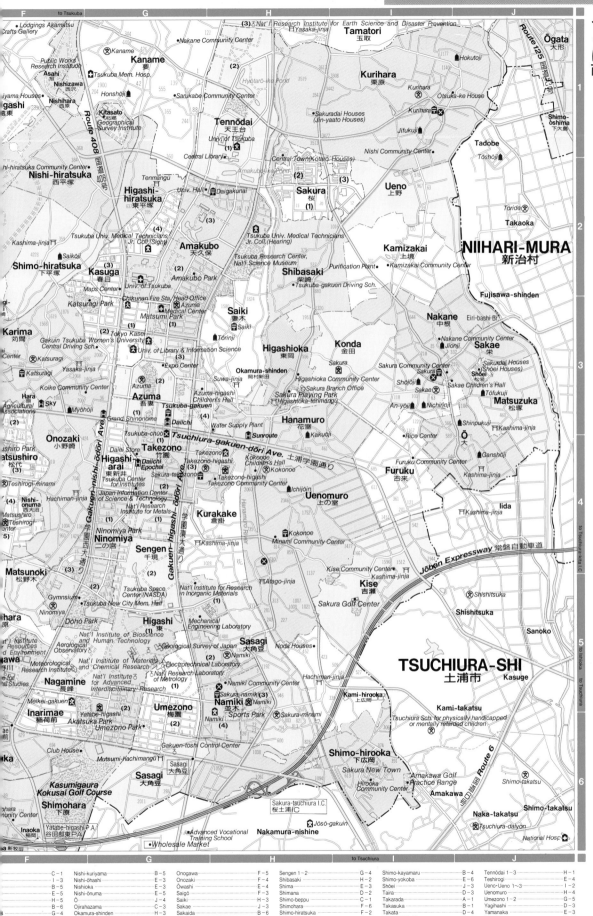

	C–1	Nishi-kuriyama	B–5	Onogawa	F–5	Sengen 1–2	G–4	Shimo-kayamaru	B–4	Tennōdai	H–1
	I–3	Nishi-ōhashi	E–3	Onozaki	F–4	Shibasaki	H–2	Shimo-yokoba	E–6	Teshirogi	E–4
	B–5	Nishioka	E–3	Ōwashi	E–3	Shima	D–2	Shōei	J–3	Ueno·Ueno 1~3	I–2
	E–5	Nishi-ōnuma	E–5	Saigō	F–3	Shimana	D–2	Taira	D–3	Uenomuro	H–4
	H–5	Ō	J–4	Saiki	H–3	Shimo-beppu	C–1	Takarada	A–1	Umezono 1–2	G–5
	B–6	Ojirahazama	C–3	Sakae	J–3	Shimohara	F–6	Takasuka	B–1	Yagihashi	D–3
	G–4	Okamura-shinden	H–3	Sakaida	B–6	Shimo-hiratsuka	E–2	Takata	D–3	Yamanaka	E–3
	F–1	Omonoi	E–2	Sakaimatsu	B–6	Shimo-hirooka	I–6	Takezono 1–3	G–4	Yatabe	C–4
	F–2	Onigakubo	D–1	Sasagi	G–6	Shimo-kawarazaki	C–2	Tateno	E–5	Yoko-machi	I–3

首都高速道路図

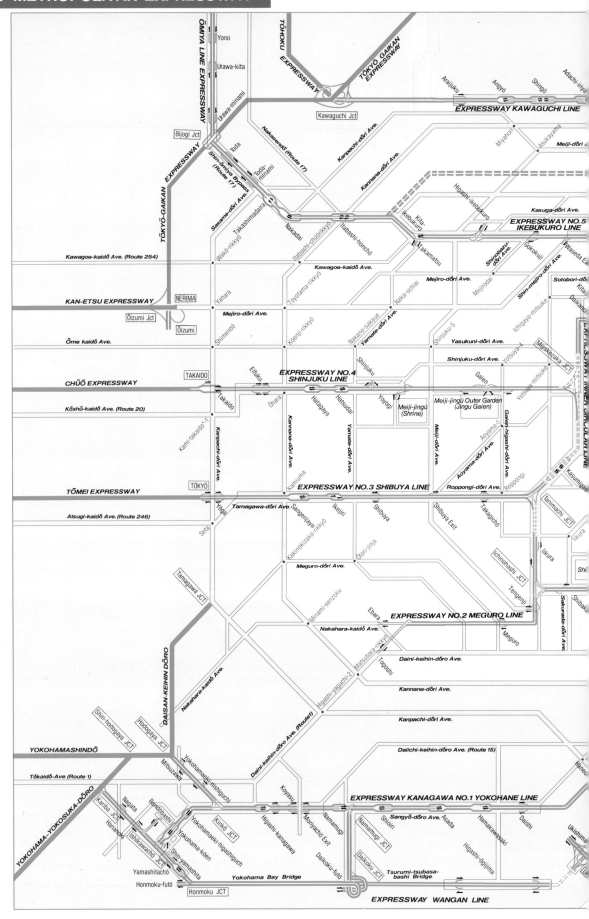

首都高速道路図

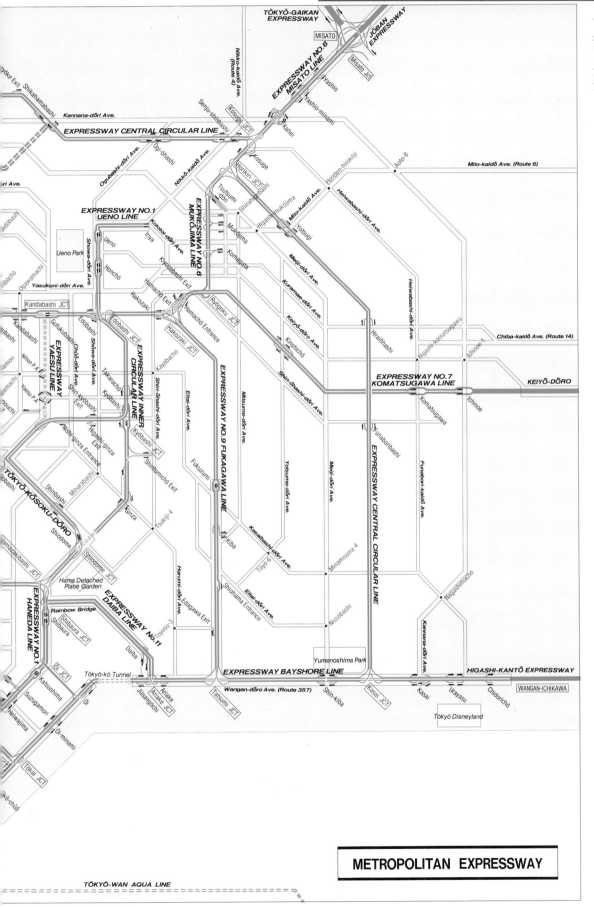

METROPOLITAN EXPRESSWAY

1:250,000

0   2.5   5   7.5km

東京周辺図（Ⅰ）

GUNMA

SAITAMA

TOKYO

to Fujioka

to Saku

Nakazato-mura
中里村

Manba-machi
万場町

Mt.Kanōyama

Mt.Temiezuyama

Mt.Futagoyama

Shigasaka Tunnel

Mt.Tsukayama

Tsuchisaka Tunnel

Mt.Jōminesan

Mt.Shiraishiyama

Kakkaku Dam

Mt.Kannon-yama

Kannako I.C.

Shimokubo Dam

Kamiizumi-mura
神泉村

Yoshida-machi
吉田町

Kosaido Saitama

Mt.Ryogamisan
両神山

Ryōkami-mura
両神村

Ogano-machi
小鹿野町

Tōtō-Saitama

Union Ace

Mt.Fudōsan

Saitama-kokusai

Mt.Hodosan

Mission Hills

Mt.Hafusan

Minano
Minano-machi
皆野町

Higuchi

Nagatoro
Nagatoro-machi
長瀞町

Hodosan-jinja

Nagatoro Valley
長瀞
Kami-nagatoro

Yorii-machi
寄居町

Chichibu Kokusai
Seibu-chichibu

Hanazono-machi
花園町

KAN-ETSU EXPWY

Minoyama Park

Nihongi Pass

Mt.Dōdairasan

Tōkyō Astronomical
Dodoira Observatory

Musashi-kyūryō
Tokigawa-mura
都幾川村

CHICHIBU-SHI
秩父市

CHICHIBU
秩父

Sadamine Pass

Chichibu

Kuroya

Onohara

Ashigakubo

Seibu Chichibu Line

Shōmaru Tunnel

Shōmaru Pass
Shōmaru

Ogose-machi
越生町

Okumusashi

Kuroyama-santaki Fa

Mt.Mitsuminesan

Mt.Kumakurayama

Mt.Yodake

Mt.Shiraishiyama

Nakatsukyō Gorge

Site of Tochimoto Checkpoint

Futase Dam
Mitsumine-dōro
三峰道路

Ōtaki-mura
大滝村

Mitsumine-jinja
三峰神社

Chichibuko Lake

Nakatsu

Mt.Minoguchi

Shiroku

Arakawa-mura
荒川村

Chichibu Railway

Chichibu-takagawa

Urayamaguchi

Urayama Dam

Hashidate Limestone Cave

Chichibu Sakurako Lake

Kagemori

Yokoze-machi
横瀬町

Mt.Bukozan
武甲山

Takayama-fudōson

Nishi-agano

Neno-gongen

Agano

Higashi-agano

Naguri-mura
名栗村

Takedera

Musashi

Mt.Tenmokusan

MT. KUMOTORIYAMA
雲取山

Mt.Ōborayama
Sanjōnoyū

Aoiwa Limestone Cave

Ishiyama-jinja

Nippara Limestone Cave
日原鍾乳洞

Mt.Takanosuyama

Mt.Kawanoriyama

Mt.Bōnomine

Ozawa Pass

HANN
飯能

Nagun Gorge

Hannō

Tōkyō Bir

ŌME-SHI
青梅市

Okutama-machi
奥多摩町

Okutama

Hinoharu

Ōme-kaidō 青梅街道

Ogōchi Dam

Hatonosu

Ikusabata

Sawai

Mitake

Futamatao

Ishigamimae

Ōme-tetsudō Park

Ōme

Hinatawada

Tabayama-mura
丹波山村

Tabagawa River

Okutamako Lake

Mt.Gozen-yama

Mt.Mitakesan

Mitake-jinja
御岳神社

Mt.Ōtakesan

Yoshino-baigō (Ume grove)

Yōzawa Limestone Cave

Otake Limestone Cave

Hinode-machi
日の出町

Mt.Daibosatsurei
大菩薩嶺

Daibosatsu Pass

Kosuge-mura
小菅村

Mt.Mitōzan

Tsuru Pass

Kazahari Pass

Mt.Bazukariyama

Musashi-itsukaichi

Itsukaichi L.

Nishiaki... Sta

Itsukaichi

Imakuma-jinja

AKIRUNO
あきる

Kazunogawa Dam

Akigawa River

Hinohara-mura
檜原村

Mt.Kariyoseyama

HACHIŌJI-
八王子

TŌKYŌ

Mt.Gongenyama

Kanayama

Sakagawa River

Mt.Shōtosan

Lake Sagami

Higashi-Sagami

Wada Pass

TAKAOSAN
高尾山

Mt.Jinbasan

Mt.Momokurayama

Mt.Ogiyama

Uenoharamachi
上野原町

to Sagamiko I.C.

to Otsu

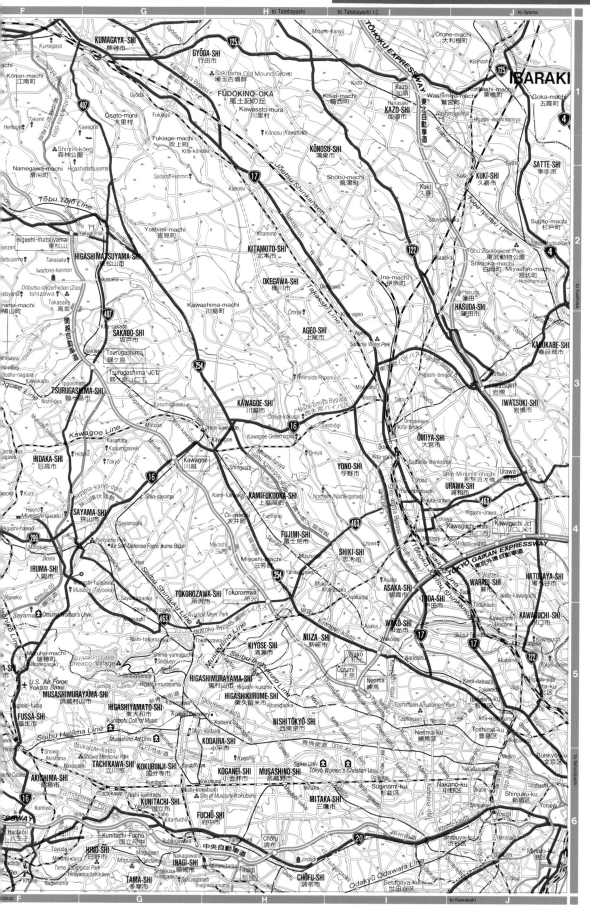

東京周辺図（Ⅰ）

東京周辺図（II）

1:250,000

0　2.5　5　7.5km

A　B　C　D　E

Chiyogawa-mura 千代川村　Sōdo
Friendship　Tamamura
Sashima-machi 猿島町　Ishige-machi 石下町　Minami-ishige
Sakai-machi 境町
Goka-machi 五霞町
Shin-tōkyō
Niihari-mura 新治村
Yuma-mura
Univ. of Tsukuba
Tsuchiura 土
Kantetsu-Jōsō Line
Kokai River
Kinugawa River
Minami-tsukuba
Tsukuba Science City

Iwai-shi 岩井市
SATTE-SHI 幸手市
Sugito-machi 杉戸町
Sekiyado-machi 関宿町
Ōtone
Mitsukaidō-dōro 水海道道路
Nakazuma
TSUKUBA-SHI つくば市
Sakura-tsuchiura 桜土浦
Kasumigaura-kokusai

Himenomiya
Chiba (Kawama)
Shin-tōkyō
Kita-mitsukaido
MITSUKAIDŌ-SHI 水海道市　Mitsukaido
Yatabe 谷田部
Yatabe-higashi 谷田部東
Yawara-mura 谷和原村
Tsukuba　Ibaraki
Jōyō
Kukizaki-machi 茎崎町
USHIK 牛

KASUKABE-SHI 春日部市
Fujinoushijima
Shōwa-machi 庄和町
Minami-sakurai
Kawama
Josō
Kokinu
Ina-machi 伊奈町
Toride-kokusai
Ushiku 牛久
Kinnodai
Takesato
Nanakodai
Chiba (Noda)
NODA-SHI 野田市
Murasaki (Sumire)
Murasaki (Ayame)
Nodashi Public
Atago
Yawara 谷和原
Shin-moriya
Moriya 守谷
Moriya-machi 守谷町
Minami-moriya
Togashira
Inatoi
Onabake
RYŪ
Ryūgasaki Line

SAITAMA
Matsubushi-machi 松伏町
Rinsenji
Ōbukuro
Kita-koshigaya Public
Umesato
Ōtone-Chūsan
Science Univ. of Tōkyō
Unga
Kashiwa 柏
Shin-ōtonebashi 新大利根橋
TORIDE-SHI 取手市
Shin-toride
Terahara
Nishi-torine
Tone
Fujishiro
Fujishiro-machi 藤代町
Sanuki
Ireji

Kita-koshigaya
Shimizu Park
Shimizukoen
Kasukabe
Yagisaki
Hisaizu-jinja
KOSHIGAYA-SHI 越谷市
Koshigaya
YOSHIKAWA-SHI 吉川市
Yoshikawa
Edogawadai
Hatsuishi
Nagareyama 流山
Toyoshiki
Kashiwa
Asia Toride
Tone
Toride
Chūō Gakuin Univ.
Jōban Line
ABIKO-SHI 我孫子市
Higashi-abiko
Minami-abiko
Kita-kashiwa

Musashino Line
Sengendai
Kawaguchi-higashi 川口東
Kita-koshigaya
Gamō
Yoshikawa
Shin-koshigaya
Misato
NAGAREYAMA-SHI 流山市
Nagareyama
Nagareyama-Heiwadai
Minami-nagareyama
Shin-matsudo
Abiko
Teganuma Lake
Abiko
Kohoku
Fusa
Kioroshi

Tōkyō Gaikan Expressway 東京外環自動車道
Kawaguchi-higashi
Sōka 草加
Matsubaradanchi
Galkan-Misato-nishi 外環三郷西
SŌKA-SHI 草加市
Ōsaka
MISATO-SHI 三郷市
Misato 三郷
Heiwadai
Minami-nagareyama
Hiregasaki
Kita-kogane
Masuo
Sakasai
Kita-kashiwa
Shin-kashiwa
Shōnan-machi 沼南町
Fujigaya

Takenotsuka
YASHIO-SHI 八潮市
Yatsuka
Mabashi
Reitaku Univ.
Takayanagi
Shiroi-machi 白井町
Funabashi
INZAI-SHI 印西市
Narashino

Nishiaraishuku
Daishimati
Nishi-arai
Adachi-ku 足立区
Kita-matsudo
Tokiwadaira
Gokō
Motoyama
Mutsumi
Konbu
Chiba New Town Chūō
Sōbu (Sōbu)
Katsuenji
Izumi

MATSUDO-SHI 松戸市
Matsudo Public
Shin-yahashira
Kūnigiyama
Ichikawaono
KAMAGAYA-SHI 鎌ヶ谷市
Kamagaya-daibutsu
Futawamukōdai
Kokusai Ladies
Nakayama
Hokusōkaihatsu Railway
Shin Keisei Line
Shin-matsudo
Kōya
Higashi-matsudo
Kamagaya 鎌ケ谷
Misaki
YACHIYO-SHI 八千代市
Yachiyo Public
Yachiyo-midorigaoka
Murakami
Toyō-katsutadai
Yūkari

Komagome
Kita-senju
Arakawa-ku 荒川区
Mikawashima
Minami-senju
Katsushika-ku 葛飾区
Aoto
Keisei-takasago
ICHIKAWA-SHI 市川市
Funabashihōten
Tsukada
Takifudo
Takanekōdan
FUNABASHI-SHI 船橋市
Hasama
Kita-narashino
Narashino
Keisei-owada
Katsutadai
Shizu
Nabata
Nippori
Ueno Park
Koiwa
Ichikawa
Moto-yawata
Nishi-funabashi
Narashino-dai
Maebara
Keisei Railway
Chiyodai
Yotsu
Keisei
Bunkyō-ku 文京区
Taito-ku 台東区
Asakusa
Hikifune
Shin-koiwa
Edogawa-ku 江戸川区
Higashi-funabashi
Kaijin
Tsukada
NARASHINO-SHI 習志野市
Hanamigawa-ku 花見川区
Miyanogi 宮野木
Iidabashi
Chiyoda-ku 千代田区
Akihabara
Sumida-ku 墨田区
Hirai
Ōshiage
Wangan-ichikawa 湾岸市川
Toyotaku
Futamata-shinmachi
Shin-funabashi
Makuhari-hongō
Chiba-kita 千葉北
Inage-ku 稲毛区
CHIBA-SHI 千葉市

Koto-ku 江東区
Chūō-ku 中央区
Minato-ku 港区
Hamarikyu (Garden)
Shiomi
URAYASU-SHI 浦安市
Ichikawa-shiohama
Shin-urayasu
Wangan-narashino 湾岸習志野
Wangan-makuhari 湾岸幕張
Makuhari Shin-kemigawa
Wangan-chiba 湾岸千葉

TŌKYŌ
Arakawa-Kakōko Bridge
Shinkiba
Arakawa River

Route markers: 408, 354, 16, 4, 6, 356, 296, 14

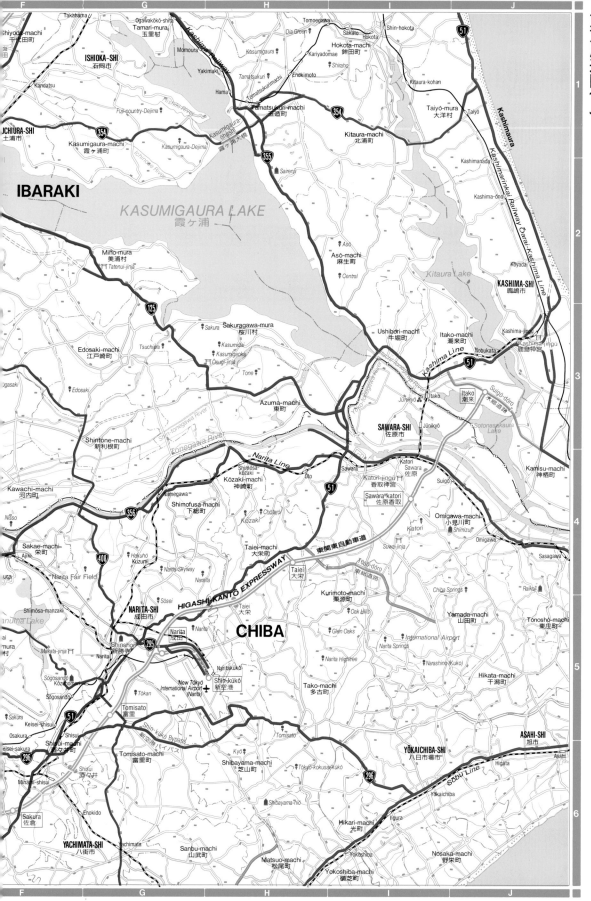

東京周辺図（Ⅱ）

1 : 250,000

0　2.5　5　7.5km

東京周辺図 (Ⅲ)

to Hach

to Kōfu I.C

to Kawaguchiko

to Kawaguchiko

to Fuji I.C

YAMANASHI

KANAGAWA

SHIZUOKA

CHŪO EXPRESSWAY 中央自動車道

Mt. Takigoyama
Hashikura
Magi
Hatsukari 初狩
Ōtsuki Jct 大月Jct
Ōtsuki 大月
Ōtsuki
Mt. Ogiyama
Otsuki
Nishi-Hachiōji
Dangōzaka 談合坂
Uenohara-machi 上野原町
Uenohara 上野原
Fujino 藤野
Higashi Ōhampi
Sagamiko 相模湖
Biidani
Mt. Takadosan 高尾山
Yakuōin
20

ŌTSUKI-SHI 大月市
Mt. Kuratakeyama
Saruhashi
Yoshū-kaidō
Tsuru
Yanagawa
Shōsu
Uenohara
Fujino-machi 藤野町
Sagamiko Picnic Land
Kamakura
Sagamiko
Sagamiko-machi 相模湖町
412
Tsukui-machi 津久井町
413

Mt. Tsurugadoyayama
Chūō-Tsuru
139
Tsuru 都留
Ōsaka
Tsuru-muramachi
Fuji Kyūkō Railway
Take One
Yunosawa
Yamura 谷村
Inch-katsura
TSURU-SHI 都留市
Tsuru
Mt. Nabatakakeyama
Dōshi
Mt. Akakuragatake
Akiyama-mura 秋山村
Akiyama
Sagamiko
Mt. Yakeyama
Nagatake
Kiyokawa-mura 清川村
Nakatsu Gorge

FUJIYOSHIDA-SHI 富士吉田市
Mt. Mishōtaiyama 御正体山
Mt. Torinomuneyama
Dōshi-mura 道志村
Mt. Omuroyama 大室山
Mt. Azegamaruyama
Mt. Hinokiboramaru
Mt. Hirugatake 鰭ヶ岳
Mt. Tanzawayama 丹沢山
Mt. Mitsumineyama
Nanase

Oshino-mura 忍野村
113
Mt. Ishiwariyama
Mt. Komotsurushiyama
Higashi-tanzawa Citizen's Forest
Mt. Ōyama 大山
Afuri-Jinja
Ōyama-fudo
ISEH 伊

Hotel Mountain Fuji
Yamanakako Lake
Yamanakako-mura 山中湖村
Mikuni Pass
Mt. Gongen-yama
Nakagawa
Tanzawake Lake
Mitsumata Dam
HADANO-SHI 秦野市
Yebitsu Pass
Ohatano
Isehara

Kagosaka Pass
Myōjin Pass
Mt. Furōzan
Mt. Onoyama
Yamakita-machi 山北町
Taiheiyo Club Sagami
Odawara (Matsuda)
Check Mate
Shibusawa
Hadano
Hatano
Hatano
Minamoto-no Sanetomo Mound
Tsurumakionsen
Tōkaidaigakumae

Fuji-kōen
138
Higashi-Fuji
Fuji Greenhill P.
Fuji Health
Oyama-chō 小山町
246
Ayusa
Yaga
TŌMEI EXPRESSWAY 東名高速道路
Higashi-yamakita
Matsuda-machi 松田町
Matsuda
Kaisei-machi 開成町
Sagami-kaneko
Kaisei
Kayama
Ōi-Matsuda 大井松田
Ōi-machi 大井町
Nakai 中井
Nakai-machi 中井町
Hadano-Nakai 秦野中井
Hiratsuka-Fujimi
Lakewood

Fuji-Oyama
Taiyo
Suruga-oyama
Shōtendō
Ashigara
Tōmei-Fuji
Sakawa Royal
Mt. Yaguradake
Ashigara Pass
Ashigara-jinja
Daiyūzan
Izu-hakone Daiyūzan Line
Kamiso
Sōga-jinja
255
Ninomiya-machi 二宮町
Ninomiya
1

GOTENBA-SHI 御殿場市
Tōmei-Oyama
Ashigara
Odakyū Family Land
MINAMIASHIGARA-SHI 南足柄市
Mt. Kintokiyama 金時山
Saijōji
Chōsen-jin
Tsukahara
Sagami-numata
Sōseiji
Ashigara
Gotenba Line
Isoga
Kōzu
Setano Bypass 西湘バイパス
Sakawa River

Taiheyo (Gotenba)
Uraku Gotenba
Minami-gotenba
Fuji-Gotenba
Gotenba 御殿場
Fuji
Mt. Kintokiyama
Myōjingatake 明神ヶ岳
HAKONE 箱根
1
Ashigara
Kazamatsuri
Odawara-jō
Iriuda
ODAWARA-SHI 小田原市
135

469
Komakado 駒門
Busshanto
Minami-gotenba
Nagao Pass
Sengoku
Gotenba
Tawaraishi
Gōra
Kowakidani Yunohana
Dōgayama
Hakoneyumoto
Tōnosawa
Hakone-Yumoto
Ōdawara-Yumoto
Hakone Railway
Nebuk

Five Hundred
Susono
246
Iwadani
Susono 裾野
SUSONO-SHI 裾野市
Komakado
Kojiri Pass
Tōmei-Gotenba
Dai-Hakone
Hakone-Kōen
Ōwakidani
Gōra
Kowakidani
Mt. Hakoneyama 箱根山
Hakone-machi 箱根町
Hakone-jinja
Mt. Futagoyama
Hakone-shindō 箱根新道
Hakone Turnpike 箱根ターンパイク
Manazuru-dō 真鶴道路
Odawarajō
Mt. Hoshigayama
Nebuk

Nagaizumi-chō 長泉町
Ashinoko Skyline 芦ノ湖スカイライン
1
Site of Checkpoint
Hakone Pass
Mt. Kurakake
Mt. Taikanzan
Hakonoen
Ashinoko Lake
Mt. Taikanzan
Yugawara 湯河原
Manazu
Manatsuru-machi 真鶴町

SHIZUOKA
Susono-Bypass
Susono
1
Site of Yamanaka Castle
Granfields
Yugawara Parkway 湯河原パークウェイ
Oku-Yugawara
Yugawara
Yugawara-machi 湯河原町
Yugawara
C. Manazurumisaki

Numazu 沼津
MISHIMA-SHI 三島市
Kannami
Jikkoku Pass 十国峠
Kannami
C. Manazurumisaki

Nagaizumi-chō 長泉町
Mishima
Mishima-toge

to Fuji I.C
to Fuji

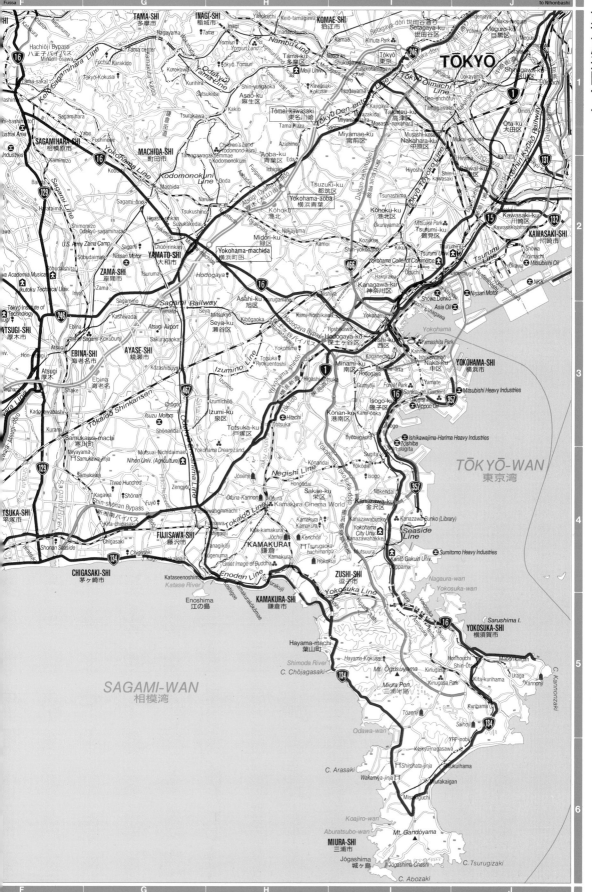

東京周辺図（Ⅳ）

1：250,000

0　2.5　5　7.5km

Rainbow Bridge
Minato-ku 港区
Kōtō-ku 江東区
Museum of Marine Science
Keiyō Line
Maihama
Tōkyō Disneyland
東京ディズニーランド

Kemigawahama
Keisei-inson Line
Sōbu Line
Inagekaigan
Chiba Univ.
Nishi-chiba
Higashi-chiba
Tsuga
Inage Seashore Park
Mihama-ku 美浜区
Chibaminato
Midorigahama
Chiba

Ōta-ku 大田区
Tōkyō Monorail
TŌKYŌ
Chiba Port
Hon-chiba
Chūō-ku 中央区
Soga
Chiba Daigaku

Tenkūbashi
Tōkyō International Airport (Haneda)
Haneda-kūkō
Kawasaki Steel

Arakawa River
TŌKYŌ-WAN
東京湾
Goi Thermal Power Plant
Yōrōgawa River
Kosumo Oil
Shōwa Denkō
Chiba Thermal Power Plant
Hamano

General Sekiyu
132
KAWASAKI-SHI 川崎市
Ube Industries
16
Goi
Yawatajuku

KANAGAWA
Tōkyō-wan Aqua Line
東京湾アクアライン
Mitsui Chemicals
297
Kazusa-murakami
ICHIHARA-SHI 市原市
Kodomo-no-kuni
Amaariki

Idemitsu Kōsan
Ichihara 市原
Uchibō Line
Anesaki Thermal Power Plant
Kazusa-mitsumata

Anesaki
Anezaki-jinja
Kazusa-yamada
Genjiyama
Chiba P.

Sumitomo Chemical
Ichihara 市原
Tatano Classic
Anesaki
Kōfūdai
Chiba-shinnihon
Ichihara-keikyū
Chihara

Nagaura
Tōkyōwan
Yawata
New Nansō
Nansō
Umatate

Obitsu River
Iwane
SODEGAURA-SHI 袖ケ浦市
Tateyama Expressway
館山自動車道
Anesaki-sodegaura 姉崎袖ケ浦
Chiba-kōsaido
Kazusa-ushiku

Sodegaura
Higashi-kiyokawa
Higashi-yokota
Yokota
Taiheiyō
Tsu

Sodegaura IC 袖ケ浦IC
Kururi Line
409
Lotte Minayoshidai
Kazusa-kawama
Kazusa-tsurumai

KISARAZU-SHI 木更津市
Kisarazu
Kisarazu-kita 木更津北
Makuta
Chiba Lakeside
Kazusa-k

Kisarazu JCT 木更津JCT
Matiya
Takataki Dam
Takataki

Nippon Steel
Shimogōri
Satomi

Kisarazu-minami 木更津南
Yanagawa Dam
Kisarazu
Obitsu
The C.C. Japan
Itabu

16
Aohori
410
Tawarada
Tsukizaki

Kimitsu
127
Kururi

C. Futtsumisaki
Hasunuma Seashore Park
Kazusa-ōkubo

Mt. Mifuneyama
Hirayama
Kimitsu
Yōrōkeikoku

C. Isonezaki
Ōnuki
Mt. Ōtsukayama
KIMITSU-SHI 君津市
Kazusa
Yoro

C. Kannonzaki
Sanukimachi
Mt. Kanōzan 鹿野山
Mt. Fujisan
Kazusafuji
Kazusa-matsuoka
Mt. Daifukuzan
Yōrō Gorge 養老渓谷

Mt. Kanōzan 鹿野山
Jinnai
The Kanōzan
Boso Skyline
Kazusa-kameyama

Mother-bokujō Farm
マザー牧場
Kameyama Dam
465

Angel
465
Kazusa-minato
Minato River
Mishima Dam
房総スカイライン
Mt. Sekisor

FUTTSU-SHI 富津市
Sōkyū
Mt. Takagoyama
Toyofusa Dam
Mt. Motokiyosumiyama

Futtsu-Tateyama Expw.
Tōkyō Car Ferry
Takeoka
Mt. Nokogiriyama 鋸山
Mt. Atagoyama
Kagihara
Mt. Kiyosum 清澄山
Kiyosur
清澄寺

Hama-kanaya
Mt. Nokogiriyama 鋸山
Nihondera
Kinone Pass
Hota
Yokone Pass
KAMOGAWA-SHI 鴨川市
Amatsuke
天

C. Myōshōzaki
Kyonan-machi 鋸南町
Awato
Awa-amat

東京周辺図（Ⅳ）

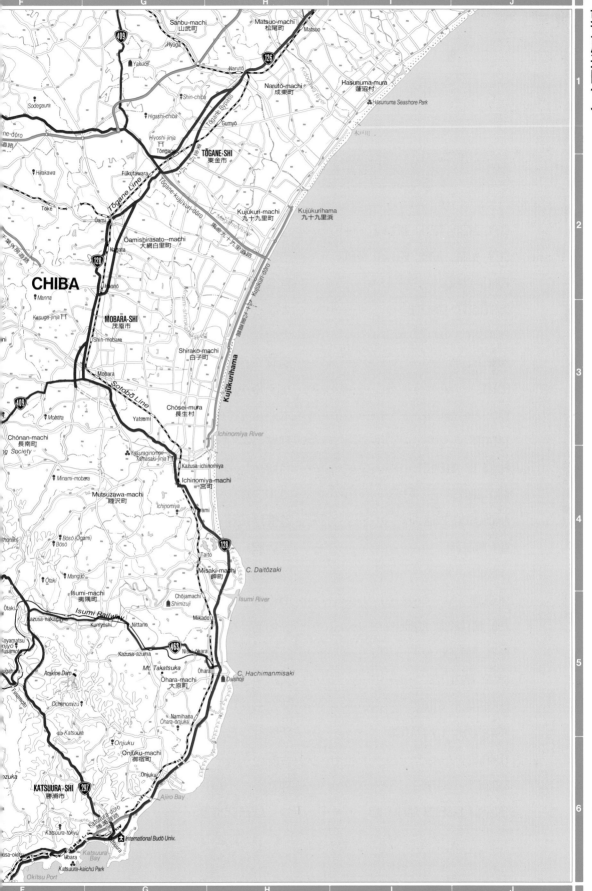

INFORMATION

CITY, WARD, TOWN, VILLAGE ·············市区町村·············113

CITY, WARD, TOWN, VILLAGE OFFICE·········市区町村役場·············116

PUBLIC OFFICE ·····················官公署·············117

UNIVERSITY, COLLEGE ···············大学·············117

EMBASSY ·························大使館·············119

HOSPITAL ·························病院·············119

HOTEL ···························ホテル·············120

HALL ···························ホール·············121

THEATER ·························劇場·············122

PLACE OF INTEREST ···············名所·············123

GOLF COURSE ·····················ゴルフ場·············123

AMUSEMENT PARK ···················遊園地·············123

ART MUSEUM ·····················美術館·············124

LIBRARY·························図書館·············124

MUSEUM ·························博物館·············125

ZOO, BOTANICAL GARDEN ···············動物園，植物園·············125

PARK, GARDEN ·····················公園·············125

SPORT FACILITES ·················スポーツ施設·············126

DEPARTMENT STORE ···············デパート·············126

NEWSPAPER, T.V.STATION ·········新聞社，放送局·············127

TEMPLE·························寺院·············127

SHRINE ·························神社·············128

TSUKUBA RESEACH FACILITIES ·········つくば研究機関·············128

CITY, WARD, TOWN, VILLAGE
市区町村

PLACE NAME	名 称	MAP INDEX
Abiko-shi	我孫子市	106・D-4
Adachi-ku	足立区	106・A-5
Ageo-shi	上尾市	105・H-3
Aikawa-machi	愛川町	109・F-2
Akiruno-shi	あきる野市	106・E-6
Akishima-shi	昭島市	105・F-6
Akiyama-mura	秋山村	108・C-1
Amatsukominato-machi	天津小湊町	110・E-6
Ami-machi	阿見町	106・E-2
Arakawa-ku	荒川区	105・A-5
Arakawa-mura	荒川村	104・B-3
Asahi-ku	旭区	109・H-3
Asahi-shi	旭市	107・J-5
Asaka-shi	朝霞市	105・I-4
Asao-ku	麻生区	109・H-1
Asō-machi	麻生町	107・I-2
Atsugi-shi	厚木市	109・F-3
Ayase-shi	綾瀬市	109・G-3
Azuma-machi	東町	107・H-3
Bunkyō-ku	文京区	105・J-6
Chiba-shi	千葉市	110・E-1
Chichibu-shi	秩父市	104・C-2
Chigasaki-shi	茅ヶ崎市	109・G-4
Chiyoda-ku	千代田区	106・A-6
Chiyoda-machi	千代田町	107・F-1
Chiyokawa-mura	千代川村	106・C-1
Chōfu-shi	調布市	105・H-6
Chōnan-machi	長南町	111・F-3
Chōsei-mura	長生村	111・G-3
Chūō-ku	中央区(東京都)	106・A-6
Chūō-ku	中央区(千葉市)	110・E-1
Dōshi-mura	道志村	108・C-2
Ebina-shi	海老名市	109・F-3
Edogawa-ku	江戸川区	106・B-6
Edosaki-machi	江戸崎町	107・G-3
Fuchū-shi	府中市	105・H-6
Fujimi-shi	富士見市	105・H-4
Fujino-machi	藤野町	108・D-1
Fujisawa-shi	藤沢市	109・G-4
Fujishiro-machi	藤代町	106・E-3
Fukiage-machi	吹上町	105・G-1
Funabashi-shi	船橋市	106・C-6
Fussa-shi	福生市	105・F-5
Futtsu-shi	富津市	110・B-5
Goka-machi	五霞町	105・J-1
Gotenba-shi	御殿場市	108・A-4
Gyōda-shi	行田市	105・H-1
Hachiōji-shi	八王子市	105・E-6
Hadano-shi	秦野市	108・D-3
Hakone-machi	箱根町	108・C-5
Hamura-shi	羽村市	105・F-5
Hanamigawa-ku	花見川区	106・D-6
Hannō-shi	飯能市	104・E-4
Hasuda-shi	蓮田市	105・J-2
Hasunuma-mura	蓮沼村	111・I-1
Hatogaya-shi	鳩ヶ谷市	105・J-4
Hatoyama-machi	鳩山町	105・F-2
Hayama-machi	葉山町	109・H-5
Hidaka-shi	日高市	105・F-4
Higashichichibu-mura	東秩父村	104・D-2
Higashikurume-shi	東久留米市	105・H-5
Higashimatsuyama-shi	東松山市	105・G-2
Higashimurayama-shi	東村山市	105・H-5
Higashiyamato-shi	東大和市	105・G-5
Hikari-machi	光町	107・I-6
Hino-shi	日野市	105・G-6
Hinode-machi	日の出町	104・E-5
Hinohara-mura	檜原村	104・D-5
Hiratsuka-shi	平塚市	109・F-4
Hodogaya-ku	保土ヶ谷区	109・I-3
Hokota-machi	鉾田町	107・I-1
Hōya-shi 保谷市→Nishitōkyō-shi 西東京市		105・H-5
Ichihara-shi	市原市	110・E-2
Ichikawa-shi	市川市	106・C-5
Ichinomiya-machi	一宮町	111・G-4
Inage-ku	稲毛区	106・E-6
Ina-machi (Saitama)	伊奈町(埼玉県)	105・I-2
Ina-machi (Ibaraki)	伊奈町(茨城県)	106・D-3
Inagi-shi	稲城市	105・G-6
Inba-mura	印旛村	107・F-5
Inzai-shi	印西市	106・E-5
Iruma-shi	入間市	105・F-4
Isehara-shi	伊勢原市	108・E-3
Ishige-machi	石下町	106・C-1
Ishioka-shi	石岡市	107・G-1
Isogo-ku	磯子区	109・I-3
Isumi-machi	夷隅町	111・G-5
Itabashi-ku	板橋区	105・J-5
Itako-machi	潮来町	107・J-3
Itsukaichi-machi 五日市町→Akiruno-shi あきる野市		
Iwai-shi	岩井市	106・B-2
Iwatsuki-shi	岩槻市	105・J-3
Izumi-ku	泉区	109・H-3
Kaisei-machi	開成町	108・D-4

Kamagaya-shi	鎌ヶ谷市	106・C-5
Kamakura-shi	鎌倉市	109・H-5
Kamifukuoka-shi	上福岡市	105・H-4
Kamiizumi-mura	神泉村	104・C-1
Kamisu-machi	神栖町	107・J-4
Kamogawa-shi	鴨川市	110・D-6
Kanagawa-ku	神奈川区	109・I-2
Kanazawa-ku	金沢区	109・I-4
Kashima-shi	鹿嶋市	107・J-2
Kashiwa-shi	柏市	106・C-4
Kasukabe-shi	春日部市	105・J-3
Kasumigaura-machi	霞ヶ浦町	107・G-1
Katsushika-ku	葛飾区	105・B-5
Katsuura-shi	勝浦市	111・F-6
Kawachi-machi	河内町	107・F-4
Kawagoe-shi	川越市	105・H-3
Kawaguchi-shi	川口市	105・J-5
Kawamoto-machi	川本町	105・F-1
Kawasaki-ku	川崎区	109・J-2
Kawasaki-shi	川崎市	109・J-2
Kawasato-mura	川里村	105・H-1
Kawashima-machi	川島町	105・H-2
Kazo-shi	加須市	105・I-1
Kimitsu-shi	君津市	110・D-5
Kisai-machi	騎西町	105・I-1
Kisarazu-shi	木更津市	110・B-3
Kita-ku	北区	105・J-5
Kitamoto-shi	北本市	105・H-2
Kitaura-machi	北浦町	107・I-1
Kiyokawa-mura	清川村	108・E-2
Kiyose-shi	清瀬市	105・H-5
Kodaira-shi	小平市	105・H-5
Koganei-shi	小金井市	105・H-6
Kōhoku-ku	港北区	109・I-2
Kokubunji-shi	国分寺市	105・G-6
Komae-shi	狛江市	109・I-1
Kōnan-ku	港南区	109・I-3
Kōnan-machi	江南町	105・F-1
Kōnosu-shi	鴻巣市	105・H-1
Koshigaya-shi	越谷市	106・A-4
Kosuge-mura	小菅村	104・A-5
Kōtō-ku	江東区	106・A-6
Kōzaki-machi	神崎町	107・H-4
Kujūkuri-machi	九十九里町	111・H-2
Kuki-shi	久喜市	105・J-2
Kukizaki-machi	茎崎町	106・E-2
Kumagaya-shi	熊谷市	105・G-1
Kunitachi-shi	国立市	105・G-6
Kurihashi-machi	栗橋町	105・J-1
Kurimoto-machi	栗源町	107・I-4
Kyonan-machi	鋸南町	110・B-6
Machida-shi	町田市	109・G-1
Manatsuru-machi	真鶴町	108・D-6
Matsubushi-machi	松伏町	106・A-3
Matsuda-machi	松田町	108・D-4
Matsudo-shi	松戸市	106・C-5
Matsuo-machi	松尾町	107・H-6
Meguro-ku	目黒区	109・J-1
Midori-ku	緑区(横浜市)	109・H-2
Midori-ku	緑区(千葉市)	110・E-2
Mihama-ku	美浜区	110・D-1
Miho-mura	美浦村	107・G-2
Minami-ku	南区	109・I-3
Minamiashigara-shi	南足柄市	108・C-4
Minano-machi	皆野町	104・C-1
Minato-ku	港区	105・J-6
Misaki-machi	岬町	111・H-4
Misato-shi	三郷市	106・B-4
Mishima-shi	三島市	108・A-6
Mitaka-shi	三鷹市	105・H-6
Mitsukaidō-shi	水海道市	106・C-2
Miura-shi	三浦市	109・I-6
Miyamae-ku	宮前区	109・H-1
Miyashiro-machi	宮代町	105・J-2
Miyoshi-machi	三芳町	105・H-4
Mizuho-machi	瑞穂町	105・F-5
Mobara-shi	茂原市	111・G-3
Moriya-machi	守谷町	106・C-3
Moroyama-machi	毛呂山町	104・E-3
Motono-mura	本埜村	107・F-4
Musashimurayama-shi	武蔵村山市	105・F-5
Musashino-shi	武蔵野市	105・H-6
Mutsuzawa-machi	睦沢町	111・G-4
Nagaizumi-chō	長泉町	108・A-6
Nagara-machi	長柄町	111・F-3
Nagareyama-shi	流山市	106・B-4
Nagatoro-machi	長瀞町	104・D-1
Naguri-mura	名栗村	104・D-4
Naka-ku	中区	109・I-3
Nakahara-ku	中原区	109・I-1
Nakai-machi	中井町	108・D-4
Nakano-ku	中野区	105・J-6
Namegawa-machi	滑川町	105・F-2
Narashino-shi	習志野市	106・D-6
Narita-shi	成田市	107・G-5
Narutō-machi	成東町	111・H-1
Nerima-ku	練馬区	105・I-5
Niihari-mura	新治村	106・E-1
Niiza-shi	新座市	105・H-5
Ninomiya-machi	二宮町	108・E-4
Nishi-ku	西区	109・I-3
Nishitōkyō-shi	西東京市	105・H-5

Noda-shi·················野田市········106・B-3
Nosaka-machi···········野栄町········107・I-6
Ōamishirasato-machi·····大網白里町·····111・G-2
Odawara-shi············小田原市······108・D-5
Ogano-machi···········小鹿野町······104・B-2
Ogawa-machi···········小川町········104・E-2
Ogose-machi···········越生町········104・E-3
Ōhara-machi···········大原町········111・G-5
Ōi-machi (Kanagawa)·····大井町(神奈川県)·····108・D-4
Ōi-machi (Saitama)·····大井町(埼玉県)····105・H-4
Ōiso-machi············大磯町········109・F-4
Okegawa-shi···········桶川市········105・H-2
Okutama-machi··········奥多摩町······104・C-4
Ōme-shi···············青梅市········104・E-4
Omigawa-machi·········小見川町······107・I-4
Ōmiya-shi·············大宮市········105・I-3
Onishi-machi··········鬼石町········104・B-1
Onjuku-machi··········御宿町········111・G-6
Ōno-mura 大野村→Kashima-shi 鹿嶋市
Ōsato-mura···········大里村········105・G-1
Oshino-mura··········忍野村········108・A-3
Ōta-ku··············大田区········109・J-1
Ōtaki-machi··········大多喜町······111・F-5
Ōtaki-mura··········大滝村········104・A-3
Ōtone-machi·········大利根町······105・I-1
Ōtsuki-shi·········大月市········108・B-1
Oyama-chō·········小山町········108・B-4
Ranzan-machi········嵐山町········105・F-2
Ryōkami-mura········両神村········104・B-2
Ryūgasaki-shi·······龍ヶ崎市······106・E-3
Sagamihara-shi······相模原市······109・F-1
Sagamiko-machi······相模湖町······108・D-1
Saiwai-ku··········幸区·········109・J-1
Sakado-shi·········坂戸市········105・G-3
Sakae-ku···········栄区·········109・H-4
Sakae-machi········栄町·········107・F-4
Sakai-machi········境町·········106・A-1
Sakura-shi·········佐倉市········107・F-6
Sakuragawa-mura·····桜川村········107・H-3
Samukawa-machi······寒川町········109・F-3
Sanbu-machi········山武町········107・G-6
Sashima-machi·······猿島町········106・B-1
Satte-shi··········幸手市········105・J-1
Sawara-shi·········佐原市········107・I-3
Sayama-shi·········狭山市········105・G-4
Sekiyado-machi······関宿町········106・B-2
Setagaya-ku········世田谷区······109・I-1
Seya-ku············瀬谷区········109・H-3
Shibayama-machi·····芝山町········107・H-6
Shibuya-ku·········渋谷区········105・J-6

Shiki-shi···········志木市········105・I-4
Shimofusa-machi·····下総町········107・G-4
Shinagawa-ku········品川区········109・J-1
Shinjuku-ku·········新宿区········105・J-6
Shintone-machi······新利根町······107・G-3
Shirako-machi·······白子町········111・G-3
Shiraoka-machi······白岡町········105・J-2
Shiroi-machi········白井町········106・D-5
Shiroyama-machi·····城山町········108・E-1
Shisui-machi········酒々井町······107・F-6
Shōbu-machi·········菖蒲町········105・I-2
Shōnan-machi········沼南町········106・D-4
Shōwa-machi·········庄和町········106・A-3
Sodegaura-shi·······袖ヶ浦市······110・C-3
Sōka-shi············草加市········106・A-4
Suginami-ku·········杉並区········105・I-6
Sugito-machi········杉戸町········105・J-2
Sumida-ku···········墨田区········106・A-6
Susono-shi··········裾野市········108・B-6
Tabayama-mura·······丹波山村······104・B-5
Tachikawa-shi·······立川市········105・G-6
Taiei-machi·········大栄町········107・H-4
Taitō-ku············台東区········106・A-6
Taiyō-mura··········大洋村········107・I-1
Takatsu-ku··········高津区········109・I-1
Tako-machi··········多古町········107・H-5
Tama-ku·············多摩区········109・H-1
Tama-shi············多摩市········105・G-6
Tamagawa-mura·······玉川村········104・E-2
Tamari-mura·········玉里村········107・G-1
Tamatsukuri-machi···玉造町········107・H-1
Tanashi-shi 田無市→Nishitōkyō-shi 西東京市·····105・H-5
Toda-shi············戸田市········105・I-4
Tōgane-shi··········東金市········111・H-1
Tokigawa-mura·······都幾川村······104・E-2
Tokorozawa-shi······所沢市········105・G-4
Tomisato-machi······富里町········107・G-6
Tone-machi··········利根町········106・E-4
Tōnoshō-machi·······東庄町········107・J-5
Toride-shi··········取手市········106・D-3
Toshima-ku··········豊島区········105・J-5
Totsuka-ku··········戸塚区········109・H-3
Tsuchiura-shi·······土浦市········107・F-1
Tsukuba-shi·········つくば市······106・D-2
Tsukui-machi········津久井町······108・E-1
Tsuru-shi···········都留市········108・B-2
Tsurugashima-shi····鶴ヶ島市······105・F-3
Tsurumi-ku··········鶴見区········109・I-2
Uenohara-machi······上野原町······108・C-1
Urawa-shi···········浦和市········105・J-4

Urayasu-shi	浦安市	106・B-6
Ushibori-machi	牛堀町	107・I-3
Ushiku-shi	牛久市	106・E-2
Wakaba-ku	若葉区	110・E-1
Wakō-shi	和光市	105・I-5
Warabi-shi	蕨市	105・J-4
Washimiya-machi	鷲宮町	105・I-1
Yachimata-Shi	八街市	107・G-6
Yachiyo-shi	八千代市	106・D-5
Yamada-machi	山田町	107・J-5
Yamakita-machi	山北町	108・C-4
Yamanakako-mura	山中湖村	108・A-3
Yamato-shi	大和市	109・G-2
Yashio-shi	八潮市	105・B-4
Yawara-mura	谷和原村	106・C-2
Yōkaichiba-shi	八日市場市	107・I-6
Yokohama-shi	横浜市	109・J-3
Yokoshiba-machi	横芝町	107・I-6
Yokosuka-shi	横須賀市	109・J-5
Yokoze-machi	横瀬町	104・D-3
Yono-shi	与野市	105・I-4
Yorii-machi	寄居町	104・D-1
Yoshida-machi	吉田町	104・B-2
Yoshikawa-shi	吉川市	106・B-4
Yoshimi-machi	吉見町	105・G-2
Yotsukaidō-shi	四街道市	106・E-6
Yugawara-machi	湯河原町	108・D-6
Zama-shi	座間市	109・G-2
Zushi-shi	逗子市	109・I-4

CITY, WARD, TOWN, VILLAGE OFFICE
市区町村役場

PLACE NAME	名称	MAP INDEX
Adachi Ward Office	足立区役所	45・F-6
Akiruno City Office	あきる野市役所	84・D-4
Akishima City Office	昭島市役所	58・C-4
Arakawa Ward Office	荒川区役所	43・F-4
Bunkyō Ward Office	文京区役所	13・F-5
Chiyoda Ward Office	千代田区役所	4・E-2
Chōfu City Office	調布市役所	66・D-5
Chūō Ward Office	中央区役所	7・F-4
Edogawa Ward Office	江戸川区役所	48・D-4
Fuchū City Office	府中市役所	57・F-4
Fussa City Office	福生市役所	85・G-3
Hachiōji City Office	八王子市役所	62・E-5

Hamura City Office	羽村市役所	86・C-4
Higashikurume City Office	東久留米市役所	81・H-4
Higashimurayama City Office	東村山市役所	80・C-4
Higashiyamato City Office	東大和市役所	83・H-4
Hino City Office	日野市役所	60・E-3
Hinode Town Office	日の出町役場	91・G-3
Hinohara Village Office	檜原村役場	92・E-5
Inagi City Office	稲城市役所	69・G-2
Itabashi Ward Office	板橋区役所	37・I-4
Kanagawa Prefectural Office	神奈川県庁	98・C-2
Katsushika Ward Office	葛飾区役所	47・G-4
Kita Ward Office	北区役所	41・F-5
Kiyose City Office	清瀬市役所	77・C-3
Kodaira City Office	小平市役所	79・F-3
Koganei City Office	小金井市役所	55・H-4
Kokubunji City Office	国分寺市役所	54・D-3
Komae City Office	狛江市役所	67・H-5
Kōtō Ward Office	江東区役所	18・D-3
Kunitachi City Office	国立市役所	56・C-3
Machida City Office	町田市役所	72・E-2
Meguro Ward Office	目黒区役所	22・E-3
Minato Ward Office	港区役所	8・E-2
Mitaka City Office	三鷹市役所	53・F-4
Mizuho Town Office	瑞穂町役場	87・G-4
Musashimurayama City Office	武蔵村山市役所	82・D-3
Musashino City Office	武蔵野市役所	52・B-3
Naka Ward Office	中区役所	98・C-2
Nakano Ward Office	中野区役所	31・F-4
Nerima Ward Office	練馬区役所	39・H-5
Nishi Ward Office	西区役所	97・G-4
Nishitōkyō City Office	西東京市役所	76・B-5
Okutama Town Office	奥多摩町役場	92・D-3
Ōme City Office	青梅市役所	89・F-4
Ōta Ward Office	大田区役所	24・E-5
Setagaya Ward Office	世田谷区役所	27・F-3
Shibuya Ward Office	渋谷区役所	29・F-4
Shinagawa Ward Office	品川区役所	20・E-4
Shinjuku Ward Office	新宿区役所	11・F-4
Suginami Ward Office	杉並区役所	33・F-3
Sumida Ward Office	墨田区役所	17・I-5
Tachikawa City Office	立川市役所	59・H-5
Taitō Ward Office	台東区役所	14・E-4
Tama City Office	多摩市役所	71・H-3
The Tōkyō Metropolitan Government	都庁	10・E-5
Toshima Ward Office	豊島区役所	35・F-3
Tsukuba City Office	つくば市役所	100・C-5
Yokohama City Office	横浜市役所	98・C-3

PUBLIC OFFICE
官公署

PLACE NAME	名 称	MAP INDEX
Agency for Cultural Affairs	文化庁	4・D-6
Agency of Industrial Science and Technology	工業技術院	4・E-6
Agency of National Resources and Energy	資源エネルギー庁	4・E-6
Bank of Japan	日本銀行	6・C-4
Board of Audit	会計検査院	4・D-6
Cabinet Office	内閣府	4・D-6
Fair Trade Commission	公正取引委員会	4・D-6
Fisheries Agency	水産庁	4・E-6
Food Agency	食糧庁	4・E-6
Forestry Agency	林野庁	4・E-6
Geihinkan (State Guesthouse)	迎賓館	8・A-3
Housing and Urban Development Corporation	住宅・都市整備公団	4・D-2
Japan External Trade Organization	日本貿易振興会(JETRO)	8・C-2
Japan Highway Public Corporation	日本道路公団	4・D-6
Japan National Tourist Organization	国際観光振興会(JNTO)	5・G-6
Japan Railway Construction Public Corporation	日本鉄道建設公団	4・C-5
Kokusai Denshin Denwa Co., Ltd.	国際電信電話	10・E-6
Local Food Agency Office	食糧事務所	100・C-5
Maritime Safety Agency	海上保安庁	4・E-5
Meteorological Agency	気象庁	5・F-3
Metropolitan Expressway Public Corporation	首都高速道路公団	4・E-6
Ministry of Agriculture, Forestry and Fisheries	農林水産省	4・E-6
Ministry of Economy, Trade and Industry	経済産業省	4・E-6
Ministry of Education, Culture, Sports, Science, and Technology	文部科学省	4・D-6
Ministry of Environment	環境省	4・E-6
Ministry of Finance	財務省	4・D-6
Ministry of Foreign Affairs	外務省	4・D-6
Ministry of Health, Labour and Welfare	厚生労働省	4・E-6
Ministry of Justice	法務省	4・E-5
Ministry of Labor	労働省	4・E-6
Ministry of Land, Infrastructure and Transport	国土交通省	4・E-5
Ministry of Public Management, Home Affairs, Posts and Telecommunications	総務省	4・E-6
Mint Bureau	大蔵省造幣局	35・G-4
National Archives	国立公文書館	4・E-3
National Diet Bldg.	国会議事堂	4・D-5
National Diet Library	国立国会図書館	4・D-5
National Personnel Authority	人事院	4・E-5
National Police Agency	警察庁	4・E-5
National Public Safety Commission	国家公安委員会	4・E-5
National Tax Administration Agency	国税庁	4・D-6
Patent Office	特許庁	4・D-6
Plant Quarantine Station	植物検疫所	98・E-2
Printing Bureau	大蔵省印刷局	8・C-2
Public prosecutors Office	検察庁	4・E-5
Regional Legal Affairs Bureau	法務局	100・C-4
Small and Medium Enterprise Agency	中小企業庁	4・E-6
Social Insurance Agency	社会保険庁	4・E-6
Supreme Court	最高裁判所	4・D-5
Teito Rapid Transit Authority	帝都高速度交通営団	14・D-4
Tōkyō District Court	東京地方裁判所	4・E-5
Tōkyō High Court	東京高等裁判所	4・E-5
Tōkyō Labor Standards Bureau	東京労働基準局	13・F-6
Tōkyō Regional Immigration Bureau	東京入国管理局	5・F-3
Tōkyō Regional Legal Affairs Bureau	東京法務局	5・F-3
Yokohama District Court	横浜地方裁判所	98・C-2

UNIVERSITY, COLLEGE
大 学

PLACE NAME	名 称	MAP INDEX
Aoyama Gakuin	青山学院大学	29・H-4
Asia	亜細亜大学	52・D-5
Bunka Women's	文化女子大学	28・D-2
Chūō	中央大学	70・D-2
Daitō Bunka	大東文化大学	36・D-3
Ferris Jogakuin	フェリス女学院大学	98・E-3
Gakushūin	学習院大学	34・E-5
Hitotsubashi	一橋大学	56・C-2
Hōsei	法政大学	4・C-2
Hoshi Coll. of Pharmacy	星薬科大学	20・C-3
International Christian	国際基督教大学	53・F-6
Japan Coll. of Social Work	日本社会事業大学	77・B-5
Japan Women's	日本女子大学	12・B-4
Japan Women's Coll. of Physical Education	日本女子体育大学	26・A-3
Japanese Red Cross Coll. of Nursing	日本赤十字看護大学	29・I-4
Jikei Univ. Sch. of Medicine	東京慈恵会医科大学	8・D-2
Jissen Women's Jr. Coll.	実践女子大学	60・E-3
Juntendō	順天堂大学	13・H-6
Kagawa Nutrition Coll.	女子栄養大学	35・J-2
Keiō	慶応大学	9・F-3
Keisen Jogakuen	恵泉女学園大学	71・G-6
Kitazato	北里大学	9・F-5

Kōgakuin	工学院大学	10・E-5
Kokugakuin	国学院大学	29・H-4
Kokushikan	国士館大学	27・F-3
Komazawa	駒沢大学	27・G-4
Kunitachi Coll. of Music	国立音楽大学	59・G-2
Kyōrin	杏林大学	53・G-3
Kyōritsu College of Pharmacy	共立薬科大学	8・E-2
Kyōritsu Women's	共立女子大学	5・F-2
Library & Information Science	図書館情報大学	101・G-3
Luthear Gakuin	ルーテル学院大学	53・F-6
Meiji	明治大学	5・F-2
Meiji Gakuin	明治学院大学	9・G-5
Meisei	明星大学	61・G-6
Musashi	武蔵大学	39・I-4
Musashi Institute of Technology	武蔵工業大学	27・H-6
Musashino Academia Musicae	武蔵野音楽大学	39・J-4
Musashino Art	武蔵野美術大学	78・C-3
Musashino Joshi Gakuin	武蔵野女子学院大学	76・C-5
Nihon (Art)	日本大学(芸術学部)	39・J-4
Nihon (Bioresource Sciencis)	日本大学(生物資源科学部)	27・H-3
Nihon (Comm.)	日本大学(商学部)	26・D-5
Nihon (Econ.)	日本大学(経済学部)	5・F-1
Nihon (Head Office)	日本大学(本部)	4・C-3
Nihon (Law)	日本大学(法学部)	4・E-1
Nihon (Lit.& Sci.)	日本大学(文理学部)	26・E-2
Nihon (Med.)	日本大学(医学部)	37・H-5
Nihon (Sci. & Engin.)	日本大学(理工学部)	5・G-2
Nihon Bunka	日本文化大学	65・H-3
Nippon Coll. of Physical Education	日本体育大学	27・G-5
Nippon Medical	日本医科大学	13・G-3
Nippon Veterinary and Zootechnical	日本獣医畜産大学	52・D-5
Nishō-Gakusha	二松学舎大学	4・D-3
Ōbirin College	桜美林大学	74・B-4
Ochanomizu Women's	お茶の水女子大学	12・C-3
Ōtsuma Women's	大妻女子大学	4・C-3
Rikkyō	立教大学	34・D-4
Risshō	立正大学	20・D-3
Science Univ. of Tōkyō	東京理科大学	11・J-2
Seijō	成城大学	26・C-5
Seikei	成蹊大学	52・C-2
Seisen Women's	清泉女子大学	20・D-2
Senshū	専修大学	4・E-2
Shibaura Institute of Technology	芝浦工業大学	9・G-3
Shirayuri Women's	白百合大学	67・G-1
Shōwa	昭和大学	20・B-5
Shōwa Coll. of Pharmaceutical Science	昭和薬科大学	73・G-1
Shōwa Women's	昭和女子大学	27・H-2
Sōka	創価大学	63・F-3
Sophia	上智大学	4・B-4
St. Luke's Coll. of Nursing	聖路加看護大学	7・F-4
Sugino Women's	杉野女子大学	20・C-2
Taishō	大正大学	35・G-2
Takachiho Univ. of Commerce	高千穂商科大学	33・G-5
Takushoku	拓殖大学	12・D-4
Tama	多摩大学	71・J-3
Tama Univ. of Arts	多摩美術大学	27・G-6
Tamagawa	玉川大学	75・G-5
Teikyō	帝京大学	37・I-3
The Nippon Dental	日本歯科大学	4・D-2
The Univ. of the Air	放送大学	12・D-3
Tōhō	東邦大学	25・F-4
Tōhō Gakuen	桐朋学園大学	67・H-2
Tōkai	東海大学	28・D-5
Tōkyō College of Pharmacy	東京薬科大学	70・B-3
Tōkyō Dental Coll.	東京歯科大学	4・E-1
Tōkyō Electrical Engineering	東京電機大学	5・G-2
Tōkyō Engineering	東京工科大学	65・G-4
Tōkyō Gakugei	東京学芸大学	55・F-3
Tōkyō Institute of Technology	東京工業大学	23・I-3
Tōkyō Kasei	東京家政大学	37・J-3
Tōkyō Kasei Gakuin	東京家政学院大学	64・E-5
Tōkyō Keizai	東京経済大学	55・F-4
Tōkyō Medical	東京医科大学	11・G-4
Tōkyō Medical & Dental	東京医科歯科大学	13・H-6
Tōkyō Metropolitan	東京都立大学	70・B-4
Tōkyō Metropolitan Institute of Technology	東京都立科学技術大学	60・B-4
Tōkyō Music	東京音楽大学	35・F-5
Tōkyō Nat'l Univ. of Fine Art & Music	東京芸術大学	14・C-3
Tōkyō Union Theological Seminary	東京神学大学	53・F-6
Tōkyō Univ. Mercantile Marine	東京商船大学	18・D-5
Tōkyō Univ. of Agriculture	東京農業大学	26・E-4
Tōkyō Univ. of Fisheries	東京水産大学	9・I-4
Tōkyō Univ. of Foreign Studies	東京外国語大学	57・J-4
Tōkyō Univ. of Agri. & Engin.	東京農工大学	57・F-3
Tōkyō Univ. of Art and Design	東京造形大学	94・C-3
Tōkyō Women's Christian	東京女子大学	32・B-2
Tōkyō Women's Coll. of Physical Education	東京女子体育大学	56・B-2
Tōkyō Women's Medical	東京女子医科大学	11・H-3
Tōyō	東洋大学	13・F-3
Tsudajuku	津田塾大学	78・E-4
Tsukuba	筑波大学	101・H-1
Ueno-gakuen	上野学園大学	14・E-3
Univ. of Electro-Communications	電気通信大学	66・D-4
Univ. of Sacred Heart	聖心女子大学	29・J-5
Univ. of Tōkyō	東京大学	13・H-4
Wakō	和光大学	75・H-4
Waseda	早稲田大学	11・G-2

EMBASSY
大使館

PLACE NAME	名称	MAP INDEX
Argentine	アルゼンチン	8・E-4
Australia	オーストラリア	8・E-4
Austria	オーストリア	8・D-4
Bangladesh	バングラデシュ	22・E-2
Belgium	ベルギー	4・B-4
Brazil	ブラジル	8・B-5
Canada	カナダ	8・B-4
China	中華人民共和国	8・D-4
Denmark	デンマーク	29・G-6
Egypt	エジプト	22・B-3
Ethiopia	エチオピア	9・G-5
Federal Republic of Germany	ドイツ連邦共和国	8・E-5
Finland	フィンランド	8・E-5
France	フランス	8・E-5
Greece	ギリシャ	8・D-4
Her Britannic Majesty	イギリス	4・D-3
India	インド	4・D-2
Indonesia	インドネシア	20・C-2
Iran	イラン	8・E-4
Iraq	イラク	8・B-4
Itely	イタリア	8・E-3
Korea	大韓民国	8・E-4
Malaysia	マレーシア	29・F-6
Mexico	メキシコ	4・C-5
Mongolia	モンゴル	28・E-5
Nepal	ネパール	27・H-5
Netherlands	オランダ	8・D-2
New Zealand	ニュージーランド	28・E-5
Nigeria	ナイジェリア	22・E-2
Pakistan	パキスタン	8・E-4
Peru	ペルー	29・H-4
Philippines	フィリピン	8・D-3
Poland	ポーランド	9・H-5
Romania	ルーマニア	8・D-5
Russian Federation	ロシア連邦	8・D-3
Saudi Arabia	サウジアラビア	8・D-3
Singapore	シンガポール	8・D-4
South Africa	南アフリカ	4・C-4
Spain	スペイン	8・D-3
Sri Lanka	スリランカ	9・G-4
Switzerland	スイス	8・D-5
Thailand	タイ	20・C-2
Turkey	トルコ	29・F-2
United States of America	アメリカ合衆国	8・C-2
Viet Nam	ベトナム	28・D-4

HOSPITAL
病院

PLACE NAME	名称	MAP INDEX
Akiru	公立阿伎留病院	84・B-4
Aoto Hosp. attached to Jikei Univ. Sch. of Medicine	慈恵医大青戸分院	47・F-3
Aoyama	青山病院	29・G-4
Arakawa Maternity	都立荒川産院	43・F-2
Asoka	あそか病院	18・B-3
Cancer Institute	癌研究会附属病院	35・G-3
Civic Hospital	町田市民病院	72・D-1
Dōai Memorial	同愛記念病院	17・H-6
Fussa	福生病院	85・G-2
Hachiōji Children's Hospital	都立八王子小児病院	62・E-6
Hikarigaoka	光が丘総合病院	39・F-2
Hino Municipal Hospital	日野市立総合病院	60・C-3
Hiroo	都立広尾病院	29・J-5
Hitachi	東京日立病院	13・I-6
Hosp. attached to Kyōrin Univ.	杏林大学附属病院	53・G-3
Hosp. of Printing Bureau	印刷局東京病院	41・G-5
Inagi Municipal Hospital	稲城市立病院	68・E-3
Itabashi Chūō	板橋中央総合病院	37・G-3
Itabashi Hosp. attached to Nihon Univ.	日本大学附属病院	37・H-5
Itabashi Hosp. attached to Teikyō Univ.	帝京大学附属病院	37・I-3
Iwakura	岩倉総合病院	48・B-3
JR Tōkyō General Hosp.	JR東京総合病院	28・D-1
Japan Red Cross Medical Service Center	日赤医療センター	29・I-4
Jikei Medical	慈恵医大付属病院	8・D-2
Jikei Univ. Sch. of Medicine No3	慈恵医大第三病院	67・G-3
Juntendō	順天堂医院	13・H-6
Kantō Chūō	関東中央病院	26・E-4
Kantō Post & Telecommunications	関東通信病院	20・D-1
Karasuyama Hosp. Attached to Shōwa Univ.	昭和大烏山病院	26・B-3
Kawakita	河北総合病院	33・G-3
Keiō Univ.	慶応大学病院	11・H-5
Keiyū	警友病院	98・D-2
Kiyose Children's	都立清瀬小児病院	77・B-5
Komagome	都立駒込病院	13・G-2
Kōsei	佼成病院	31・I-4
Kōsei Chūō	厚生中央病院	22・C-1
Kugayama	久我山病院	26・B-2
Matsuzawa	都立松沢病院	26・C-2
Medical Center attached to Tōkyō Medical Coll.	東京医大医療センター	64・C-3
Medical Center for the Severely Handicapped	都立療育センター	56・D-2
Met. Bokutō	都立墨東病院	17・I-3

Met. Ebara ·· 都立荏原病院 ·········24・C-2
Metropolitan Fuchū ·· 都立府中病院 ·········56・E-2
Metropolitan Neurological Hospital ················ 都立神経病院 ·········56・E-2
Minamitama ··· 南多摩病院 ···········62・E-6
Mishuku ·· 三宿病院 ··············22・D-4
Mitsui Memorial Hosp. ···································· 三井記念病院 ·········5・I-1
Musashino Red Cross ···································· 武蔵野赤十字病院 ···52・E-4
Nakano ··· 中野総合病院 ·········31・G-4
Nat'l Children's ·· 国立小児病院 ·········27・G-2
Nat'l Musashi ·· 国立武蔵病院 ·········79・F-2
Nat'l Ōji ··· 国立王子病院 ·········40・C-2
Nat'l Ōkura ··· 国立大蔵病院 ·········26・D-5
Nat'l Tōkyō Medical Service Center ············· 国立東京医療センター ···23・G-6
National Cancer Center ································· 国立がんセンター ····7・G-5
National Hosp. Medical Service Center ··········· 国立病院医療センター 11・G-2
National Sanatoria Murayama Hospital ·········· 国立療養所村山病院 ···82・E-4
National Sanatoria Tama Zenseien ··············· 国立療養所多磨全生園 81・F-3
National Sanatoria Tōkyō ······························ 国立療養所東京病院 ···77・B-5
National Tachikawa ······································· 国立立川病院 ·········59・G-5
Nerima ·· 練馬総合病院 ·········39・J-4
Nihon Univ. Hospital ····································· 駿河台日大病院 ······5・G-2
Nippon Express ··· 日本通運東京病院 ····12・C-3
Nippon Medical ··· 日本医大付属病院 ····13・H-3
Nippon Medical Sch. Tama-Nagayama
Hosp. ··· 日医大多摩永山病院 ···71・H-3
Ogikubo ·· 荻窪病院 ··············32・D-2
Ōkubo ··· 都立大久保病院 ······10・E-4
Okutama ·· 奥多摩病院 ···········92・D-3
Ōme Municipal Hospital ································· 青梅市立総合病院 ····89・G-5
Ōmori Red Cross ·· 大森赤十字病院 ······24・E-3
Ōtsuka ·· 都立大塚病院 ·········35・H-4
Police Hospital ·· 東京警察病院 ·········4・D-1
Saiseikai ··· 済生会中央病院 ······8・E-3
San-ikukai ·· 賛育会病院 ···········17・G-4
Self-defence Force Central Hosp. ··················· 自衛隊中央病院 ······27・H-2
Shiseikai 2nd ·· 至誠会第二病院 ······26・B-4
Shitaya ··· 下谷病院 ··············14・E-2
Shōwa ·· 昭和大学病院 ·········20・B-5
Shōwa ·· 公立昭和病院 ·········79・H-3
Social Insurance Chūo Hosp. ························· 社会保険中央病院 ····10・E-3
St. Luke's International Hospital ···················· 聖路加国際病院 ······7・F-4
Tachikawa ··· 共済立川病院 ·········59・H-6
Taitō ·· 都立台東病院 ·········15・G-2
Tamagawa ·· 日産厚生会玉川病院 ···27・F-6
Ṭamagawa ·· 多摩川総合病院 ······66・E-4
Tanashi ··· 田無病院 ··············76・C-3
Tōhō Univ. ·· 東邦大学大橋病院 ····22・B-5
Tōkyō Communications ·································· 東京通信病院 ·········4・C-2
Tōkyō Kyōsai ·· 東京共済病院 ·········22・C-2
Tōkyō Medical & Dental ································· 東京医科歯科大病院 ···13・H-6

Tōkyō Medical Coll. Hosp. ···························· 東京医科大学病院 ·····10・E-5
Tōkyō Police Hosp. Tama Branch Hosp. 警察病院多摩分院 ···54・D-5
Tōkyō Senbai ·· 東京専売病院 ·········8・E-3
Tōkyō Women's Med. Coll. ···························· 東女医大第二病院 ····42・C-2
Tōkyō Women's Medical ································· 東京女子医大病院 ····11・H-3
Tōkyū ··· 東急病院 ··············24・C-1
Tonan ··· 社会保険都南病院 ····21・F-4
Toranomon ·· 虎の門病院 ···········8・C-2
Toshima ·· 都立豊島病院 ·········37・H-4
Tsukiji Maternity ·· 都立築地産院 ·········7・F-3
Tsukuba Mem. Hosp. ···································· 筑波記念病院 ·········101・G-1
Tsukuba-gakuen Hosp. ································· 筑波学園病院 ·········100・D-5
Umegaoka ··· 都立梅ケ丘病院 ······27・F-2
Univ. of Tōkyō Hosp. ··································· 東京大学付属病院 ····13・H-5
Yokohama Central Hosp. ······························ 横浜中央病院 ·········98・D-3
Yokohama City Univ. ····································· 横浜市大附属病院 ····98・B-5
Yokohama Red Cross ···································· 横浜赤十字病院 ······98・E-6

HOTEL
ホテル

PLACE NAME	名 称	MAP INDEX

Akasaka Prince ·· 赤坂プリンス ··········4・C-5
Akasaka Shanpia ··· 赤坂シャンピア ·······8・C-3
Akasaka Tōkyū ·· 赤坂東急 ··············4・C-5
Akihabara Washington ·································· 秋葉原ワシントン ····5・H-2
Asakusa View ·· 浅草ビュー ···········15・F-3
B & B Shibuya ·· ビーアンドビー渋谷 ···22・C-5
Capital Tōkyū ··· キャピトル東急 ······4・C-6
Center City ··· センターシティ ······34・E-3
Century Hyatt ··· センチュリーハイアット
Nat'l Tōkyō Medical Service Center ·········· 10・E-5
Century Southern Tower ······························ 小田急サザンタワー ···28・D-1
Cojima ·· コジマ ·················14・C-3
Daiichi Hotel Tōkyō ······································ 第一ホテル東京 ······8・D-1
Daiichi Inn Ōmori ··· 第一イン大森 ·········25・G-3
Daisan Hotel ··· 第三ホテル ···········96・C-4
Diamond ·· ダイヤモンド ·········4・C-4
Edmont ··· エドモント ···········4・D-1
Fairmont ·· フェアーモント ······4・D-3
Ginza Daiichi ·· 銀座第一 ··············7・F-5
Ginza Nikkō ·· 銀座日航 ··············7・F-6
Ginza Tōkyū ··· 銀座東急 ··············7・F-5
Gotanda Chisan ··· 五反田チサン ·········20・D-5

Grand Palace	グランドパレス	4・E-2
Haneda Tōkyū	羽田東急	25・H-6
Hankyū	阪急	20・E-4
Harumi Grand	晴海グランド	7・I-3
Hilltop	山の上	5・F-2
Holiday Inn Tōkyō	ホリディ・イン東京	98・D-2
Holiday Inn Yokohama	ホリディ・イン横浜	6・E-3
Hotel Kaiyō	ホテル海洋	10・E-3
Hotel Rich Yokohama	ホテルリッチ横浜	96・C-3
Ibis	アイビス	8・C-4
Imperial	帝国	5・F-6
International Sightseeing	国際観光	5・G-4
Juraku	聚楽	5・G-2
Kayabachō Pearl	茅場町パール	6・D-3
Kayū-kaikan	霞友会館	4・D-3
Keiō Plaza	京王プラザ	10・E-5
Kudan-kakan	九段会館	4・E-2
Listel	リステル	11・G-4
Marroad Inn Akasaka	マロウドイン赤坂	8・C-3
Marroad Inn Tōkyō	マロウドイン東京	57・H-4
Meguro Gajoen	目黒雅叙園	22・D-1
Metropolitan	メトロポリタン	34・E-4
Miel Parque	メルパルク	8・E-2
Mita Miyako	三田都	9・F-4
Mitsui Urban	三井アーバン	7・F-6
Miyako Hotel Tōkyō	都ホテル東京	9・F-5
New Grand	ニューグランド	98・D-2
New Meguro	ニューメグロ	22・E-3
New Ōtani	ニューオータニ	4・B-4
New Takanawa Prince	新高輪プリンス	9・H-5
Ōkura	オークラ	8・D-2
Ōta Daiichi	大田第一	24・E-2
Pacific Tōkyō	パシフィック東京	9・H-5
Palace	パレス	5・F-4
President Aoyama	プレジデント青山	8・B-4
Roppongi Prince	六本木プリンス	8・D-3
Royal Park	ロイヤルパーク	6・C-2
Ryōgoku Pearl	両国パール	17・I-6
Seaside Edogawa	シーサイド江戸川	49・J-5
Shiba Park	芝パーク	8・E-2
Shibuya Tōbu	渋谷東武	29・F-4
Shibuya Tōkyū Inn	渋谷東急イン	29・G-4
Shinjuku New City	新宿ニューシティ	10・E-6
Shinjuku Prince	新宿プリンス	11・F-4
Star Hotel Tōkyō	スターホテル東京	10・E-4
Suidōbashi Grand	水道橋グランド	13・G-6
Sunroute Shibuya	サンルート渋谷	29・F-5
Sunroute Tōkyō	サンルート東京	28・D-1
Sunroute Yokohama	サンルート横浜	96・C-4
Sunshine Prince	サンシャインプリンス	35・F-4

Takanawa	高輪	9・G-4
Takanawa Prince	高輪プリンス	9・H-5
Takanawa Tōbu	高輪東武	9・H-5
The Hotel Yokohama	ザ・ホテル 横浜	98・D-2
Tōkyō	東京	9・G-4
Tōkyō Garden Palace	東京ガーデンパレス	13・H-6
Tōkyō Grand	東京グランド	9・F-2
Tōkyō Hilton	東京ヒルトン	10・E-5
Tōkyō Marriott Hotel	東京マリオットホテル	17・H-4
Tōkyō Prince	東京プリンス	8・E-2
Tōkyō Station	東京ステーション	5・H-5
Tōkyō Sunny Side	東京サニーサイド	18・D-3
Tōkyō Washington	東京ワシントン	10・E-6
Tōkyō Yayōi-kaikan	東京弥生会館	13・I-4
Tōkyō Zennikkū	東京全日空	8・C-3
Toranomon Pastral	虎の門パストラル	8・D-2
Tsukuba Sunroute	つくばサンルート	101・H-3
U-Port	ゆうぽうと	20・D-3
Yaesu Fujiya	八重洲富士屋	6・E-5
Yōkō Akasaka	陽光赤坂	8・C-3
Yokohama Bay Sheraton-Hotel & Towers	横浜ベイシェラトン	96・C-3
Yokohama Kokusai	横浜国際	96・D-4
Yokohama Plaza	横浜プラザ	96・D-2
Yokohama Tōkyū	横浜東急	96・C-3
Yomiuri Land	よみうりランド	69・H-4
Yūbin-chokin-kaikan	郵便貯金会館	98・D-2

HALL
ホール

PLACE NAME	名称	MAP INDEX

Adachi Culture Hall	足立区文化会館	45・F-4
Akishima Shiminkaikan Hall	昭島市民会館	58・C-3
Asahi Seimei Hall	朝日生命ホール	10・E-5
Asakusa Public Hall	浅草公会堂	15・G-4
Chiyada Public Hall	千代田区公会堂	4・E-2
Chōfu Central Community Center	調布市中央公民館	66・D-4
Chōfu Civic Welfare Hall	調布市民福祉会館	66・D-4
Chūō kaikan Hall	区立中央会館	7・F-4
EXPO Center	エキスポセンター	101・G-3
Edogawa Culture Center	江戸川文化センター	48・D-4
Fuchū Shiminkaikan Hall	府中市民会館	59・G-3
Fussa Shiminkaikan Hall	福生市民会館	85・H-3

Ginza Gas Hall	銀座ガスホール	7・F-5
Hachiōji Shiminkaikan Hall	八王子市民会館	63・F-6
Hibiya Public Hall	日比谷公会堂	4・E-6
Hikifune Culture Center	曳船文化センター	16・E-3
Izumi Hall	いずみホール	54・D-4
Kanagawa Kenmin Hall	神奈川県民ホール	98・D-2
Kanagawa Prefectural Youth Center	神奈川県立青少年センター	97・G-4
Kannai Hall	関内ホール	98・D-2
Kita Public Hall	北区公会堂	41・F-5
Kiyose Civic Center	清瀬市民センター	77・C-4
Koganei Public Hall	小金井市公会堂	55・H-4
Komaba Eminence	こまばエミナース	22・B-5
Komae Welfare Hall	狛江市福祉会館	67・G-6
Kōtō Culture Center	江東文化センター	18・D-3
Kōtō Public Hall	江東公会堂	18・B-3
Kudan-kaikan Hall	九段会館	4・E-2
Machida Civic Hall	町田市民ホール	72・E-2
Meguro Public Hall	目黒区公会堂	22・E-3
Met.Children's Houses	東京都児童会館	29・G-4
Miel Parque Hall	東京郵便貯金ホール	8・E-2
Musashimurayama Shiminkaikan Hall	武蔵村山市民会館	82・D-3
Musashino Public Hall	武蔵野公会堂	52・D-2
NHK Hall	NHKホール	29・F-4
Nakano Culture Center	中野文化センター	31・G-3
Nakano Public Center	中野公会堂	31・G-3
Nakano Sun Plaza Hall	サンプラザホール	31・F-4
Nerima Culture Center	練馬文化センター	39・H-4
Nihon Seinenkan Hall	日本青年館	11・H-6
Nippon Budōkan Hall	日本武道館	4・E-2
Ōme Shiminkaikan Hall	青梅市民会館	88・D-4
Ōta Ward Hall	大田区民会館	24・D-3
Ōta Ward Plaza	大田区民プラザ	24・C-4
Parthenon Tama	パルテノン多摩	71・F-4
Ryōgoku Public Hall	両国公会堂	17・I-6
Setagaya Ward Hall	世田谷区民会館	27・F-3
Shibuya Public Hall	渋谷公会堂	29・F-4
Shinjuku Culture Center	新宿文化センター	11・G-4
Sōgetsu-kaikan Hall	草月会館	8・B-3
Suginami Public Hall	杉並公会堂	32・E-3
Suijō Concert Hall	不忍池水上音楽堂	14・C-4
Sun Pearl Arakawa	サンパール荒川	43・F-4
Suntory Hall	サントリーホール	8・C-3
Tachikawa Shiminkaikan Hall	立川市民会館	59・H-5
Tama Community Center	多摩市公民館ホール	71・H-3
Tama Training Center	多摩教育センター	59・H-6
Tanashi Shiminkaikan Hall	田無市民会館	76・B-4
Tōkyō Kōsei Nenkin-kaikan Hall	東京厚生年金会館	11・G-4
Tōkyō Metropolitan Festival Hall	東京文化会館	14・D-3
Tōkyō Workers Welfare Hall	東京都勤労福祉会館	6・E-4
Tsukuba New City Mem.Hall	筑波新都市記念館	101・F-5
U-Port Hall	東京簡易保険ホール	20・D-3
Yakult Hall	ヤクルトホール	8・D-1
Yamaha Hall	ヤマハホール	7・F-5
Yamano Hall	山野ホール	28・D-1
Yotsuya Public Hall	四谷公会堂	11・H-4

THEATER
劇場

PLACE NAME	名称	MAP INDEX
Aoyama Theater	青山劇場	29・G-4
Bunkamura	Bunkamura	29・F-5
Geijutsuza Theater	芸術座	5・F-6
Haiyūza Theater	俳優座劇場	8・C-4
Hakuhinkan Theater	博品館劇場	7・F-6
Hōshō Noh Theater	宝生能楽堂	13・G-6
Imperial Theater	帝国劇場	5・F-5
Kabukiza Theater	歌舞伎座	7・F-5
Kanze Noh Theater	観世能楽堂	28・E-5
Kita Roppeita Noh Theater	喜多六平太能楽堂	20・C-2
Meijiza Theater (Under Construction)	明治座	6・B-2
National Noh Theater	国立能楽堂	29・F-1
National Theater of Japan	国立劇場	4・D-4
Nissei Theater	日生劇場	5・F-6
Sanbyakunin Theater	三百人劇場	12・E-2
Shinbashi Enbujō Theater	新橋演舞場	7・F-5
Shinjuku Koma Theater	新宿コマ劇場	11・F-4
Shinohara Engeijō Theater	篠原演芸場	40・E-4
Suzumoto Engeijō Theater	上野鈴本演芸場	14・D-4
The Globe Theater	グローブ座	10・E-3
Tōkyō Takarazuka Theater	東京宝塚劇場	5・F-6
Umewaka Noh Theater	梅若能楽堂	31・H-2
Yarai Noh Theater	矢来能楽堂	11・I-2

PLACE OF INTEREST
名所

PLACE NAME	名称	MAP INDEX
Central Wholesale Market	中央卸売市場	7・G-4
China Town	中華街	98・D-2
Ferry Terminal	フェリーターミナル	19・I-4
Foreigner's Cemetery	外人墓地	98・E-2
Geihinkan(State Guesthouse)	迎賓館	8・A-3
Grand Pier	大桟橋	98・C-1
Hikawa-maru	氷川丸	98・D-2
International Passenger Terminal	国際旅客ターミナル	98・C-1
Marine Tower	マリンタワー	98・D-2
Mullion	マリオン	5・F-6
National Astronomical Observatory	国立天文台	53・G-5
Shinjuku Center Bldg.	新宿センタービル	10・E-5
Shinjuku Mitsui Bldg.	新宿三井ビル	10・E-5
Shinjuku NS Bldg.	新宿NSビル	10・E-5
Shinjuku Nomura Bldg.	新宿野村ビル	10・E-5
Shinjuku Sumitomo Bldg.	新宿住友ビル	10・E-5
Sunshine City	サンシャインシティ	35・F-4
TOC Bldg.	TOCビル	20・C-3
Tōkyō City Air Terminal	東京シティエアターミナル	6・D-2
Tōkyō International Airport	東京国際空港	25・J-5
Tōkyō International Trade Center	東京国際貿易センター	7・I-4
Tōkyō Stock Exchange	東京証券取引所	6・C-3
Tōkyō Tower	東京タワー	8・E-3
World Trade Center Bldg.	貿易センタービル	8・E-2
Yamate Anglican Church	山手聖公会	98・D-3
Yamate Cathoric Church	山手カトリック教会	98・E-3
Yokohama Customhouse	横浜税関	98・C-2
Yushima Seidō	湯島聖堂	13・I-6

GOLF COURSE
ゴルフ場

PLACE NAME	名称	MAP INDEX
Akabane Golf Club	赤羽ゴルフクラブ	40・B-1
Fuchū Country Club	府中カントリークラブ	70・D-4
GMG Hachiōji Golf Course	GMG八王子ゴルフコース	62・A-1
Kasumigaura Kokusai Golf Course	霞ケ浦国際ゴルフコース	101・F-6
Koganei Country Club	小金井カントリークラブ	55・H-2
Musashino Golf Club	武蔵野ゴルフクラブ	62・D-2
Ōme Golf Club	青梅ゴルフクラブ	89・F-3
Sakuragaoka Country Club	桜ケ丘カントリークラブ	71・J-2
Shōwa-no-mori Golf Course	昭和の森ゴルフコース	58・C-3
Sōbu Country Club	相武カントリークラブ	64・D-5
Tachikawa International Country Club	立川国際カントリー倶楽部	84・E-2
Tama Country Club	多摩カントリークラブ	68・D-3
Tōkyō Birdy Club	東京バーディクラブ	93・H-2
Tōkyō Itsukaichi Country Club	東京五日市カントリー倶楽部	91・G-6
Tōkyō Kokusai Country Golf Club	東京国際カントリーゴルフ場	74・B-1
Tōkyō Yomiuri Country Club	東京よみうりカントリークラブ	69・F-4
Yomiuri Golf Club	よみうりゴルフ倶楽部	69・G-4

AMUSEMENT PARK
遊園地

PLACE NAME	名称	MAP INDEX
Akigawabashi Riverbed Park	秋川橋河川公園	90・D-4
Arakawa-yūen Ground	荒川遊園	42・B-1
Hanayashiki Amusement Park	浅草花屋敷	15・G-3
Kodomonokuni Natural Park	こどもの国	73・I-1
Kōrakuen Recreation Ground	後楽園遊園地	13・F-5
Pony Land Park	ポニーランド	48・D-1
Tamateck Amusement Park	多摩テック	60・E-6
Tōkyō Summerland	東京サマーランド	84・B-5
Toshimaen	豊島園	39・G-4
Yomiuri Land	よみうりランド	69・H-4

ART MUSEUM
美術館

PLACE NAME	名 称	MAP INDEX
Asakura-chōsokan Gallery	朝倉彫塑館	14・C-1
Bridgestone Mus. of Arts	ブリヂストン美術館	6・D-4
Chihiro Iwasaki Memorial Gallery	いわさきちひろ絵本美術館	38・D-5
Emperor Meiji Memorial Picture Gallery	聖徳記念絵画館	11・H-5
Gotō Art Musuem	五島美術館	27・G-6
Gyokudō Museum of Art	玉堂美術館	93・F-3
Hatakeyama Collection	畠山記念館	9・G-6
International Museum of Print Arts	国際版画美術館	73・F-2
Itabashi Art Gallery	板橋区立美術館	36・B-4
Japanese Sword Museum	刀剣博物館	28・D-2
Meguro Art Gallery	目黒区美術館	22・D-2
Met.Teien Mus. of Art	東京都庭園美術館	9・F-6
Murauchi Home Center Museum of Art	村内美術館	63・G-4
Mus. of Calligraphy	書道博物館	14・D-2
Nat'l Museum of Western Art	国立西洋美術館	14・D-3
National Museum of Modern Arts	国立近代美術館	4・E-3
Nerima Art Gallery	練馬区立美術館	39・G-4
Nezu Institute of Fine Art	根津美術館	8・C-5
Nihon Mus. of Calligraphy	日本書道美術館	37・G-4
Ōkura Shūkokan Museum	大倉集古館	8・D-2
Ōme Municipal Museum	青梅市立美術館	88・D-5
Ōta Mem.Museum of Art	太田記念美術館	29・F-3
Ryūshi Mem. Museum	龍子記念館	24・E-3
Seikadō Library	静嘉堂文庫展示館	26・E-6
Setagaya Art Gallery	世田谷区立美術館	26・E-5
Shōtō Mus. of Art	区立松濤美術館	29・F-5
Suntory Mus. of Art	サントリー美術館	8・B-3
Tōkyō Fuji Museum of Art	創価大富士美術館	63・F-3
Tōkyō Met. Museum of Modern Arts	東京現代美術館	18・C-4
Tōkyō Met.Museum of Photography	東京都写真美術館	22・C-1
Tōkyō Metropolitan Art Museum	東京都美術館	14・D-3
Tomioka Art Musuem	富岡美術館	25・F-2
Toy Museum	おもちゃ美術館	31・F-3
Ueno Royal Mus.	上野の森美術館	14・D-4
Yamatane Mus. of Art	山種美術館	4・D-3
Yokohama Museum of Art	横浜美術館	97・F-1
Yokoyama Taikan Memorial Gallery	横山大観記念館	14・C-4

LIBRARY
図書館

PLACE NAME	名 称	MAP INDEX
Akishima Library	昭島市民図書館	58・E-4
Arakawa Library	荒川区立荒川図書館	42・E-4
Edogawa Kasai Library	江戸川区立葛西図書館	49・G-4
Fuchū Central Library	府中市立中央図書館	57・F-4
Fussa Central Library	福生市立中央図書館	85・H-4
German Culture Center	ドイツ文化センター	8・B-3
Hachiōji Central Library	八王子市立中央図書館	62・E-6
Higashikurume Central Library	東久留米市立中央図書館	81・H-4
Higashimurayama Central Library	東村山市立中央図書館	80・C-4
Higashiyamato Central Library	東大和市立中央図書館	83・H-4
Hino Central Library	日野市立中央図書館	60・D-4
Hōya Shimo-hōya Library	保谷市立下保谷図書館	76・E-2
Int'l Library of Children's Literature	国際子ども図書館	14・D-2
Kanagawa Prefectural Library	神奈川県立図書館	97・G-2
Katsushika Library	葛飾区立葛飾図書館	46・E-3
Kiyose Central Library	清瀬市立中央図書館	77・B-4
Kodaira Central Library	小平市立中央図書館	79・F-3
Koganei Library	小金井市立図書館	55・H-4
Kokubunji Koigakubo Library	国分寺市立恋ヶ窪	54・D-3
Komae Central Library	狛江市立中央図書館	67・H-5
Kōtō Fukagawa Library	江東区立深川図書館	18・C-4
Kunitachi Central Library	国立市立中央図書館	56・C-3
Machida Central Library	町田市立中央図書館	73・F-3
Mitaka Library	三鷹市立三鷹図書館	53・F-4
Musashino Central Library	武蔵野市立中央図書館	52・C-3
Nakano Library	中野区立中野図書館	31・G-3
National Diet Library	国会図書館	4・D-5
Nerima Shakujii Library	練馬区立石神井図書館	38・D-4
Ōme Central Library	青梅市立中央図書館	88・D-4
Ōta Library	大田区立大田図書館	24・B-3
Shibuya Central Library	渋谷区立中央図書館	29・F-3
Shinagawa Library	品川区立品川図書館	21・F-3
Shinjuku Central Library	新宿区立中央図書館	10・D-2
Suginami Central Library	杉並区立中央図書館	33・F-3
Sumida Azuma Library	墨田区立あずま図書館	17・F-3
Sumida Terashima Library	墨田区立寺島図書館	16・D-4
Tama Library	多摩市立図書館	71・H-3
Tanashi Central Library	田無市立中央図書館	76・B-5
Tōkyō Met.Central Library	都立中央図書館	8・E-5
Toshima Central Library	豊島区立中央図書館	35・G-4
Tsukuba Central Library	つくば市立中央図書館	101・G-3
Yokohama City Library	横浜市立図書館	97・H-2

MUSEUM
博物館

PLACE NAME	名 称	MAP INDEX
Communications Museum	通信総合博物館	5・G-3
Daimyō Clock Museum	大名時計博物館	14・C-2
Edo Tokyo Museum	江戸東京博物館	17・I-6
Fukagawa Edo Museum	深川江戸資料館	18・C-4
Hasseiden Museum	八聖殿	99・H-5
Japan Modern Literature Library	日本近代文学館	22・A-6
Kanagawa Mus. of Modern Literature	神奈川近代文学館	98・E-2
Kanagawa Prefectural Museum	神奈川県立博物館	98・B-2
Koishikawa Botanical Garden	小石川植物園	12・E-3
Medical Culture Hall	医学文化館	88・E-3
Metropolitan Modern Literature Museum	都近代文学博物館	22・A-6
Mus. of Maritime Science	船の科学館	21・I-1
Museum of Gas	ガスの博物館	19・F-5
NHK Broadcasting Museum	NHK放送博物館	8・D-2
Nat'l Park for Nature Study	国立自然教育園	9・F-6
Nat'l Science Museum	国立科学博物館	101・H-2
National Museum	東京国立博物館	14・D-3
National Science Museum	国立科学博物館	14・D-3
National Shōwa Memorial Museum	昭和館	4・E-2
Racing Mem. Museum	競馬記念館	98・E-5
Science & Technology Museum	科学技術館	4・E-3
Science Museum	文化資料館	97・G-2
Shinjuku Gyoen Garden	新宿御苑	11・G-5
Silk Center	シルクセンター	98・C-3
Subway Museum	地下鉄博物館	49・H-4
TEPCO Electric Energy Museum	東電力館	29・F-4
Takao Natural Science Museum	高尾自然科学博物館	64・A-3
The Furniture Museum	家具の博物館	7・I-3
Transportation Museum	交通博物館	5・H-2
Yamate Data Museum	山手資料館	98・E-3

ZOO, BOTANICAL GARDEN
動物園，植物園

PLACE NAME	名 称	MAP INDEX
Edogawa Natural Zoo	区立自然動物園	49・G-5
Hamura-shi Zoological Park	羽村市動物公園	86・E-4
Inokashira Natural Park	井の頭自然文化園	52・D-3
Itabashi Children Zoo	区立子供動物園	37・I-4
Itabashi Freshwater Fish Aquarium	区立淡水魚水族館	37・I-4
Kasai Seaside Aquarium	葛西臨海水族園	49・J-5
Makino Memorial Garden	牧野記念庭園	38・B-4
Man-yō Botanical Garden	国分寺万葉植物園	54・E-5
Medical Plant Garden	薬用植物園	78・A-3
Nogeyama Zoo	野毛山動物園	97・H-3
Shinagawa Aquarium	しながわ水族館	21・G-6
Takao Animal and Plant Park	高尾自然動物植物園	94・C-3
Tama Zoological Park	東京都多摩動物園	61・F-5
Tsukuba Botanical Garden	実験植物園	101・H-2
Ueno Zoo	東京都上野動物園	14・C-3
Yomiuri Land Seawater Aquarium	よみうりランド海水水族館	69・H-4

PARK, GARDEN
公園

PLACE NAME	名 称	MAP INDEX
Akatsuka Park	赤塚公園	36・C-3
Ariake Tennis-no-mori Park	有明テニスの森公園	19・G-5
Arisugawanomiya Memorial Park	有栖川宮記念公園	8・E-5
Asukayama Park	飛鳥山公園	41・G-5
Baji Park	馬事公苑	27・F-4
Dōhō Park	洞峰公園	101・F-5
Former Furukawa Garden	旧古河庭園	41・H-6
Fujimidai Park	富士見台公園	70・B-4
Fujimori Park	富士森公園	65・F-1
Hamarikyū Garden	浜離宮庭園	7・H-5
Hibiya Park	日比谷公園	5・F-6
Higashi-ayase Park	東綾瀬公園	45・H-4
Hikarigaoka Park	光が丘公園	39・F-2
Hirayama-jōshi Park	平山城址公園	70・B-2
Honmoku Civic Park	本牧市民公園	99・H-6
Horikiri-shōbuen Garden	堀切菖蒲園	47・G-6
Inokashira Park	井の頭公園	52・D-2
Jindai Botanical Garden	神代植物公園	66・D-2
Jōhoku Central Park	城北中央公園	37・F-5
Kamon-yama Park	掃部山公園	97・G-2
Kasai Recreation Park	レクリエーション公園	49・I-3
Kinshi Park	錦糸公園	17・H-3
Kinuta Park	砧公園	26・E-5
Kitanomaru Park	北の丸公園	4・E-2
Kiyosumi Garden	清澄庭園	18・C-4
Koganei Park	小金井公園	55・I-2
Koishikawa Kōrakuen Garden	小石川後楽園	13・F-6
Kōkyo-higashi-gyoen Park	皇居東御苑	5・F-3

Kōkyo-mae-hiroba Park ·············· 皇居前広場 ·············· 5・F-5
Komaba Park ·············· 駒場公園·············· 22・A-6
Komazawa Olympic Park·············· オリンピック公園·············· 27・H-4
Kyū-Shibarikyū Garden ·············· 旧芝離宮庭園 ·············· 9・F-2
Kyū-Yasuda Garden·············· 旧安田庭園·············· 17・I-6
Meiji Park ·············· 明治公園·············· 29・G-2
Meiji-jingū Gaien Park ·············· 明治神宮外苑·············· 11・H-6
Minato-no-mieruoka Park ·············· 港の見える丘公園·············· 98・E-2
Mizumoto Park ·············· 水元公園·············· 46・B-2
Mogusaen Garden ·············· 百草園·············· 61・I-5
Mukōjima-Hyakkaen Garden ·············· 向島百花園·············· 16・D-4
Musashino Park ·············· 武蔵野公園·············· 57・J-2
Nat'l Park for Nature Study·············· 国立自然教育園 ·············· 9・F-6
Negishi Forest Park ·············· 根岸森林公園·············· 98・D-6
Nogawa Park ·············· 野川公園·············· 66・A-2
Noyama-kita Park·············· 野山北公園·············· 82・C-2
Ōi Wharf Central Park ·············· 大井ふ頭海浜公園·············· 21・H-5
Rikugien Garden ·············· 六義園·············· 12・E-1
Rinshi-no-mori Park ·············· 林試の森·············· 20・A-3
Roka-kōshun-en ·············· 芦花恒春園·············· 26・C-3
Sankeien Garden ·············· 三渓園·············· 99・G-5
Sayama Park ·············· 狭山公園·············· 80・A-3
Shakujii Park ·············· 石神井公園·············· 38・C-4
Shiba Park ·············· 芝公園·············· 8・E-3
Shinjuku Central Park ·············· 新宿中央公園·············· 10・E-5
Shinjuku Gyoen Garden ·············· 新宿御苑·············· 11・G-5
Shinozaki Park·············· 篠崎公園·············· 48・D-2
Shōwa Memorial Park ·············· 昭和記念公園·············· 59・F-3
Sumida Park ·············· 隅田公園·············· 17・F-5
Tetsugakudō Park ·············· 哲学堂公園·············· 30・E-2
Tōkyō Port Wild Bird Park ·············· 東京港野鳥公園·············· 25・H-3
Toyama Park ·············· 戸山公園·············· 11・F-3
Tsukuba EXPO Mem. Park ·············· 筑波科学万博記念公園
·············· 100・D-3
Ueno Park·············· 上野公園·············· 14・D-3
Ukima Park ·············· 浮間公園·············· 40・A-1
Wadabori Park ·············· 和田堀公園·············· 33・G-5
Yakushiike Park ·············· 薬師池公園·············· 74・E-4
Yamashita Park ·············· 山下公園·············· 98・D-2
Yokohama Park ·············· 横浜公園·············· 98・C-3
Yoyogi Park ·············· 代々木公園·············· 28・E-3
Yumenoshima Park ·············· 夢の島公園·············· 19・F-2
Zenpukuji Park·············· 善福寺公園·············· 32・B-2

SPORT FACILITIES
スポーツ施設

PLACE NAME	名称	MAP INDEX

Ariake Tennis-no-mori Park ·············· 有明テニスの森公園··· 19・G-5
Bunka Gymnasium ·············· 文化体育館·············· 98・C-3
Chichibunomiya Memorial Rugby Stadium 秩父宮ラグビー場··· 8・B-5
Edogawa Speedboat Racecourse ·············· 江戸川競艇場·············· 49・F-5
Heiwajima Speedboat Racecourse ·············· 平和島競艇場·············· 25・G-3
Higashifushimi Ice Arena·············· 東伏見アイスアリーナ76・E-4
Jingū Baseball Stadium ·············· 神宮球場·············· 11・I-6
Keiōkaku Cycling Stadium ·············· 京王閣競輪場·············· 66・D-6
Kōdōkan ·············· 講道館·············· 13・G-5
Kokugikan ·············· 国技館·············· 17・I-6
Komazawa Olympic Park·············· 駒沢オリンピック公園 27・H-4
Nat'l Nishigaoka Stadium ·············· 国立西ケ丘競技場·············· 40・C-4
Nat'l Yoyogi Gymnasium ·············· 国立代々木競技場·············· 29・F-4
National Stadium ·············· 国立競技場·············· 11・H-6
Nippon Budōkan Hall ·············· 日本武道館 ·············· 4・E-2
Ōi Race Course ·············· 大井競馬場·············· 21・G-6
Shinagawa Ice Arena ·············· 品川アイスアリーナ·············· 20・E-2
Tachikawa Cycling Stadium ·············· 立川競輪場·············· 59・H-4
Tamagawa Speedboat Racecourse·············· 多摩川競艇場·············· 57・H-5
Tatsumi International Swimming Pool ····· 辰巳国際水泳場·············· 19・F-3
Tōkyō Dome ·············· 東京ドーム·············· 13・F-6
Tōkyō Metropolitan Stadium ·············· 東京都体育館·············· 29・F-1
Tōkyō Racetrack ·············· 東京競馬場·············· 57・G-5
Yokohama Stadium ·············· 横浜スタジアム·············· 98・C-3

DEPARTMENT STORE
デパート

PLACE NAME	名称	MAP INDEX

Daimaru Dept. Store Tōkyō Shop ·············· 大丸東京店 ·············· 5・G-4
Hankyū Dept. Store Sukiyabashi Shop ··· 数奇屋橋阪急 ·············· 6・E-5
Isetan Dept. Store Kichijōji Shop ·············· 伊勢丹吉祥寺店·············· 52・D-2
Isetan Dept. Store Main Shop ·············· 伊勢丹本店·············· 11・F-4
Isetan Dept. Store Tachikawa Shop ·············· 伊勢丹立川店·············· 59・H-5
Keiō Dept. Store ·············· 京王百貨店·············· 11・F-5
Keiō Dept. Store Seisekisakuragaoka
Shop ·············· 京王聖蹟桜ケ丘店·············· 71・H-1
Kintetsu Dept. Store Tōkyō Shop ·············· 近鉄東京店·············· 52・D-2

Matsuya Dept. Store Asakusa Shop ······ 松屋浅草店 ·············· 15・G-4
Matsuya Dept. Store Ginza Main Shop ··· 松屋銀座本店 ··········· 6・E-5
Matsuzakaya Dept. Store Ginza Shop ··· 松坂屋銀座店 ··········· 7・F-5
Matsuzakaya Dept. Store Ueno Shop ······ 松坂屋上野店 ·········· 14・D-5
Matsuzakaya Dept. Store Yokohama Shop 松坂屋横浜店 ············ 98・B-3
Mitsukoshi Dept. Store Ginza Shop ····· 三越銀座店 ·············· 7・F-5
Mitsukoshi Dept. Store Ikebukuro Shop 三越池袋店 ············· 34・E-3
Mitsukoshi Dept. Store Main Shop ······ 三越本店 ················· 6・C-4
Mitsukoshi Dept. Store Shinjuku Shop ··· 三越新宿店 ············· 11・F-5
Mitsukoshi Dept. Store Sunshine Shop ··· サンシャイン三越 ······ 35・F-4
Mitsukoshi Dept. Store Yokohama Shop 三越横浜店 ············· 96・C-3
Odakyū Dept. Store ·························· 小田急百貨店 ··········· 11・F-5
Odakyū Dept. Store Machida Shop ······· 小田急町田店 ··········· 72・E-2
Pritemps Ginza Dept. Store ··············· プランタン銀座店 ····· 6・E-5
Seibu Dept. Store Ikebukuro Shop ········ 西武池袋店 ············· 34・E-4
Seibu Dept. Store Shibuya Shop ·········· 西武渋谷店 ············· 29・F-5
Sogō Dept. Store Tōkyō Shop ·············· そごう東京店 ··········· 5・F-5
Sogō Dept. Store Yokohama Shop ········· 横浜そごう ············· 96・C-2
Takashimaya Dept. Store Shinjuku Shop ··· 高島屋新宿店 ·········· 28・E-1
Takashimaya Dept. Store Tachikawa Shop 立川高島屋 ············· 59・H-5
Takashimaya Dept. Store Tamagawa Shop 玉川高島屋 ············· 27・F-6
Takashimaya Dept. Store Tōkyō Shop ··· 高島屋東京店 ··········· 6・D-4
Takashimaya Dept. Store Yokohama Shop 横浜高島屋 ············· 96・C-3
Tōbu Dept. Store ··························· 東武百貨店 ············· 34・E-3
Tōkyū Dept. Store Kichijōji Shop ········· 東急吉祥寺店 ··········· 52・D-2
Tōkyū Dept. Store Machida Shop ·········· まちだ東急 ············· 72・E-2
Tōkyū Dept. Store Main Shop ··············· 東急本店 ················· 29・F-5

TEMPLE
寺院

PLACE NAME	名称	MAP INDEX
Araiyakushi	新井薬師	31・F-3
Daienji	大円寺	22・D-1
Fukagawa-fudōson	深川不動尊	18・D-4
Gokokuji	護国寺	12・B-3
Gōtokuji	豪徳寺	27・F-3
Haijima-daishi	拝島大師	58・B-4
Honmonji	本門寺	24・D-3
Hōsenji	宝仙寺	31・H-3
Jindaiji	深大寺	66・D-2
Jōshinji	浄真寺	27・H-5
Kan-eiji	寛永寺	14・D-2
Kishibojin	鬼子母神	34・E-5
Kisshōji	吉祥寺	13・G-2
Meguro-fudō	目黒不動	22・E-1
Sanpōji	三宝寺	38・C-4
Sengakuji	泉岳寺	9・G-4
Sensōji	浅草寺	15・G-3
Shibamata-taishakuten	柴又帝釈天	46・E-2
Takahata-fudōson	高幡不動尊	61・G-4
Takaosan-yakuōin	高尾山薬王院	94・C-3
Tanashisan-Sōjiji	田無山総持寺	76・C-4
Togenuki-jizō	とげぬき地蔵	35・H-3
Tōkyō-daibutsu	東京大仏	36・B-4
Tsukiji-honganji	築地本願寺	7・F-4
Zōjōji	増上寺	8・E-2

NEWSPAPER, T.V.STATION
新聞社，放送局

PLACE NAME	名称	MAP INDEX
Asahi Newspaper	朝日新聞社	7・G-5
Bunka Broadcasting	文化放送	11・I-4
Fuji TV	フジテレビ	9・J-1
NHK Broadcasting Center	NHK	29・F-4
Nippon Keizai Newspaper	日本経済新聞社	5・G-3
Nippon TV Network	日本テレビ	4・C-3
TV Asahi	テレビ朝日	8・C-3
TV Tōkyō	テレビ東京	8・D-3
The Mainichi Newspapers	毎日新聞社	5・F-3
The Yomiuri Newspaper	読売新聞社	5・G-3
Tōkyō Broadcasting System (TBS)	東京放送	8・B-3

SHRINE
神 社

PLACE NAME	名 称	MAP INDEX
Asakusa-jinja	浅草神社	15・G-3
Atago-jinja	愛宕神社	8・D-2
Hie-jinja	日枝神社	4・C-5
Higashifushimi-inari-jinja	東伏見稲荷神社	76・D-5
Kameido-tenmangū	亀戸天満宮	18・A-3
Kanda-myōjin	神田明神	5・G-1
Meiji-jingū	明治神宮	28・E-2
Mitake-jinja	御嶽神社	92・E-3
Nezu-jinja	根津神社	13・H-3
Ōkunitama-jinja	大国魂神社	57・F-4
Ōmiya-hachimangū	大宮八幡宮	33・G-5
Ōtori-jinja	大鳥神社	22・D-1
Shinagawa-jinja	品川神社	21・F-3
Shōin-jinja	松陰神社	27・G-3
Suitengū	水天宮	6・C-2
Tomioka-hachimangū	富岡八幡宮	18・D-4
Torigoe-jinja	鳥越神社	15・F-5
Toyokawa-inari	豊川稲荷	8・B-3
Yaho-tenmangū	谷保天満宮	56・C-3
Yasukuni-jinja	靖国神社	4・D-2
Yushima-jinja	湯島神社	13・I-5

TSUKUBA RESEARCH FACILITIES
つくば研究機関

PLACE NAME	名 称	MAP INDEX
Aerological Observatory	高層気象台	101・G-5
Electotechnical Laboratory	電子技術研究所	101・G-5
Fruit Tree Research Station	果樹試験場	100・E-5
Geographical Survey Institute	国土地理院	101・G-1
Geological Survey of Japan	地質調査所	101・G-5
Japan Automobil Research Institute Inc.(JARI)	自動車研究所	100・E-2
Japan Information Center of Science & Technology	科学技術情報センター	101・G-4
Japan International Research Center for Agricultural Sciences	国際農林水産業研究センター	100・E-4
Mechanical EngineeringLaboratory	機械技術研究所	101・G-5
Meteorological ResearchInstitute	気象研究所	101・F-5
Nat'l Agriculture ResearchCenter	農業研究センター	100・D-6
Nat'l Center for Seeds & Seedings	種苗管理センター	100・E-4
Nat'l Food Research Institute	食品研究所	100・D-6
Nat'l Institute for Advanced Interdiscitilinary Research	産業技術融合領域研究所	101・G-5
Nat'l Institute Research in Inorganic Laboratory	無機材料研究所	101・G-5
Nat'l Institute for Resources & Environment	資源環境技術総合研究所	101・F-5
Nat'l Institute of Agricultural Engineering	農業工学研究所	100・D-5
Nat'l Institute of Animal Health	家畜衛生試験場	100・D-6
Nat'l Institute of Bioscience & Human Technology	生命工学工業技術研究所	101・G-5
Nat'l Institute of Health	予防衛生研究所	100・D-4
Nat'l Institute of Materials & Chemical Reseach	物質工学工業技術研究所	101・G-5
Nat'l Institute of Sericultural Entomological Science	蚕糸・昆虫農学研究所	100・E-4
Nat'l Research Institute for Earth Science & Disaster Prevention	防災科学技術研究所	101・H-1
Nat'l Research Institute for Metals	金属材料研究所	101・G-4
Nat'l Research Laboratory of Metrology	計量研究所	101・G-5
Public Works Research institute	土木研究所	101・F-1
Tsukuba Space Center (NASDA)	筑波宇宙センター	101・G-5

TOKYO METROPOLITAN ATLAS

SHOBUNSHA
3-1 Kōji-machi Chiyoda-ku Tokyo 102-8238, JAPAN
Phone：03-3556-8111

Fourteenth Published Jan. 2001

Copyright © Shobunsha Publications, Inc. 1991

ISBN4-398-20103-3

This map is based on the 1:25,000, 1:50,000 scale topographical map
and 1:200,000 scale regional map published by the Geographical
Survey Institute, approval under the article 30 of the surveying Law.
(Approval number KAN-SHI No.233 1999)

Art Direction：ATELIER DESKA

Printed in Japan

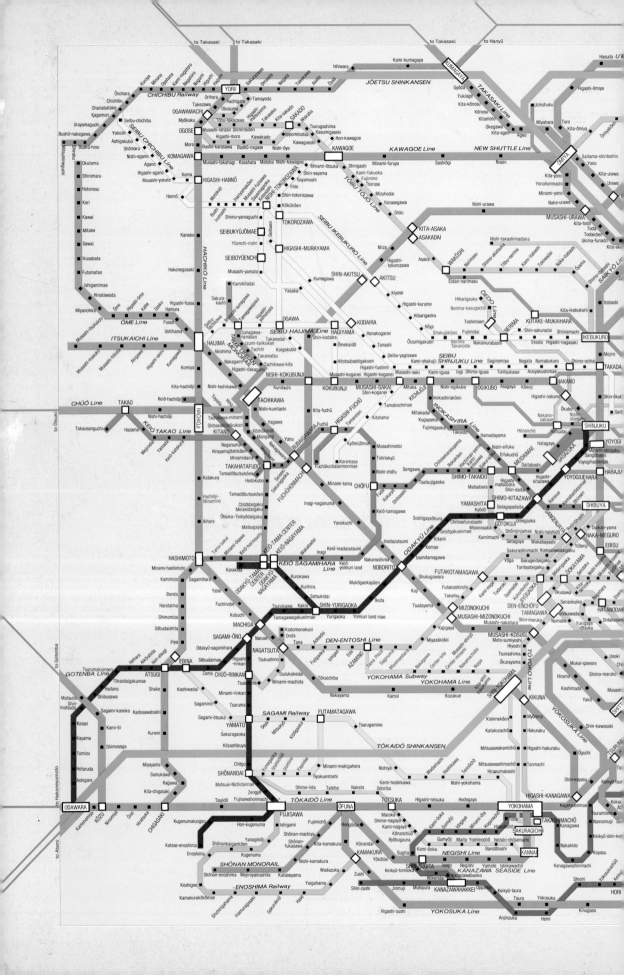